GA

HELGA TAWIL-SOURI AND DINA MATAR

(EDITORS)

Gaza as Metaphor

HURST & COMPANY, LONDON

First published in the United Kingdom in 2016 by
C. Hurst & Co. (Publishers) Ltd.,
41 Great Russell Street, London, WC1B 3PL
© Helga Tawil-Souri, Dina Matar and the Contributors, 2016
All rights reserved.
Printed in India

Distributed in the United States, Canada and Latin America by
Oxford University Press, 198 Madison Avenue, New York, NY 10016,
United States of America.

The right of Helga Tawil-Souri, Dina Matar and the Contributors to be identified
as the authors of this publication is asserted by them in accordance with
the Copyright, Designs and Patents Act, 1988.

A Cataloguing-in-Publication data record for this book
is available from the British Library.

978-1-84904-624-4 *paperback*

www.hurstpublishers.com

This book is printed on paper from registered sustainable
and managed sources.

CONTENTS

NARRATING GAZA

THINKING GAZA

LIST OF ILLUSTRATIONS

A family in Gaza City enjoys a picnic on the beach, one of the few options left to most families in Gaza unable to escape the siege by Tanya Habjouqa.

A group of children playing above the rubble of their home, which has been destroyed, during the war on Gaza by Omar El Qattaa.

The receding Armistice line of 1949 shrinking the area of the Gaza Strip by 200 km² to its present size. Israel unilaterally imposed another buffer zone reducing the area of the Strip by a further 20 percent. Source: Salman Abu Sitta, *Atlas of Palestine 1917–1966*, Palestine Land Society, London, 2010.

Girls painting Gaza Sea Port by Omar El Qattaa.

Palestinian youth practise parkour on Gaza beach by Omar El Qattaa.

'Tomorrow I Will Be Fine.' Palestinian students at the UNRWA school in Canada Camp, Rafah, 1988 by Randa Shaath.

INTRODUCTION

GAZA AS METAPHOR

Helga Tawil-Souri and Dina Matar

[Gaza] equals the history of an entire homeland, because it is more ugly, impoverished, miserable, and vicious in the eyes of enemies. Because it is the most capable, among us, of disturbing the enemy's mood and his comfort. Because it is his nightmare. Because it is mined oranges, children without a childhood, old men without old age and women without desires. Because of all this it is the most beautiful, the purest and richest among us and the one most worthy of love.

Mahmoud Darwish, 'Silence for Gaza.'[1]

No matter when, where, and to whom the word is uttered, 'Gaza' immediately evokes a plethora of metaphors: Open-air Prison, Terror, Resistance, Poverty, Occupation, Siege, Trauma, Bare Humanity. Conversely, a plethora of terms also invoke Gaza: Crisis, Grief, Exception, Refugees, Nationalism, Destitution, Tunnels, Ruin, Persistence.

Metaphors pervade our lives and our thinking. They turn up everywhere, in stories, plays, films, news, politics and everyday life. Metaphors are figures of speech, sometimes standing for something abstract. A metaphor can serve as a symbol, a parallel, a relationship, a connection, an example. It helps us make sense of the unfamiliar and transfer meaning from what is a complex phenomenon to something more easily understood, or vice versa. A metaphor is also a question of distance, identifying something as

1

being the same as some unrelated thing, perhaps for rhetorical effect, or for making clear a sense of continuity or proximity.

Gaza also increasingly seems to stand at a distance, territorially sealed, subsisting in conditions hard to comprehend, politically marginalized, subjected to ongoing forms of violence, segregated behind stereotypes and misunderstandings.

As Gaza becomes increasingly physically inaccessible, perhaps the easiest way to bring it closer — to grasp it, to humanize it, maybe even to change it — is through metaphors. Equally, the more life becomes unsustainable from within Gaza, the easier it becomes to think of that as a metaphor as well. As one author writes, while inside his house under the non-stop barrage of drone, warship, tank and F16 bombings in the midst of the summer 2014 Israeli war: '[You] presume […] to be a microcosm of the trembling, boiling world outside.'[2]

Gaza has many historical narratives assigned to it, some of them peculiar. It is said to be a pivotal point on the way to larger imperial desires and yet the place where no invading force has been able to fully quell or control its people. It took Alexander the Great three arduous tries to crumble the walls around the old city of Gaza, and from there make his way to Egypt. Napoleon, who saw Gaza as 'the outpost of Africa, the door to Asia,' fared no better.[3] By some accounts, Gaza was the site of Samson's degeneration, a story that echoes into Israel's contemporary weakness – whether a weakness of its military might to dispose of Gaza, or a weakness of morality in still attempting to do just that. Gaza is also the site of the world's failure, a stubborn presence of colonialism, and an obdurate reminder of the world's unwillingness (or, more kindly, incapability) to solve the 'Palestine problem.' Gaza is also, undoubtedly, the story of political resistance, of an unbreakable will to fight, not only for its own survival, but for everyone's humanity. Gaza is increasingly marginalized: rendered outside of meaningful political negotiations and a future Palestinian state, severed from the West Bank and the rest of the world, a space beyond the law, beyond reach, sometimes it seems beyond consideration. Yet Gaza continuously and tenaciously reinstates its centrality: to the Palestinian cause, and to the unfinished struggle for national dignity everywhere. Gaza remains a vivid and painful contemporary example of the violence and enmity of modern warfare, and the ability to endure its violence.

INTRODUCTION

Explaining Gaza

The term 'Gaza' requires some specificity, as it is interchangeably used to denote two overlapping geographic entities.

First, there is Gaza the city, tucked along the South-Eastern Mediterranean, inhabited for more than five thousand years, and which continues to be a vibrant urban center. In recent history, Gaza City served as the first seat-of-government of the Palestinian Authority from 1993 to 1996, and then of Hamas from 2007 until the present moment. Within its municipal boundaries live about a million Palestinians, making it, bar none, the largest Palestinian city in the Palestinian Territories.

Second, there is the 'Gaza Strip,' which is a territorial-political outcome of the 1948 war. The entirety of the Strip can seem to be a 40-kilometer-long urban sprawl inside of which eight refugee camps-turned-cities bleeding into neighboring cities are dotted by small towns, shrinking farmland, palm oases, and abandoned settlements. It's a tiny place, crammed with 1.8 million people who are isolated from the rest of the world behind an 11-kilometer-long border with Egypt and 51-kilometer-long military buffer zone with Israel.

Often, it is this larger domain, only a little more than 360 square kilometers — the Gaza *Strip* — that is pronounced as a series of outlandish statistics. More than two-thirds of the population is made up of refugees; 70% live in poverty; 20% live in 'deep poverty'; just about everybody has to survive on humanitarian hand-outs; adult unemployment hovers around 50% give or take a few percentage points; 60% of the population is under the age of 18. This is the Gaza where on a good day there is no electricity 'only' 20 hours a day; where, before the latest Israeli military operation, in summer 2014, there was already a shortage of 70,000 homes; where 60% of the population suffers from food insecurity; where 95% of piped water is below international quality standards; where every child aged 8 or younger has already witnessed three massive wars. This is the Gaza which includes some of densest places on earth: the Shati (Beach) refugee camp in which more than 87,000 residents live in 0.52 square kilometers; the Jabaliya camp — the largest — which covers an area of 1.4 square kilometers that more than 110,000 refugees call home (not including the tens of thousands who took refuge in the camp during the summer 2014 bombing campaign). One can be dumbfounded by Gaza's sheer statistical impossibility. But numbers often conceal more than they expose; besides, numbers are not helpful in providing the context of Gaza's lived realities, its history, the political field that has rendered it a fabricated 'Strip' of disasters.

Gaza — the city and the Strip — today is hermetically-sealed: the flow of people, goods, as well as medicines, fuel, and electricity is tightly controlled by Israel, all the while subjected to various forms of military and political violence. As in any other place, Gaza's changes are dynamic. But the conditions imposed on the territory and the people that live in it are man-made.

By thinking of Gaza through an allegory or a comparison, a metaphor can help bring Gaza's lived reality closer into focus. Gaza is described along a spectrum of increasingly worsening conditions, from Israel's backyard as a cheap labor pool and captive market to an open-air prison. However, as Ariella Azoulay explains in this volume there was no original crime committed by Palestinians when they were first corralled and locked-up in what became the Gaza Strip in order for the metaphor of a penitentiary to hold — although it is the term that the Israeli military has officially ascribed to the Gaza Strip since 2005. Or, as Darryl Li writes in this volume, Gaza has not only become 'a space in which the "pure" conditions of laboratory experimentation are best approximated,' but has also been transformed into a zoo. Said Shehadeh pushes the metaphor further as he expounds on the psychological impacts of the latest war: Gaza is not a zoo but a torture chamber. Glenn Bowman turns to bodily metaphors of disease to posit Gaza as a 'cyst' which is quarantined into a life constantly exposed to death. Although they may focus our attention invariably on territorial, political, or psychological factors, these metaphors address the qualitative shift of Israeli policies and levels of violence since the mid-2000s. This beckons a question: can Gaza keep being (re)produced and squeezed as something beyond, worse than what it already is? In fact, as the contributors who speak to the Palestinian — and originally Gazan — form of resistance, *sumud*, highlight, both the metaphors of prisons and torture chambers have historical purchase. However, as Sherene Seikaly and Haidar Eid note, also in this volume, Gazans' original sin was to be born Palestinian, and, over the years, to refuse, as would anyone, to be colonized, subjugated, and humiliated.

Gaza is often talked of and imagined as a political entity that is 'exceptional' for its poverty, over-crowdedness, isolation, and violence. Historical facts tell us differently. First, Gaza remains occupied by Israel.

INTRODUCTION

Second, the violence waged on Gaza is not simply in the exceptional moments of kinetic 'operations' but on an everyday basis through a range of policies that are at the heart of Zionism and the colonial practices of the Israeli state. Third, Gaza is part of the Palestinian (hi)story.

Despite the 2005 disengagement, Israel maintains direct control over Gaza. Israel continues to control Gaza's air and maritime space, six of the seven land crossings (the seventh, along the border with Egypt, is the only one Palestinians are permitted to use, and is rarely open), and the flow of trade, water, electricity, monetary currency, communication networks, identity cards and permits, medicine, building materials, and so much more. Israel continues to occupy Gaza through on-the-ground military incursions and through its technologies that seal Gaza: unmanned aerial drones, CCTV cameras, remote-controlled bulldozers and boats, F-16s and Apache helicopters constantly buzzing overhead, and not only during times of heightened violence or explicit warfare. The limits and stunted mobility of Gaza are actively produced by Israel. Gaza is sealed with a buffer zone manned by military sensors, remote-controlled cameras mounted with made-to-kill artillery, and padded with electrified fences and concrete walls, created and enforced and expanded by the Israeli military, stretching as much as 3 kilometers into the Gaza Strip in certain areas, and encompassing, in total, 44 percent of Gaza's entire land mass. Gaza is continuously and violently rendered smaller — not only because one can't get out, but because there is less and less space on the inside. But small here is not just a size, it is a condition. As Ilana Feldman writes in this volume, restrictions on Palestinian movement that have isolated the inhabitants of Gaza from the rest of the world, impeding their ability to live full lives, impairing the Palestinian political community, increasing distance, distrust, and ultimately division between the West Bank and Gaza (let alone the rest of the Palestinians in Israel and beyond) are just part and parcel of the process of isolation that began with the creation of the 'Strip' in 1948.

Concomitant to territorial, aerial, and maritime enclosure is the range of socio-economic and psychological impacts of the process of rendering Gaza isolated, impoverished, marginalized, always on the edge of collapse. As many of the contributors contend, this is not Gaza's 'natural' condition, nor a result of an abstract humanitarian crisis, but of policies practiced for decades to render Gaza marginal, to render its inhabitants, in the words of Haidar Eid, 'unwanted Palestinians.' As importantly, each violent outburst on the part of the Israeli military is a moment in a much longer trajectory of colonialism and occupation. There is no doubt that Israel plays the lead role here, but by no means are others immune from blame, critique, and responsibility, both inside and outside the Palestinian nation: Egypt of course, but all other neighboring and regional countries, the entire international community of states and institutions, Palestinian elites, and, more recently, the Palestinian Authority.

As Salman Abu Sitta notes, already in 1948 Palestinians were subject to aerial bombardments and imprisoned as they attempted to return to their homes across what was first an imaginary line and over the years has come to serve as hard border. Hundreds of thousands of masses of Palestinians were expelled from historic Palestine into the Gaza Strip (among other places too), in order to isolate them and prevent them from returning to their homes and families. Israeli military operations have been ongoing since the Gaza Strip was first created — and even during Egyptian control. The practices of sealing the territory, of depleting the economy, of razing infrastructure, of attempting to break people's wills, have been ongoing for decades and are all means to disempower Gaza. Israel seems to be trying to make Gaza incompetent, trivial, negligible. This is inevitably a political move to sever Gaza — from the West Bank, from Palestinians inside Israel, from Palestinians anywhere, from any future of Palestine, whatever that may be. The project of attempting to render Gaza politically marginal has been ongoing for decades, almost a century. And in that, Gaza fares no different than Palestine as a whole — both the land and its peoples.

If Gaza seems awash in apocalyptic metaphors, it is also, resolutely, a site of life and resistance. In the contributions by Helga Tawil-Souri, Khaled Hroub, and Selma Dabbagh, for example, the largesse of Gazan life is highlighted, focusing our eyes on Gaza as a site brimming with life and an insatiable will to survive, and even find new love. It is also a place where resistance to power and to processes of exclusion comes in different cultural forms, such as poetry, fiction, images and new historical critiques as Atef Alshaer, Dina Matar and Ilan Pappé write in this volume.

Discursive tools, too, are employed to keep a distance from understanding and unearthing this history. Metaphors, such as Gaza's perpetual vulnerability, destitution, its need for the 'drip-feed' of international aid and the 'benevolence' of Arab states has also come to define Gaza, as have processes of structural and discursive externalization through which its Palestinian inhabitants have come to be treated as the

Palestinian 'other,' and through which it is seen as a negative space, or as a special kind of place that is, in essence, a problem.

Gaza has always been and remains a problem for Israel; as Tawil-Souri, Azoulay, Li, Bowman, and others write in this collection, Gaza will remain a 'menace' to Israel, a blemish on its image, an eyesore it cannot keep hiding from the world — or, to turn an earlier metaphor on its head, it is that there are and continue to be Palestinian refugees (and so many of them) that remains evidence of a crime. Of course this menace is not simply one that arises out of the threat of Hamas rocket fire into Israeli areas, for example, which is the excuse Israel has been using more recently to justify its repeated violence and incursions. As is argued through the volume, Israel has used various forms of justification to isolate and quell Gaza for decades, all of which have had to do with, ultimately, preventing Palestinians from returning to their original homes, keeping them fragmented, in the hope that these processes would thwart — and eventually completely quell — the desire for return, liberation, or, quite simply, freedom.

The history of Gaza's resistance to occupation is well known and rehearsed in some of the essays in this volume. Gaza is the place from which the first Palestinian guerrilla operation inside Israel was mounted in 1955, resulting in an Israeli reprisal raid against an Egyptian military barracks north of Gaza City. From Gaza, too, came some of the key leaders of Fatah, the dominant faction of the Palestine Liberation Organization. Gaza is also the place from which the first Palestinian *intifada* of 1987 began and where Hamas and other Islamist factions first took root. In Gaza, as Atef Alshaer, Nimer Sultany, Ramzy Baroud and other writers in this volume attest to, resistance is a historical inevitability, an existential necessity. The everyday actions and practices to resist and exist have also come to define Gaza's relationship with Israel, as Li, Matar, Shehadeh, Alshaer and others in this volume demonstrate, as has, of course, Israel's violence against it.

The latest military onslaught in July and August 2014, codenamed Operation Protective Edge by the Israeli military, was the latest manifestation of this violence, making it the longest and most vicious of the three devastating 'wars' waged on Gaza since 2008. It left over two thousand Palestinians dead, mostly civilians, over eleven thousand injured, and whole-scale destruction of neighborhoods and infrastructure, and further propelled Gaza into the realm of unsustainability. As some of the contributions in this volume highlight, such violence is not the merely repetition of new forms of military violence waged since Israel's disengagement in 2005, but part of the ongoing policy to subjugate, subdue, silence, and erase Palestinians (see Sultany, Pappé, Seikaly, Eid, and Matar in this volume).

There is no question that this latest campaign — combined with the two previous ones — has weighed on Gaza's people — and perhaps, the images of that ferocity have helped increase sympathy or solidarity. Over the past decade, more and more Gazans have expressed helplessness and a sense of loss; more have been injured and maimed, more express a desire to escape. At the same time, this last war reminded many that Gaza is both part and parcel of the Palestinian condition and Palestinians' ongoing resistance. What this highlighted is not metaphorical at all: Gaza remains an existential question for Palestinians, in every sense of the word.

Writing metaphor

This volume was born in the midst of the ferocious attacks launched by Israel against Gaza on 8 July 2014 out of a desire to record, historicize and render Gaza accessible. The essays and interventions in this volume are written by an array of people — journalists, writers, doctors, UN agency officials, academics from a variety of disciplines — who engage with and problematize realities, representations and renderings of Gaza. The essays are eclectic in style and mode of presentation; some are reflexive and personal while others are interpretive and discursive. All the essays use metaphors as discursive and conceptual entry points to interrogate the realities of Gaza, to excavate, contextualize and make visible the effect of Israel's settler colonial project, among other forces, on Gaza and its people.

In other words, we use metaphors here to enter into a conversation with Gaza in order to understand its joys and sorrows, its defeats and triumphs, its hopes and aspirations. We use Gaza as metaphor to ask how the place, its practices, its people, its culture and its historical processes can help us understand the contemporary condition of Palestinians, in particular, and the condition of dispossession, in general. Through metaphor, we address what Gaza and its people tell us about their lives and histories and what their (hi)stories contribute to our understanding of exception, inequality, dispossession, biopolitics, and necropower, along with other terms which we rely on to make sense of our world.

INTRODUCTION

In a sense, the collection asks and answers the following question: what do the metaphors for which Gaza stands expose and obscure? What can Gaza tell us about the meta-moments of history that continue to shape what it means to be a Palestinian, to be human? The hope is to interject the realities of Gaza into our metaphors as we also figuratively assert the world into Gaza, and in the process, convey an understanding about the mechanics of the world and the practices of the people within it.

The first section of the volume, *Living Gaza*, reflects on Gaza's everyday conditions, during moments of heightened violence, in their aftermath, and across time. We are introduced to some of the ways — and the reasons — of Gaza's continuous will to survive, even as destruction is waged on streets and buildings, deep within individual psyches, across the social collective, and against a political solution. What becomes clear is the breadth of the existential crisis that Gaza faces, explicitly brought up by Said Shehadeh and Pierre Krähenbühl and echoed in the book's subsequent sections. Somewhere between the illogic and incomprehension of the violence waged, suffered through, and survived, it becomes clear that Gaza is not a humanitarian crisis but a man-made one. Not only that, but the condition Gaza finds itself in is not purely an academic, or indeed metaphorical, exercise, as Mouin Rabbani, also in this volume, argues, but inflicted through well-calculated policies which stem from a strategy of continued separation and fragmentation of Palestinians, as well as an attempt by Israel to deflect attention from its continued occupation. As the contributors in this section elucidate, Gazans continue to seek their dignity and rights, even as they struggle against worsening conditions and a degradation of what is 'normal.' The resilience that later chapters will speak to more explicitly is already apparent in this section. It comes up, for example, in the mundane as Naim al Khatib describes the 'suicide mission' of taking one's kid to the bathroom during days and nights under a military assault. The complexity — and the difficulty — that is Gaza also emerges in Helga Tawil-Souri's essay which argues that Gaza is equally a productive site.

The essays in *Placing Gaza* contextualize how Gaza has come to be. These essays argue that the sequestration and isolation of Gaza have emerged over time through specific policies, and thus show how the *Nakba* is not simply a historical remnant, but a catastrophe still lived in the present. Although Israel's cycles of military-waged destruction have increased over the past decade, and it now deploys 'immobility as a lethal weapon,' as Ilana Feldman argues, Gaza's territorial production has been an ongoing process — and not driven entirely by Israel alone. As Jehad Abu Salim notes, the borders from within Gaza imagined as reaching from 'fence to fence' speaks to the fact that the 'fence' is not simply a contemporary form of fortification, but a metaphor serving as 'a constant reminder of the rupture caused by the 1948 war.' Early Zionist and Israeli policies, along with the help of Egypt, have long thwarted Palestinians' return to their homes, erected borders around them, and prevented them both territorial contiguity and national unity. Glenn Bowman provides comparison of what Salman Abu Sitta calls originally 'imaginary lines' (as they neither ever directly overlaid onto the Armistice lines, nor were ever agreed upon) to the 'borders' that emerged in the West Bank after the *Nakba*. Bowman suggests that the mechanisms and tools which Israel had imposed on Gaza are already in place in the West Bank — a spectre shared among some of the other contributors as well. The attempt by Palestinians in the 1940s and 1950s to return home provides a background against which to understand the emergence of Gaza's underworld of tunnels, which Khaled Hroub describes as an allegory of contradictory forces: the power of love, political incomprehensibility and absurdity, Palestinians' journeys to nowhere, and the magic of resistance.

Fortified behind fences, weapons, walls, restrictions, drones, and constant-surveillance, Gaza seems equally isolated behind a veil of misunderstanding and misrepresentation. The essays in the *Narrating Gaza* section reflect on attempts to represent, humanize, and even universalize Gaza (Dabbagh); the legitimacy that is derived through near-repetitive images that normalize Gaza as a site of violence (Matar); and the discursive tools necessary to unshackle the hegemonic hold over Gaza as well as the military might imposed upon it by Israel (Ilan Pappé). These essays also reflect on the role of memory, literature, poetry, images, and words more generally, in keeping a struggle alive, and contending both with the inevitability of a (violent) struggle, as Alshaer argues by dissecting poetry. If for Alshaer, the violence of colonialism is met with violent resistance, Pappé advocates an alternative narrative that can challenge the Israeli sword. Both agree, along with Matar, that the discursive portrayals of Israeli violence as aberrations or isolated cases are not *ad hoc* responses to Palestinian violence, but incremental policies of attempting to silence Palestinians that are 'as old as the Zionist presence in Palestine itself,' in the words of Pappé. As such, the essays reflect on how Gaza is a site of ongoing resistance, or, as Dabbagh writes: 'There is a Gaza in all of us, the idea of continuing to fight for what one believes to be morally and legally compelling, even if all odds are against you.' This is echoed by Ramzy Baroud and contributions in the other sections.

As a space of temporal and political destabilization, Gaza speaks to the larger Palestinian predicament. *Thinking Gaza* is comprized of essays that look at Gaza with a larger world view, whether historically, comparatively, or otherwise. Darryl Li suggests that Gaza is 'the lowest rung in a territorially segregated hierarchy of subjugation that encompasses Palestinians' as a product of an ongoing process of 'controlled abandonment' that seems likely to remain intact and is increasingly paralleled in the West Bank. Ariella Azoulay further contextualizes the isolation of Gaza into what she terms a 'concentration-place' tracing its roots back to practices of slavery and imperialism. She makes clear that the territorial and rhetorical tools used against Palestinians, and in particular against those who became 'refugees,' have worked to erase the very process which rendered them as such. The process is equally one which attempts to deprive those victims of the freedom to produce meaning of their condition. This is further echoed in a heartfelt piece by Sara Roy in which she claims that the continuously unheard entreaty that all Palestinians are seeking is quite simply the quest for human dignity. If there is a sense of déjà vu, Nimer Sultany problematizes it by pointing to the structural relationships of recursive power dynamics, and critiquing attempts at perceiving certain moments as exceptional, lest they render other periods normal. Sultany describes how Palestinians are trapped, asked to choose between the 'normality' of oppression and the 'exceptionality' of spectacular suffering. These conditions of violence, as Sherene Seikaly suggests, are familiar. The scenes of Gaza during and in the aftermath of the summer 2014 assault, are but an instance in a now century-long confrontation with colonialism. But Seikaly, like a handful of the contributors, seems to hold out a sliver of hope, which emanates from within the Palestinian condition itself: an inimitable resistance and ongoing struggle for decolonization.

Each of the essays in the volume speaks to a particular metaphor, but they all speak to each other, thus setting in motion a conversation with the particularities of Gaza, thus making evident its symbolic and real significance in the twenty-first century. The contributions also speak to Gaza as a real place, an inseparable part of Palestine's past, present, and future. As editors of this volume, we hope it can be seen as a step towards political action, or, an engagement with Gaza which, in the words of the poet Mahmoud Darwish, does 'not compel people to cool contemplation, but rather to explosion and a collision with reality.'[4]

LIVING GAZA

GAZA AS LARGER THAN LIFE

Helga Tawil-Souri

This obscure feeling that you had as you left Gaza, this small feeling must grow into a giant deep within you. It must expand, you must seek it in order to find yourself, here among the ugly debris of defeat [...]

Ghassan Kanafani, Letter from Gaza[1]

A Giant Deep Within

There are almost two million people living in Gaza: a plethora of individual lives and experiences, each one of them unique. Two million dreams, life histories, desires and fears. Two million unique fingerprints and sets of eyes, two million unique voice intonations. Two million personalities, overflowing within a tiny piece of land. Each one of them makes do despite structures of scarcity and violence imposed on them. They not only exist, they live; and, despite conditions that make it nigh impossible, sometimes they thrive too. Gaza has profit-seekers and entrepreneurs, artists and dancers, marathon runners and surfers, chefs and bakers, translators and smugglers, criminals and lovers, teachers and preachers, photographers and kite-flyers, aspiring doctors and vegetarians.

There are two million experiences of survival and creativity that are, given the conditions hindering them, extraordinary. That daily practice of resourcefulness and improvisation makes Gaza large. Gaza is crowded with commitments; commitments to keep learning, to wake up everyday, to seek shreds of normality in a hellhole, to keep struggling: whether struggling simply to survive, to keep loving, or to keep fighting. That too is grandeur.

Gaza is almost two million stories of getting by with limited resources, making do with a life defined by dispossession, violence, and war; two million ways of practicing steadfastness and resolve, and of doing so individually and collectively day in and day out, year after year after year. There is no doubt that sometimes it means losing one's sense of sanity, sometimes it means starving, freezing to death, being maimed or bombed or falling into a state of paralysis; but it also means learning to pick up the rubble and starting over, or, as in some cases, using the rubble as parkour platform.[2] Gaza is a voluminous will to live.

Gaza is productive, often only in a survivalist form of recycling and re-using, but sometimes too in creating something new. Gaza learns to use every piece of fabric, every shred of blue and white UNRWA canvas bags, every drop of used cooking oil and transform it, respectively, into an item of clothing, a 'wall' in a house, fuel for a modified engine. Gaza is little kids sneaking a peek behind a window or a curtain while their mouth is still full of toothpaste, because there are no bathrooms, because there is no 'proper time' to brush your teeth, because you do what you can when you can and where you can. Because in Gaza, you have to improvize. Even what is misunderstood from the outside as merely or innately violent is itself generative, creative, a necessary outcome of resisting the overbearing structural violence of occupation and collective imprisonment, for example, the tunnels, Qassam rockets, website hacks, drug trafficking. Like the parkour performers, Gaza has learned to engage with the environment by navigating it by movement around, across, through, over, and under its features. Schools are turned into shelters. Destroyed settlements are turned into eerie playgrounds and places to escape the daily grind. Living rooms are turned into internet cafés. Playgrounds are turned into political parade grounds. In Gaza nothing goes to waste.

A lot of planning must take place in Gaza, even if most of it can only be done on an ad-hoc and daily basis, because it's never certain whether there will be electricity, food, water, whether your classmate or teacher will be alive tomorrow. Gaza demonstrates an implicit vitality, where nearly two million people continuously make productive use of the available, even if scarce and outdated, technical, natural, and symbolic resources. Gaza has schools, universities, cultural hubs, police stations, prisons, orchards, factories, printing presses.

Gaza continues to teem with literature, poetry, photography. Much of it has formed the backbone of Palestinian literary and artistic genius for decades. But its genius, its largeness, is that despite conditions of a near-impossible 'normal life,' these continue and are generated anew. A young girl garners more than a thousand followers on Instagram.[3] New poetic and art forms emerge: some in translation[4]; some remain relatively unknown, circling only with a network of family and friends.[5] Despite being severed from the world, and the world from Gaza, it tries to consume the latest trends, coopt what it likes, create its own satires. It balks against its marginalization. In the middle of the 2014 war, people all over the U.S. and eventually around the world, in an effort to raise awareness of Lou Gerigh's disease, videotaped themselves as an ice bucket was dumped on them. In Gaza too, journalist Ayman Aloul made a video and uploaded it to YouTube. But he called it the 'rubble challenge' as buckets of debris were dumped on him: to raise awareness that in Gaza one is bombed inside one's own home.[6] When local renditions of Pharrell Williams' *Happy* music video popped up all over the world, so too did some from Gaza.[7] When video spoofs emerged of Jean-Claude Van Damme's advertisement in which the thespian shows off his muscles by doing an 'epic split' on two Volvo trucks driving in reverse, there quickly emerged a Gazan version: a split between two cars being pushed, because in Gaza, there is often no fuel.[8] Gaza engages us — and often with deep-seated humour and ironic wit. But we must choose to listen, to hear Gaza rather than the din around it.

Gaza can be overbearingly loud. The ceaseless buzz of *zannanas*[9], the cloud-shattering booms of the F-16s, the thump-thump-thump of Apache helicopters, the stomping feet of *dabke* dancers, the calls to prayer, honking cars and mopeds, braying donkeys, and children — so many, so many, so *many* children! — and the infinite ways they fill the sound waves with their screams, squelches, squeals, arguments, giggles, tears, games, whispers. Gaza is the daily faithful discussions between neighbors, friends, and family members sitting outdoors on plastic chairs; the finely timed pounding of peeled garlic cloves in the *zibdiya*, the sizzling of eggplant slices. Gaza is the sound of a guttural $\dot{\varepsilon}$ (g). Gaza is the sound of your breath withheld when you hear the whispered whistle of a bomb's exit from the airplane's womb. Gaza is instinctively knowing to discern the roars made by violence, by military technologies, by resistance warriors and

17

those made by machinery that is puttering along: a D-9 bulldozer, a farmer's tractor, a *klashin*[10], a gunship, a surveillance drone, a building's generator, a taxi running on home-made fuel, low battery signals on your cellphone. Gaza is raucous squares and alleyways; where on the same day you encounter a wedding party and a funeral procession, a police parade and a hoard of boys playing soccer. Clapping, whistling, feet stomping, singing, chanting, praying, crying, screaming.

Gaza is bountiful to the senses. It is strikingly colourful: graffiti[11], painted walls, polyester blankets hanging as curtains and room separators, layers of rust, bright kindergartens; boats, fishing nets, the dancing reflection of dusk on the sea, the brightness of the sunset on whitewashed walls and glass windows. It is filled with vibrant ruins and remnants: veined marble traces from centuries ago; stone-washed Mamluk mosques; azures and turquoises of the icons found in Gaza's Greek Orthodox churches; pink, yellow, green and denim-coloured clothing and books screaming out from the flattened grey rubble caused by the last Israeli bombing. It is rich with smells and tastes: succulent tomatoes, spicy salads, dizzying flavoured smoke from the *argilehs*, rotting garbage, shit literally flowing on the streets, dust, sewage that rises whenever it rains, freshly pressed olive oil, fish drying out in market stalls, stale diesel fuel, watermelons, sweet sage tea, human sweat. Gaza is filled with tender voices and broad shiny smiles, with green-eyed blondes, with dark chocolate brown skin and all shades in between. Gaza radiates in the men's glittering eyes, and sun-drenched arms, gentle and soft as if floating on clouds yet strong and determined holding up the nation; Gaza is carved in the wrinkles of the faces of the aged Bedouin women who don their black and gold *thob*.

Gaza's largeness is in the patience practiced to no end. The hours waiting in the burning sun: for an UNRWA coupon, for a checkpoint, for an attempt across the border, for a hand-out, for a loaf of bread during a ceasefire, for a return to the Palestine ripped from under your grandparents' feet. The patience it takes to have your aquifers sucked dry by the Israelis on the other side of the buffer zones and no-man's lands trying to prove to themselves and to the world that only they know how to make the desert bloom while they leave you with droplets of water too salinated to make anything of. Gaza's largeness is in the patience, resolve, and immediate action it takes to deal with the abrupt, and of course unannounced, three-meter-deep flood that comes gushing into your home in the middle of a rain storm when those same people on the other side of the buffer zone had too much rain and open their dams. Gaza is the tenacity it takes to rebuild your house not once, not twice, not thrice, but dozens of times because the settlers moved in, because the camps' alleyways need to be broadened so that Israeli soldiers can swarm through more efficiently,[12] because the Philadephi Route[13] was still within eyesight of your window, because the buffer zone needs expansion, or just because.

That kind of patience and resolve is the resilience that is quintessentially Gazan. A steadfastness that is grand and generous, built as it is on solidarity, friendliness, religious and cultural roots, and a belief in historical rights and a better future. This is the same resilience practiced by bakers and doctors who refuse to raise their prices despite the siege, despite the food scarcity, despite the electricity cuts; the resilience in sharing whatever goods one has with those around her. The generosity in the abundance — of food, blankets, tea, floorspace, or conversation — that is offered to a guest no matter the poor circumstances, sweltering dust, and ruins of one's house, and, it must be said, no matter the guest's religious, political, or national affiliation.

With limited resources, and a disorder defined by dispossession, occupation, violence, and loss, two million people hold and exude a steadfastness that only increases. The constant attempt to shrink and marginalize and thwart Gaza makes it even more impressive: Gaza's methods of survival are bountiful and people's sense of life capacious. Gaza is larger than life because the will to live is monumental, the daily strength to survive is nothing short of captivating, the collective struggle is mesmerizing, the political struggle mythical. Gaza is larger than life because it continuously tells us that it is immortal.

There are ample places in the world cloaked in myths such as if one drinks from one of its fountains or sits on a particular bench then one will return. It is said that Sarajevo, Rome, and Jerusalem are cities whose attraction, if felt once, is so overpowering that you will necessarily return. Gaza is like that, and more. Because for about three-quarters of the population, Gaza is not their original home; Gaza is a strip they were forced and corralled into, like an airplane in a holding pattern within close range of the place it seeks to land. Life inside Gaza is larger than life, but Gaza is larger than itself too. Its largeness radiates outward.

GAZA AS METAPHOR

The Large Shadow

For Israel, Gaza is a menacing shadow that will not go away.

Of course, Gaza's 'menace' is predicated on the historical fact that Israel is built on the destruction of Palestine, both in the past and in the present — and which Israel does nothing to admit, recognize, or redress. The Gaza Strip was never a naturally occurring 'strip', but the outcome of multiple processes, most poignant and forceful of which were that Zionist militias and later the Israeli state herded Palestinians from towns, cities, desert oases, farmlands mostly from across southern Palestine, and kept them under lock and key, with the help of partners-in-crime including Egypt and the international community of states and institutions. That historical fact and its present-day outcomes are one way to understand Palestinians' credence that justice, or time, or God will eventually prevail on their side.[14]

Gaza's shadow looms large because Israel has never left Gaza. Israel is present and forceful all around, above, and below Gaza: in its control of airspace and the sea, in the surveillance zeppelins, UAVs, and gun boats, in the buffer zones lined with mines, infrared and gamma-ray detection machines, and robotic machine gun towers remote-controlled by soldiers tucked away in Tel Aviv or the Negev with the capability to kill on instance. The IDF's mantra of 'frictionless control'[15] only veils Israeli practices of control from afar and up-close, making any 'border' between Israel and Gaza a cruel joke imposed on those imprisoned: continuous raids, assassination strikes, intense aerial surveillance, regular wholesale invasions, and a permanent constant domination through drones, satellites, and killing machines. Borders and barriers are there to contain Gaza (and to keep out other Palestinians and others who do not want to play by Israel's rules), but they do not hold Israeli power back.[16] Israel never in actuality 'disengaged.' Moreover, Israel's presence in Gaza is not only in the moments of spectacular violence and the phantom limbs and psychological scars that thousands must learn to live with(out), but in the subtle form of killing that has become commonplace: through dietary and medical restrictions, limitations on fuel supplies and sewage pumping, pollution of fishing farms and destruction of crops. Israel imposes limitations on electricity, on internet speeds, on telecommunications infrastructure. Israel's presence is everywhere: in the biometric and profiling techniques embedded in Palestinians' ID cards, in the 'knocks' on the roof and menacing text messages, in the hijacking of radio and television signals in order to broadcast its own propaganda, and so much more. Life inside Gaza is marked and bounded by the stubborn, persistent, vehement presence of Israel in Gaza's every breath.

Gaza looms large because it remains a central aspect of the Palestinian predicament in the face of Israeli occupation and colonialism. More than that, the attempt to sever, marginalize, fragment, impoverish, and 'shrink' Gaza is part and parcel of Israel's modus operandi. It is not only despite being marginalized that Gaza remains central, but also because of it. Gaza is larger than itself, because, in other words, is it part of a larger whole.

Gaza is at the center and outcome of the manifestations of a regime in which segregation, inequality, violence (both enacted and withheld) towards Palestinians occurs all over Israel/Palestine. Gaza's production and, as importantly, its destruction, take place in a still-ongoing historical arc of Palestinian dispossession, including wholesale urban devastation that harks back to the 1930s and 1940s. Gaza, along with Jaffa, Haifa and Jerusalem, were sites where a Palestinian urban modernity was abruptly aborted by the Zionist colonial project.[17] As such, the (urban) condition of Gaza as harbouring the densest places on the planet, literally living in dark ages, floating in untreated sewage and rubble, kept on a 'diet,' with writhing infrastructures and ever-increasing forms of poverty, is a function of the ongoing 'nakbaization' of Palestine.[18] The cultural, economic, and social devastation wrought on pre-1948 Palestine are losses that Palestinians are still reeling from — and are all the more obvious in Gaza where refugees largely outnumber original inhabitants. Equally important, that devastation continues today. Gaza cannot be divorced from the ongoing context of Zionist expansion and Israeli occupation.

There is a forward (future) movement here too. Gaza demonstrates the apotheosis of Israel's policy of collective confinement and incarceration. The shadow of Gaza looms over the future of the West Bank. The Palestinian population grows in density, shifting upwards in multi-story apartment buildings and in tighter and tighter spaces, both inside those apartments and across the shrinking territory. Israeli land confiscation, expansion of military zones, settlements, construction of the wall, checkpoints, by-pass roads and buffer areas, which continue unabated, confine Palestinian growth into narrower slivers. The bubble-boom of Ramallah is perhaps the best example. The increased Judaization and de-Arabization of Jerusalem and the worsening economic conditions across Palestinian territories help increase Ramallah's density. Empty plots of land have been engulfed in multistory apartment buildings. But the city is surrounded by an ever-encroaching Israel and the latter's obstinate drive to take more and more of Palestine. Ramallah has also served as the de facto capital since the late 1990s, and now boasts nightclubs and hotels, open-air shisha lounges and entrepreneurship incubators, newly formed local and international elites, attracting NGOs and diaspora Palestinians to invest. Ramallah has become the site of the 'ingathering' of Palestinians. The same was true of Gaza in the early and mid 1990s. The structures which have rendered Gaza an open-air 'penitentiary' (in the terminology of the IDF[19]) are omnipresent around Ramallah and the West Bank. We know what the future looks like — like Gaza — it is only a question of when that future is going to be imposed.

Gaza does not go away in the Israeli imaginary because the more stringent and cruel Israel's treatment of Gaza is, the more it remains a thorn in Israel's side. Maps are drawn with concentric circles emanating out of Gaza, displaying a threat; graphics are rendered with tunnels dug like tentacles spinning outwards from the Gaza Strip into Egypt and into Israel.[20] This is a large Gaza too, often perceived as growing out of control: a cancer to be treated with chemotherapy, a woman that needs to be raped, a wilderness that needs repeated 'mowing,' a penitentiary that needs to be disciplined with ever more stringent technologies and ever-harsher 'responses.'[21] Gaza is so much larger than itself that every unborn child is already a threat. Utter עזה to almost any Israeli, and they shudder in fear and disgust.

Fortified behind fences, weapons, walls, travel restrictions, and drones, Gaza emanates beyond itself but also behind a growing veil of misunderstanding and misrepresentation. In this sense too, Gaza generates — albeit, for the most part, not of its own volition. It creates images, stereotypes, fears, assumptions. As one writer from Gaza claims, 'Gaza is consummately professional in the production of new material: cooking up new TV food, so tasty and delicious for a carefree audience. Other signs of normal life — of love, of joy, of quiet resilience, of humanity — do not make it to press.'[22] Gaza comes to stand — problematically, ahistorically, in the most racist and simplest of ways — for everything threatening, backwards, non-progressive. Gaza is emaciated, drowns in shit, lives in the dark ages, hangs on to God, seeks comfort and recourse in fundamentalist ideologies. As Gaza's conditions get worse so too does its image. Gaza is thus also discursively and symbolically productive as it becomes the other:

in relation to Tel Aviv, or Ashdod and Sderot, and equally in relation to the 'success' of Ramallah.

That representation feeds itself into a larger form. Gaza helps Israel generate and actively produce political-economic values to remain 'at war' with Gaza; it rationalizes larger 'defence' expenditures and new military technologies, generating even more forms of income, even as it also requires and produces more fear, more protection, more barriers, more techniques and technologies rendering Gaza 'small.' Gaza becomes a military test site, a marketing bonanza for Israeli surveillance and 'security' companies, an experimental case for drone warfare for others to emulate, a space wherein military men can combine their tank manoeuvres with their readings of Deleuze.[23]

Gaza is productive for Israel: it distracts from Israel's territorial-political movements in the West Bank, from Israel's attempts to fragment the Palestinian nation and thwart and prevent 'unity governments;' it distracts from Israel's exploration of natural gas reserves off the coast of Gaza, from Israel's funneling of ever more water from underneath Gaza and the West Bank. This larger than life shadow is in part actively produced by Israel as it helps to maintain the status quo, feeds into the imagined and real sense within Israeli society that it is constantly at threat itself.[24] Gaza becomes an Israeli-produced vortex that keeps pulling Israel in.

In the process, Gaza is rendered a more and more extraordinary place: a military testing ground, a social experiment in horror, a nightmare on earth. Gaza bursts at the seams, pushing its symbolism outwards from its tiny territorial confinement. In a negative sense, Gaza generates misunderstandings, misconceptions, stereotypes: the nest of terror, the backwardness of Islam, the innate violence of the Palestinian people, and so on.

But Gaza also pleads scholars, thinkers, writers, artists, and activists to go back to the study of third-world solidarity, of settler colonialism, of anti-imperial resistance, of Frere, Fanon, Lenin, Mao and Che and rethink their theoretical and political contributions all over again. Gaza demonstrates that humanity's history does not move teleologically towards progress, equality, justice, or universal rights but that those move in pocketed and uneven ways, and very often, only for some people. These are ways, too, that Gaza is generative, larger than itself. It spurs connections and begs us to think, rethink, imagine, reimagine.

Gaza is the example that pushes our (dark) scholarship and our politics, their metaphors and terminologies, to their extreme. Gaza is the embodiment of enclosure processes from land to factory to prison to expurgation and the political-economic structures that confine those on the weaker end. Gaza is where Deleuze's 'societies of control' and Foucault's 'panopticon' converge and simultaneously meet their limitations: the ideal architectural figure for modern disciplinary societies and their pervasive inclination to observe and normalize subjects' behaviours by rendering them permanently visible or legible, in the case of the latter, and where enclosure is no longer (or not only) restrained by concrete structures but by a diffuse matrix of information-gathering algorithms, in the case of the first.[25] Gaza illustrates Virilio's 'total war' where the lines between civilians and military populations are not just blurred but have been completely fractured, where everyone inside the gulag is perpetually preparing for war and is thereby denied life. Israel's 'war' in Gaza also demonstrates Virilio's claim of chrono-politics, where the control of the means of instant information, communication, and destruction is the dominant socio-political force, determined by the need for faster and faster spin-control and effective media politics.[26]

Gaza is the latest, and arguably starkest, example of Giorgio Agamben's 'state of exception' where a prolonged state of emergency translates into one government's power and where authority (here Israel) extends beyond the law, or suspends the law, and operates to deprive individuals (here Gazans) of their citizenship, thereby rendering these individuals into 'bare life' — a biological existence that can be sacrificed at anytime by a colonial power which maintains the right to kill with impunity and which has also withdrawn all moral, political, or human responsibilities for that population (here Gaza since disengagement).[27] As Achille Mbembe suggests, Agamben and Foucault's conceptions of biopower (the assemblage of disciplinary power and biopolitics — the latter being, broadly, the process by which lives become subjects of political control and calculations) are no longer sufficient to explain contemporary reconfigurations of the relations among resistance, sacrifice, and terror, or, more simply, contemporary forms of subjugation, of which Gaza is paragon, again. Mbembe argues that we live in an era of necropower (as opposed to biopower), wherein the 'technologies of destruction have become more tactile, more anatomical and sensorial' and where the choice of the sovereign power is not simply the gauging and determining of what kind of life its subjects will live, but to take life away. For Mbembe, the most 'proficient' contemporary execution of necropower is the Israeli occupation of Palestine: where 'vast populations are subjected to conditions of life conferring upon them the status of living dead.'[28]

The political violence waged by Israel against Gaza has also been understood as intentionally designed to kill or erase cities, what Stephen Graham describes as 'urbicide.'[29] Gaza is the systematic devastation of the means of living a modern urban life, a military- and man-made process of 'demodernization.' Through the forcible creation of a chaotic urban hell, Israeli violence produces the self-fulfilling prophecy of the Orientalist discourse of Arab cities: chaotic and disconnected urban worlds 'outside of the modern, figuratively as well as physically,' in the words of Derek Gregory.[30] In the process, Gaza also becomes the (very real) laboratory for new techniques of urban control, pacification, and counterinsurgency warfare. This in turn leads some scholars to declare that Gaza is the horrific future of urban warfare, where the city itself and the conditions which define it become the (new) manifestations of violence and war.[31] For Eyal Weizman, that horrific future goes further, where 'thresholds [...] are tested and pushed: the limits of the law, and the limits of violence that can be inflicted by a state and be internationally tolerated.'[32]

And so Gaza circulates and grows well beyond its confines. Gaza is larger than life because of what it tells us of the world but also because it is where a multitude of our world's processes converge: technologies of confinement, the power of the military, global capitalism, lawfare, omnipresent surveillance, modern-day colonialism, among others. And, in part because it resists, Gaza equally connects to other movements attempting to withstand and negate apartheid, settler-colonialism, neoliberalism, racism, poverty, and various forms of inequalities and exploitation. As such, Gaza emanates outwards. Gaza's shadow reaches all the way to Ferguson, Missouri, for example — in the shared histories of dispossession and continued structural violence against blacks and Gazans, in the impunity with which (white) American policemen and the Israeli military continue to assault black and Palestinian bodies, in the use of similar tactics and visuals of resistance, among other similarities.[33]

This is larger-than-life Gaza: a shadow that looms large in part because Gaza has become so (territorially) inaccessible. Most of what is seen and theorized about Gaza from the outside is about its horrors, destitution, poverty, isolation, abjection; about the immorality and impunity of Israel and the U.S.' very material participation in the support and continuation of this violence; about the silence and compliance of the international community. In short, Gaza comes to stand for the ills of our modern world. This is not Gaza *sui generis* anymore, but a metaphorical Gaza.

But if we are captivated by the horrors of Gaza, we should equally be drawn by the opposite: how grand Gaza is. And here, I return to what makes Gaza large from within its confines: the largeness of Gaza in the Palestinian — and human — struggle.

A Nation's Greatness

Gaza may force us to glimpse into the heart of darkness, but it equally reveals the heart of humanity that never gives up. Gaza is not a footnote,[34] it is the larger than life shadow of the colonizer's fear: a people that cannot be quelled.

Gaza is without a doubt the home of Palestinian resistance. There is no way to understand the history and future of Palestinian nationhood and resistance without including Gaza in that view, and without, simultaneously, reinserting the nation and resistance into Gaza. Gaza is where our resistance is strongest, our sadness most marked, our aloneness most acute, where the world's indifference is the starkest and most embittering. Gaza is expansive because, after all, it is *umm il muqqawameh* (the mother of the resistance). Gaza fights tooth and nail even when you have severed its limbs and broken its jaw. Gaza defies, it screams: you can lock us up. You can squeeze us. You can starve us. You can maim us. You can prevent others from seeing us and from touching us. But we will remain. Gaza is Palestine's willow tree. It will bend and contort, but it has yet to be broken. Gaza continues to stand at the forefront of the story of our homeland. So Gaza is larger than life because of its centrality in the Palestinian condition, not only in its ills and horrors, but in its stubborn presence.

In fact, the more Israel, the US, Egypt, the PA, others beyond Gaza, attempt to 'shrink' Gaza — to territorially contain it, to demoralize it, to marginalize its latest political and religious parties, to de-develop its economy, to keep sending its infrastructures decades and decades back, and so on — the more apparent its centrality and largeness is. This larger-than-life Gaza is precisely what the institutions of Zionism and the Israeli regime have variously tried to prevent and constantly seek to destroy, and continuously fail to do so. This larger-than-life Gaza will endure on Israel's and the world's conscience because it speaks precisely to what we Palestinians have long known: we are not going anywhere.

Gaza is larger than life: captivating, awesome, mythical, mesmerizing, extraordinary, impressive, monumental, unreal, burdensome, miraculous, and most of all, durable. Gaza is our obligation.

Of course one wonders: is it possible? Can you keep surviving? Will you forever resist? Can you remain Palestine's backbone? Can you keep on breathing life into our cause? Can you withstand the ugliness and viciousness of colonialism and militarism? Can you overcome the horrors of our world? Are you larger than life?

Yes, Gaza answers.

DIARY, 20 JULY 2014[1]

Haidar Eid

Saturday 19 July, 6pm

It is summer in Gaza. Ramadan. Families should be together, sitting on the rooftops, having *iftar*, cutting open a red, juicy watermelon, eating roasted pumpkin seeds, shelling nuts, going to the mosque, staying awake late into the night, praying. It is the time to take our children to the beach, to tease them for being too clever if they got very high marks, and to tease them for not being very clever if they did not get high marks. It is the time to visit family in Sheikh Radwan, in Rafah, in Khan Younis, to have *iftar* with brothers and sisters, and nieces and nephews. But we have not dared to leave our homes for the last twelve days.

We have to confess to our children that we cannot observe Ramadan like everyone else. We are Palestinian, so our lives are different, are forced to be different. We have land that the Israelis want. We are different, we have Israelis in our lives. We are the *goyim*, the unwanted other, the native American, the *nigger* of the American South, the *kaffir* of South Africa.

Sunday 20 July, Midnight

A black, dark summer night. No water, no electricity. The smell of smoke and fear and panic fills the night. The relentless sound of Israeli shelling: thump, thump, thump. All night long. Huge explosions in the east of Gaza,

29

in Shejaiya: the only mistake of the people there is that they live right next door to Israel and they were born into the wrong religion. So they must endure multiple explosions all night long. Ambulances are not allowed in. The Red Cross does not go in — too dangerous. So what will the people there do? Sit with their injured and dead?

That sound of non-stop explosions — it drives us mad with anger, with fear, with despair. How many are dying? How many are in pain? Where is the world? They told them to run away from there because they are going to attack, but where do you run to in Gaza? The borders are closed. It is the Israelis who want the borders closed, but it is also the Israelis who say 'run away.'

2am

Summer in Gaza. We should be walking on the shores of the beautiful Mediterranean, enjoying the cool breeze now that the sun has gone down. Young people should be playing night football, commiserating with those who supported Brazil in the World Cup, retelling every moment of excellence in Colombia's games, insulting those who supported Germany, making Spain's supporters the butt of a thousand jokes. Young people should be dancing *dabke*, staging theatre shows, planning *eid*.

But this is Gaza under Israeli bombardment and young people here have to hold on tight to the hands of their young siblings, while at the same time checking that the road is clear, that the sky is clear. Sometimes they must carry a mother, a grandmother, a baby, and they must run, run, run, quick before the drones see us! Quick before an Israeli filled with hate pulls the trigger, quick before an American-made missile blows us into the sky so that we become part of that big, yellow flame that lights up the dark, Gaza night.

4am

Can't sleep, thinking about the people being attacked. F-16s are flying next to my window! With every explosion, I wonder: Who? How many? What is their state now? Who is gone? Who is left? Where will it end? I know what death tastes like now.

DIARY, 20 JULY 2014

8am

Another sleepless night. The Israelis will not allow the Red Cross into Shejaiya! And the bombings continue with no one to pick up the bodies on the streets, no one to help the injured. Thousands of families walking into Gaza City from the north, from the east, walking away from the approaching Israeli army. Is this 1948? Or 1967?

12 noon

17 children, 18 women, 14 elderly (so far) in Shejaiya, among 60 dead. Today the Israeli war machine butchered 104; the number of those injured in Gaza so far is 3000. There is no gauze in the hospitals, no painkillers, no anesthetic for operations, no beds, no sleep for the doctors, no silence for the injured.

3pm

Random shelling and air strikes across the Gaza Strip. Eight killed in Remal, my neighborhood.

5:40pm

The words of Mark Regev pierce my incredulous ears. I look outside and see humungous billows of thick grey smoke, the same smoke that has engulfed Gaza for the last twelve days, the same smoke that has blocked out the sun and the blue Mediterranean Sea for the last twenty-four hours. This spokesman of the Israeli apartheid regime is justifying the killing of Palestinian civilians in Shejaiya because the most 'moral' army in the world dropped pamphlets to tell people to leave their homes before they bombed. 'Leave your homes or we will kill and rape you' — that's what the Haganah and the Stern Gang told my parents in 1948. My parents died dreaming of returning to their Zarnouqa. There was no satellite television then, no Facebook, no Twitter, no cell phones, no way to tell the world what was happening to them. So much technology, so much communication, so many words, so little action, so little change. Gaza oh my Gaza! Palestine, oh my Palestine! My land of sad oranges!

8pm

Another evening, another hour of Israeli bombardment of the Gaza Strip. Will Beit Hanoun and/or Beit Lahiya, in the north, witness the second massacre tonight? How many should be killed in order to convince journalists and editors in London and New York to call it a massacre?

Gaza, the Sharpeville, the Guernica of Palestine will become our Saigon! We cannot afford despair.

Signposts on the road to liberation[2]
Haidar Eid

On my notebooks from school
On my desk and the trees
On the sand on the snow
I write your name
On every page read
On all the white sheets
Stone blood paper or ash
I write your name ...
Liberty

Paul Eluard

Edward Said wrote extensively about the necessity of writing the Palestinian narrative.[3] But he also argued, very eloquently, that we were never allowed to do so. Now, we in Gaza have decided to write our narratives, sometimes with blood.

Because they leave a mark on our individual and collective consciousness, we call them martyrs. Those who took up arms or pens — Che Guevara, Ghassan Kanafani, Naji al-Ali, Dalal Mughrabi, Shadia Abu Ghazaleh, Steve Biko, Salavador Allende, Rosa Luxemburg, Patrice Lumumba, to mention but a few — have booked their places there.

But there are others, much younger, unknown to many, who have played a major role in the formation of our consciousness. They visit me every night; I see them in my dreams. I talk to them: I discuss serious issues with them, more serious than any living person can imagine.

At 139 square miles, Gaza is the largest refugee camp on earth, a daily reminder of the ongoing *Nakba*. The inhabitants of Gaza have become the most unwanted Palestinians, the black heart that no one wants to see, the 'Negroes' of the American south, the black natives of apartheid South Africa. The surplus population that the powerful, macho, white Ashkenazi Israeli cannot coexist with.

Landmarks

The years 1987, 2009, 2012 and now 2014 are signposts on the road to our liberation. But they have also been landmarks in the formation of my own consciousness, not unlike those left by the great martyrs mentioned above. 1987: Ashraf Eid, 15 years old, my cousin's son/sun. One bullet, shot by an Israeli sniper in Rafah, penetrated his small heart. It was the end of a long fasting day during the holy month of Ramadan. One bullet, the end of Ashraf's life, a mark on my consciousness.

2009: Maather Abu Znaid, 24, my student. I was teaching my first course, 'The Novel,' at al-Aqsa University in 2005 in Khan Younis. I taught two novels, one by Ghassan Kanafani and, the other, ironically, by the racist writer and Nobel Laureate V.S. Naipaul. Students know me to be 'strict' and 'stingy' in giving marks, but Maather got 92 percent, a mark I rarely award. She graduated with high honors — an intelligent student with big, expansive dreams. She wanted to further her studies, but in Gaza, dreams fly away. During the Gaza massacre of 2009, Maather was targeted and hit by a drone missile as she left her house. Her family is still trying to find parts of her body, if they ever can. That was a dream cut short. One drone missile, end of dreams; another mark on my consciousness.

2009: 44-year old Samir Muhammad was executed with a single bullet to the heart in front of his wife and children. The Israeli army refused to let an ambulance pick up his corpse for eleven days so his family had to wait for the assault to stop before they could bury him. His father, Rashid, told me in agonizing detail how he had the excruciatingly painful experience of looking at, touching, kissing and then burying the decomposed body of his son. Rashid is originally from my parents' village, Zarnouqa; he knew them well. Samir could have been me. Single bullet: Zarnouqa is not far.

2009: Muhammad Samouni, 10, was found lying next to the bodies of his mother and siblings, five days after they were killed. He would tell you what he has been telling everyone — that his brother woke suddenly after being asleep for a long time. His brother told him that he was hungry, asked for a tomato to eat and then died. A torch in the dark depths of my consciousness.

2009: Ismat, 11, and Alaa Qirm, 12, whose house in Gaza City was shelled with artillery and phosphorous bombs — bombs which burned them to death together with their father, leaving behind their fourteen-year-old sister Amira. Alone, injured and terrified, Amira crawled 500 meters on her knees to a house close by which happened to be my cousin's home. It was empty because the family had fled when the Israeli attack began. She stayed there for four days, surviving only on water. When my cousin returned to get clothes for his family, he found Amira, weak and close to death. The bodies of her siblings and father were decomposed. Another deep scar left in the depths of my consciousness.

2014: Najla al-Haj, a student at al-Aqsa University, killed with her family, in an Israeli air strike on the home of her family in Khan Younis in southern Gaza. She was talking to her university friends online just a few hours before. Hanadi, another student, as well as my 18-year-old niece Shimo, only learned of their friend's death hours later when they awoke for *suhur*, the Ramadan pre-fast meal. Hanadi went immediately to Najla's Facebook page. The last thing Najla wrote was: 'God be with us. Oh, hello martyrdom.' Najla al-Haj died with seven others from her family. One airstrike, martyrdom of an entire family; a signpost on the road back to Haifa.

Torment

The fact that these Palestinians were not born to Jewish mothers is enough reason to deprive them of their right to live equally with the citizens of the state of Israel.[4] Like the black natives of South Africa, they must be isolated in a bantustan, in accordance with the terms of the 1993 Oslo Accords. If those corralled into a cage show any resistance to this plan, they must be severely punished — sometimes by a single bullet, sometimes by missiles made in the United States, and sometimes by phosphorus bombs.

How I can contribute to make their deaths a meaningful one is the question that has been tormenting me for years. Being a teacher of resistance literature, two Palestinian novels have also left their mark: Ghassan Kanafani's *Men in the Sun* and *All That is Left to You*. In the former, we, Palestinian refugees, are the weaker party: the passive, hiding victims who dare not bang on the walls of the searingly hot tanker truck in which we are concealed.

But in *All That is Left to You*, Hamid, like me a refugee, is the Palestinian protagonist who chooses to act and become an agent of change. If this brings death, it will be a death which opens up possibilities for a better life to others.

Similarly, the offer that is given to us in Gaza and Palestine today is that we can either have a dignified death as we struggle or we can continue to live in slavery. Those who left a mark on my consciousness made the former choice and allowed us to live. The Palestinian people, and Gazans in particular, have been living an unending massacre since 1948. We can no longer negotiate about improving the conditions of oppression; it is either the full menu of rights, or nothing. And that means the end of occupation, apartheid and colonialism.

Liberation, not Coordination

At the end of the massacre of 180 people, the vast majority civilians, in November 2012, we were told that the end of the massacre would lead to the lifting of the siege. That did not happen. Now, the lifting of the siege is not enough. When this barbaric attack ends with the victory of the Palestinian people, we do not want a Palestinian Authority, nor Oslo Accords, nor 'security coordination.'

Like the previous massacres in 2009 and 2012, the current one must become a signpost on our long walk to liberation. Liberation is the antithesis of Oslo, and the racist two-state solution. Any revolutionary alternative offered by resistance on the ground must, therefore, divorce itself from all previous agreements.

The end of this genocidal war must necessarily mean the end of Oslo because, simply put, the Oslo Accords are the equivalent of slavery, as there is nothing to lose but our chains and our refugee tents.

Ashraf, Maather, Najla, Ismat, Alaa, Muhammad and Samir deserve better: a free country in which their names are signposted on the streets of Haifa, Jaffa and Zarnouqa.

GHAZEH EL SUMUD: CONFRONTING ISRAELI MASS TORTURE

Said Shehadeh

Ghazeh el sumud, meaning Gaza the symbol of steadfastness, were the words Palestinians chanted to the world and to themselves, sometimes in their sleep, as the horrifying images of torn Gazan bodies started to (re-) emerge from news outlets. Another Israeli assault on Gaza, a summer war this time. The significance of the metaphor of Gaza as the paragon of resistance, resilience, and *sumud* (steadfastness), lies in its promise to console us and, at the same time, instill us with hope that the oppressed and disempowered are not defeated. While an interesting question in its own right, this paper does not explore how the recent war in Gaza impacted us, the world outside of Gaza. Rather, it is an effort to understand the traumatic experiences of those who lived through the war and its aftermath. What I argue in the following pages is that the Israeli war on Gaza was designed to engineer trauma on a massive scale, and amounts to mass torture inflicted on the entire Gazan population. The choice of *sumud* as a metaphor for Gaza is especially apt in this context, since the concept of *sumud* was historically used to signify the capacity of Palestinian prisoners to resist torture while in Israeli prisons. Literally translating as steadfastness in the face of oppression, *sumud* is a core tenet in the 'Palestinian philosophy of confrontation' and resistance to colonial occupation in general, and particularly to torture in Israeli colonial prisons.[1]

The Summer War

On 8 July 2014 Israel launched yet another devastating war on Gaza, the fourth since 2006. Compared to previous times, this round of slaughter was the longest and most vicious, leaving over two thousand Palestinians dead, mostly civilians, over eleven thousand injured, and whole-scale destruction of neighborhoods and infrastructure. Operation Protective Edge, as it was codenamed by the Israeli military (insidiously disguising the brutality of their military assault as self-defense), was unprecedented on many levels. This was the prevalent sentiment in the testimonies of the Gazans I had the privilege of meeting and working with during and after the war, who described the human devastation to be the most severe and destructive thus far, surpassing even the 1967 war, when the Gaza strip was occupied by the Israeli military. Similarly, the initial reports from local and international relief organizations in Gaza reported that the level of destruction and killing in this war was unprecedented.[2] What was also unprecedented, as I argue in this paper, is the severity of psychological suffering intentionally inflicted on an entire population, for political purposes, mainly to break the Gaza 'model of resistance and resilience.'

Most of the post-war assessments focus predominantly on the enormous civilian death toll and injured persons, especially children, as well as the massive destruction to homes, factories, public (governmental) buildings and infrastructure. Indeed, the numbers speak for themselves: 1.8 million people, trapped in a small costal enclave of 365 square kilometers, mercilessly bombarded from the air, land and sea by the sixth strongest military in the world,[3] with no means of escape. Over 2,200 Palestinians were killed, 77 percent of whom were civilians, including 521 children and 297 women. According to a report by the Al-Mezan Center for Human Rights,[4] at least 999 of the casualties were killed in their own homes, including 329 children and 212 women. An additional 233 people were killed in the vicinity of their houses; many of whom were fleeing their homes as a result of the attacks by the Israeli military. Another report[5] found that 'many fatalities involved multiple family members, with at least 142 Palestinian families having three or more members killed in the same incident, for a total of 739 fatalities.' Beyond the enormous death toll and over 11,200 injuries, there were about half a million people, 26 percent of the population, who became internally displaced during the war as a result of the total or partial destruction of their homes.[6] The aerial bombardment systematically targeted schools (26 completely destroyed), hospitals (15 damaged, 6 shut down), factories, shopping malls, business centers, government buildings and property, mosques (161 damaged or destroyed), as well as livestock farms, and agricultural lands.[7] The deliberate and widespread targeting of the already fragile infrastructure of the Gaza Strip, including the electricity,[8] sewage and water networks, drove the entire population into a humanitarian disaster that was unprecedented in its severity and scope.

These post-war statistics regarding the human and financial costs of the war on Gaza do not fully capture the scope and depth of human suffering inflicted. To gain such an understanding, one needs to examine the psychological impact of the war, as experienced by its survivors. The psychological reality created by the 50-day military assault on Gaza is often overlooked or dismissed as an indirect and intangible consequence of the war. However, the psychological sequela of the war is neither incidental nor secondary. In fact, I contend that it is the most disturbing and ominous aspect of this war because it reveals a deliberate and systematic effort at engineering mass torture and trauma against an entire civilian population.

The psychological insights offered here stem in large part from the work I carried out with some of the Gazan children, women, and men who were seriously injured during the 50-day war on Gaza, and who were transferred to hospitals in the West Bank and East Jerusalem for medical treatment. I also draw on testimonies of individuals from the Gaza Strip I counseled over the phone during the war. As a clinical psychologist providing psychological first aid and crisis intervention to the injured Gazans and their family members accompanying them, I bore witness to testimonies of their horrifying traumatic experiences that not only left them maimed, but oftentimes also resulted in the killing of their family members. Their heart-wrenching testimonies revealed a psychological reality of horror and extreme trauma, which was imposed on the entire Gazan population. This is the true hidden casualty of this war.

In order to better understand the reality of war and its aftermath for the people of Gaza, one needs to place the recent war on Gaza in its proper historical and political context. A de-contextualized view of the post-war conditions in Gaza, when seen merely as a 'humanitarian crisis' with miscarried attempts at quantifying human suffering through war statistics, does little to capture the catastrophic experiences of the people of Gaza. Some may even argue that it distorts reality, and avoids the fact that this is a man-made disaster, deliberately and systematically inflicted by Israel on a civilian population, using the most sophisticated military technologies.

Historical Context

The Gaza Strip is often portrayed in contemporary mainstream media as a distinct geographic and political entity, exceptionalized by its 'crushing poverty, suffocating crowdedness, and mind-numbing isolation.'[9] A more accurate view of the Gaza Strip is to see it as part of the larger Palestinian nation, which includes the West Bank, historical Palestine and the Diaspora, all vexed by the Zionist colonial project in Palestine that started over a century ago. In his insightful analysis, Darryl Li suggests understanding the Gaza Strip and the West Bank as 'representing two different phases of a common process of segregation, confinement, and surveillance produced by the Zionist project.'[10] He argues that the Gaza Strip has historically been used by the Israeli occupation as a laboratory, in which colonial policies of confinement, management and control of the Palestinian population are tested and refined, later to be replicated in the West Bank. The overarching principle of the Israeli colonial policies against the Palestinians, as Li puts it, is 'continuously experimenting in search of an optimal balance between maximum control over the territory and minimum responsibility for its non-Jewish population.'[11] Following the Israeli disengagement from Gaza in 2006, and the suffocating siege that followed, this policy appears to have been highly successful. In effect, 25 percent of the global Palestinian population currently lives under Israeli control, while confined to 1.4 percent of the territory of (Mandatory) Palestine.[12]

The Gaza Strip enclosure was initially described as the world's largest prison, but this metaphor no longer applies. As Li writes, 'Israel now treats the Strip more like a zoo. For running a prison is about constraining or repressing freedom; in a zoo, the question is rather how to keep those held inside alive, with an eye to how outsiders might see them. The question of freedom is never raised.'[13] Similarly, Jeff Halper describes the Israeli treatment of Palestinians as that of 'warehousing,' which he claims is 'worse than apartheid.'[14] He adds, 'It does not even pretend to find a political framework for 'separate development,' it simply jails the oppressed and robs them of all their collective and individual rights. It is the ultimate form of oppression before actual genocide.'[15] In recent years, we have seen various mechanisms of confinement, management and control, which were tested and refined in the Gaza Strip, being replicated in the West Bank. For one, the segregation barrier — spiraling throughout the West Bank, trisecting the area, and encircling whole Palestinian cities — recreates Gaza Strip-like enclaves in the West Bank; Qalqilya is the most obvious example to date. Similarly, we have also witnessed the transformation, under international funding, of many of the West Bank checkpoints into border 'terminals,' à la Erez Crossing.

The Gaza experiment also demonstrates how the Israeli occupation modified the methods of control over the Palestinian population within such enclosures, from 'up and close' military control, to one that is 'from a distance.' Surveillance and control of the population was then adequately achieved by using airpower, as well as creating buffer zones around the separation barriers, which requires much less manpower, and reduces the risk to Israeli soldiers.[16] As the four wars on Gaza between 2006 and 2014 have demonstrated, Israel is relying predominantly on its airpower, via its fighter jets, helicopters and drones, to monitor and control the encaged Palestinian population. This policy was articulated back in 2004 by Maj. Gen. Amos Yadlin, the head of Israeli military intelligence at the time, who stated: 'Our vision of air control zeroes in on the notion of control. We're looking at how you control a city or a territory from the air when it's no longer legitimate to hold or occupy that territory on the ground.'[17]

At the outset of the 2014 war on Gaza, we seem to be stuck in a political dead-end perpetuated by racial segregation and isolation of Palestinian communities, the ever-expanding colonial settlements in the West Bank, as well as the ongoing measured military operations — punctuated by intermittent large-scale assaults on Gaza. Israel's colonial objective has been to manage rather than resolve the conflict, optimizing the policy of maximum control over the land and minimum responsibility for the Palestinians under its occupation. Palestinians, on their end, maintain their impregnable resistance to the colonial control over every aspect of their lives, whether physically, mentally, symbolically, or spiritually. The political deadlock becomes inevitable when the native's resistance is adequately met by the colonizer's control, as both parties implicitly follow the expected rules of the game set by the colonizer: exercising optimal control over the natives' physical and psychological space to manage and contain their resistance, as long as the balance of power is not seriously threatened. Within this framework, the elimination of the native's resistance was deemed largely an aspirational goal, without committing genocide proper, as is evident by the growing incitement to genocide against Palestinians, before and after the war, which has 'manifested across many levels of Israeli society.'[18] The status quo is, perhaps, best exemplified by the Israeli 8-year-siege on Gaza, whose policy was to keep Gazans on a minimal calorie count of 2279 calories per day.[19] The purpose of this was succinctly summed up by Dov Weissglass, then senior advisor of Israeli Prime Minister Ehud Olmert, as 'to put the Palestinians on a diet, but not to make them die of hunger.'[20]

A Shift in the Colonial Paradigm

The first real threat to this status quo, as I see it, has been the recent unbreakable armed resistance in Gaza that disrupted the lives of over 70 percent of Israel's population.[21] For Israelis, the threat was never an existential one, but rather a psychological one, as their illusion of safety was threatened by the primitive rockets launched from the Gaza Strip. This threat appears to have triggered a dramatic response from the current Israeli government, military, media and society at large. The collective Zionist sentiment seems to have been that of outrage over the fact that the Gazans 'broke the rules of the game' when they brought the conflict back closer to their home. Israel, it would seem, was forced to acknowledge that occupation, and the continuation of the colonial-settler project in general, came at a cost — and a hefty one indeed. Israel sustained considerable financial, physical and psychological losses, not least of which was the unexpected loss of relatively high number of soldiers, many of whom were considered the best-trained elite combatants. The effectiveness of the resistance in Gaza was unexpected and succeeded in upsetting that status quo.

The Israeli military started the bombing campaign on Gaza on an almost biennial routine, which according to Noam Chomsky 'amount[s] to shooting fish in a pond' and 'is called "mowing the lawn" in Israeli parlance.'[22] At the outset of the 2014 war on Gaza, the bombing campaign appeared to have followed a similar script to previous wars, which targeted the Gaza infrastructure, governmental buildings and personnel, social and educational institutions, as well as the homes of resistance fighters. However, unlike other wars, the Israeli aerial and artillery bombardments categorically failed to diminish or deter the resistance's rocket firing on

Israeli settlements, which have reached a radius of over 100 kilometers and affected 70 percent of the Israeli population.[23] The ground incursion on Gaza also failed to exact a military blow to the resistance, and Israeli ground troops suffered heavy losses, with scores of soldiers killed and hundreds injured. The military response that followed was arguably different from what preceded in the early days of the war, and different from previous wars. The difference was not only quantitative, measured by the enormous number of lives, homes, and infrastructure destroyed — especially in areas of Shejaiya, Khuza'a, Khan Younis, and Rafah, where wholesale devastation and massacres were committed. There was also a qualitative difference born out of the anguish and terror that followed the indiscriminate bombing of homes and residential buildings/towers, which marked all the people of Gaza as potential targets for aerial assassinations. What we witnessed in the later phases of the Israeli assault on Gaza gave early indication of a shift in the colonial paradigm, from managing and controlling the resistance, to attempts at destroying it psychologically: mainly by breaking the Palestinian psyche and the social fabric from which it draws its resilience.

This shift in the colonial paradigm was also felt by the Gazans I counseled at the hospitals. As I listened to their testimonies, reflecting out loud on their war experiences, I — like them — tried with great difficulty to make sense of this new psychological reality they were forced to live in. The struggle to comprehend the situation was not due to our limited ability to process and manage the information at hand, but rather because it was outside of what we imagined possible in our historical relationship with the Israeli occupier. The ferocity and cruelty of the aerial and artillery bombing campaign, with its wholesale indiscriminate bombardment of civilians and residential areas, and elimination of entire families, created a psychological reality of extreme unsafety, uncontrollability, and unpredictability.

Unsafety, Unpredictability and Learned Helplessness

What was it like, then, for the people of Gaza to live through this 50-day war? Drawing on testimonies from some of the children, men, and women I worked with in the aftermath of the war, I will try to describe this psychological reality, as it was conveyed to me. First, I should note that the experiences of my interlocutors were surprisingly consistent across various age groups and social strata. Indeed, this reality appears to be shared by

43

most if not all of the people in Gaza. It is best summed up by a statement I heard repeated many times from the survivors: 'nobody was safe.' There was nothing anyone could do to secure any semblance of control over whether they would survive the night or not. The incessant sound of drones hovering above their heads — locally referred to as *zanana*[24] or buzzer — served as a constant reminder of the sudden and unpredictable death that comes from the sky. This fear of a death from above became a constant and imminent threat to one's life, and worse still, to the lives of family members and loved ones. Parents were unable to fulfill their most basic and important functions: protecting their children from harm. Psychologically, this caused extreme anguish to the parents and undermined their sense of agency and self-confidence. In turn, this left the children further vulnerable to anxieties, as their primary sources of protection, their parents, were rendered helpless.

Augmenting the suffering Gazans had to endure was the repeated exposure to gruesome scenes of dead bodies, and body parts, lying in pools of blood after being torn apart by high-intensity explosives. The constant threat of Israeli bombings prevented the evacuation of bodies from the streets and homes, exposing the population to scenes of bodies in various states of decomposition for prolonged periods of time. All these gory scenes instilled intense experiences of horror in a large segment of the population. The scope of horror appears to have been designed to impose catastrophic traumas on the Palestinian population as a whole, and to induce the mental breakdown of individuals, families, and communities.

A core feature of this new psychological reality was the feeling of helplessness, forced on the entire population of Gaza. The notion is akin to Seligman's concept of *learned helplessness*. Martin Seligman's famous (or rather infamous) 1967 experiments, featured dogs that were (inadvertently) subjected to unpredictable electric shocks, while tied up, with no means of escape. They were then placed in a shuttle box comprized of two compartments separated by a low barrier, where they were subjected to electric shocks in one compartment. In this experimental model, the dogs were expected to learn the avoidance behavior of jumping over to the other side in order to escape electric shocks. However, as Seligman discovered, the dogs that were previously subjected to inescapable electric shocks failed to learn the escape behavior, and tended to lie still, and whimper. He coined the term *learned helplessness* to refer to such acquired behaviors in which one learns that there is nothing one can do when faced with loss of personal control over one's life.[25] When applied to humans, repeated traumatic experiences under situations of totalitarian control (under which people lose all control over events in their lives) conditions one to give up without trying, and ultimately lose all motivation and interest in life. Learned helplessness, therefore, results in disruptions to one's self-concept and personality. It is no surprise then that it is a cornerstone of interrogation and torture manuals, whose sole purpose is to break an individual's will to fight back and resist his interrogator.

The psychological reality of the people of Gaza during the recent war bears uncanny resemblance to Seligman's experiments: 1.8 million Palestinians trapped in a small coastal enclave of 365 square kilometers, locked in from the sea and all land borders with Israel and Egypt, mercilessly bombarded with high-intensity explosives, in an unpredictable manner for 50 days, with no possibility of escape or adequate shelter to avoid the life-threatening situation. The impossible choice Gazans were afforded was whether their family should all sleep in one room to die together if their home was bombed, or sleep in different rooms to maximize the chances of at least some family members surviving. Despite their best efforts, they were unable to predict where the next bomb might fall. The aerial and artillery bombardments were, by design, unpredictable. While such cruel experimentation on animals has (thankfully) long been outlawed in scientific circles, the 'Gaza experiment,' which engineered trauma and learned helplessness on a large human population, was de facto sanctioned by Israel and its supporters throughout this war.

Another tactic that served to engender feelings of helplessness among the Gazans has been the 'double tapping' strikes. A report by Physicians for Human Rights-Israel revealed that the Israeli military deliberately targeted paramedics and initial responders who were first to arrive at a bloodied scene of an air strike to assist the wounded, only to be bombed by a second strike a few minutes later.[26] The logic behind such war crimes, while beyond any moral reasoning, can nonetheless be understood in terms of its terror-inducing value. The message it carries to the survivors of bombings (and those who witness it) is that ambulances will not be allowed to take them to the hospital. No one will be coming to save them. Family and community members, who dare rush to their aid, will also be bombed. Both survivors and witnesses were therefore rendered helpless as they were forced to witness the carnage, without being able to do anything about it. The emotional wound inflicted by this traumatic experience was described by one of my interlocutors as a profound sense of impotence, shame and guilt.

Beyond the sense of complete loss of safety or control over one's fate, there were also deliberate disruptions to all aspects of daily life. Perhaps the gravest mass disruption was to the population's sleep habits. The bombardments by air, sea, and land seem to have been meticulously timed around the Gazans' sleep schedule, to ensure that the entire population would remain sleep deprived, night after night for days on end. During Ramadan, for example, the sustained bombings were intensified around 1am, right as people would typically go to bed, and then again after 4am, following the predawn breakfast, *suhur,* when people are expected to go back to sleep. As the war continued past the month of Ramadan, the timing of the nightly bombardment of the civilian population was adjusted to the change in the Gazans' sleep schedule, eliminating any doubt as to the reason for this particular bombing schedule: a policy of collective sleep deprivation across all of the Gaza strip. While fear of dying is enough to keep any sane person awake all night, the Israeli military also exposed the population to noxious sensory stimulations, across various modalities, including visual (illumination flares), auditory (deafening explosions), and tactile (ground-shaking explosions that rattle even the sturdiest of buildings).

In addition, the Israeli military conducted nerve-wracking psychological warfare against the people of Gaza. This included repeated harassment over the phone, text messages, and leaflets dropped from planes over their neighborhoods. Palestinian television broadcasts in Gaza were routinely intercepted to expose the population to Israeli propaganda messages.[27] At times the messages would threaten to bomb their home; at other times it would urge them to inform on resistance fighters, and betray their people;[28] and still other times would taunt the people with statements regarding the futility of resistance in the face of the might of the Israeli army.[29] According to Israeli propaganda, this was a so-called humanitarian gesture to minimize collateral damage by warning the civilian population before a pending aerial assault on their homes. In reality, these communications were part of the scare tactics aimed at instilling fear and terror. This was especially evident in light of the fact that many of the bombings came without any warning, and some warnings came without any bombings — all designed to maintain the conditions of unpredictability and uncontrollability throughout the Gaza Strip. This psychological warfare, before and after air strikes, takes on a threatening and menacing character, especially to a population left helpless in the face of these deadly assaults. One poignant example is an incident that happened with a Gazan woman I counseled while she was accompanying her relative, a young child who had been severely injured during an air strike that targeted her home. The woman, who was also traumatized by the murder of three of her family members in the same bombing attack, received a phone call from Israeli intelligence demanding she inform on resistance fighters, all while she was at a hospital in East Jerusalem. That phone call was enough to retraumatize the woman, reminding her of the atrocities she had witnessed, and the danger her family in Gaza was still in, effectively depriving her of the brief respite she had had from the war since leaving the Gaza Strip.

Policy of Mass Torture

How, then, can we explain the Israeli policy behind all these oppressive acts of physical and psychological aggression against the Palestinians in Gaza? The answer, I contend, is that it was a deliberate policy of torture executed on a massive scale against the entire population of Gaza, during the 50-day war. Torture, as defined by the UN Convention Against Torture and other Acts of Cruel, Inhuman or Degrading Treatment, or UNCAT, is:

> any act by which severe pain or suffering, whether physical or mental, is intentionally inflicted on a person for such purposes as obtaining from him or a third person information or a confession, punishing him for an act he or a third person has committed or is suspected of having committed, or intimidating or coercing him or a third person, or for any reason based on discrimination of any kind, when such pain or suffering is inflicted by or at the instigation of or with the consent or acquiescence of a public official or other person acting in an official capacity. It does not include pain or suffering arising only from, inherent in or incidental to lawful sanctions.[30]

According to the above definition, the intentional infliction of 'severe pain or suffering, whether physical or mental', involving a public official and carried out for a specific purpose, is torture.[31] I make no distinction here between physical and psychological torture. While the methods of torture may differ, subjectively the experience of severe pain and suffering for the victim is one and the same. As Hernán Reyes argues:

[T]he definition of torture is firmly based on "severe pain and suffering". The fact that this notion is qualified as being both "physical and mental" is a recognition that both aspects go together. Physical torture produces both physical and mental suffering; the same applies to psychological torture. It therefore becomes difficult to isolate psychological torture per se as a separate entity and define its different features.[32]

This view was also shared by Professor Peter Kooijmans, the UN Special Rapporteur on Torture and Other Cruel, Inhuman and Degrading Treatment or Punishment, who stated that '[t]his distinction [between physical and psychological torture] seems to have more relevance for the means by which torture is practised than for its character. Almost invariably the effect of torture, by whatever means it may have been practised, is physical and psychological…[a] common effect is the disintegration of the personality.'[33]

Thus, if we apply this framework to examine the aggregate of Israeli assaults against the Palestinian population in the Gaza Strip, as detailed above, it becomes clear that these measures constitute torture. The methods of physical and psychological torture included the following:

- Measures to induce extreme fear of death or injury
- Exposure to gory scenes of deaths and injuries, to generate feelings of intense horror and fear
- Witnessing physical or perceived harm to family members and loved ones
- Engendering feelings of extreme helplessness and dependency
- Exposure to repeated harassing messages of humiliation
- Sleep deprivation
- Sensory disruptions, such as alternating between complete darkness, after bombing the only power plant in the Gaza Strip, and cutting all the electricity supplies,[34] and then invasive exposure to illumination flares throughout the night.

Taken separately, some of these measures might seem mere forms of ill-treatment or collective punishment. However, as Reyes points out, the cumulative effects of all these methods together, used over a prolonged period of time, amplifies the pain and suffering of the torture victim.[35] He adds:

[A]ll these methods, used together, form a system deliberately designed to wear and break down, and ultimately also to disrupt the senses and personality. The effect over a prolonged period of time of this "grouping of methods" has to be considered as part and parcel of the effects of psychological torture.[36]

The perpetrator in this case is the state of Israel. Considering the meticulous planning and orchestration of these cruel measures, there can be little doubt as to Israel's intentionality. Given that torture is classified by the international conventions as a crime against humanity, and a war crime when committed during armed conflict, it is expected that Israel would not officially endorse this policy, or admit to reverting to it in its military operation against Gaza. However, Israel's military actions and public statements speak for themselves. There is ample evidence of Israel's punitive intentions toward Gaza from the surge of racist incitement to genocide, which was 'manifested across many levels of Israeli society, on both social and traditional media, from football fans, police officers, media commentators, religious leaders, legislators, and government ministers,' as well as from the messages by Israeli intelligence officers to the Gazan population — whether in the leaflets dropped from planes, the hacked television broadcasts, or the threatening phone calls and text messages.[37]

The mass torture committed against Gaza had several political objectives. Firstly, the purpose was to pound into the minds of the indigenous population — with about 20,000 tons of explosives, the equivalent of the nuclear bomb dropped by the U.S. on Nagasaki[38] — the notion that resistance to Israel's omnipresent control and dominance is futile. In the Israeli media, political pundits reframed this objective as reasserting the deterrence capabilities of the Israeli army. Another objective included gathering intelligence on the ground, by forcing individuals to inform on each other, using direct threats to their lives and the lives of their family. Finally, it is contended that the mass torture was used to punish Gazans for supporting the resistance and for not revolting against the ruling Hamas government. In effect, the intent seems to have been the breaking of the Gazans' will to fight for their freedom, which was pragmatically framed as a struggle to end the suffocating siege over the Gaza Strip. Thus, when the usual means of coercion — for example, targeting infrastructure and governmental buildings — failed to break the resistance and diminish its public support, the objective shifted to target the Gazans' psychological capacity to endure and resist. This meant applying extreme physical and psychological stress on individuals, families and entire communities, to produce large-scale mental collapse, which in turn could potentially fragment the society.

The use of torture for political purposes is well documented. For instance, Ebert & Dyck claim that '[w]hen used in a political context, torture has as its goal the creation of a *living dead* [sic], whose brokenness is intended to serve as a deterrent to others; it is a means of exercising systematic control over individuals, groups, and the entire community.'[39] Similarly, Hárdi & Kroo[40] commented on the intergenerational transmission of torture trauma and its devastating effects on victims and their community. 'The aim of torture,' they add, 'is the destruction of one's identity, the core of the personality, making the victim, and then his/her children, and the children of the children incapable of leading a "normal" daily life.'[41]

Torture is often seen as an interpersonal act of cruelty between an individual and his/her torturer(s), typically taking place in the context of interrogation. References to mass torture in literature or media are extant. Mostly, these seem to denote instances whereby a large number of people are subjected to interpersonal torture in the interrogation room. One such example is the so-called Caesar report that revealed evidence of torture and execution of tens and likely hundreds of thousands of Syrians by the Assad regime inside governmental detention centers.[42] I use the term *mass torture* to describe the intentional mass infliction of severe pain and suffering by a regime against an entire collective for the purpose of subjugation and/or punishment. One case that bears closer semblance to the Gaza model is the U.S. drone war on Pakistan, Yemen, and Somalia, where thousands of people have been killed since 2002, and hundred of thousands continue to live in fear under the constant threat of drone attacks.[43] One research project revealed the severe and longstanding impact of these measures on the physical and psychological wellbeing of people in Pakistan.[44] Metin Başoğlu analyzed these findings from a learning theory perspective and drew comparisons between torture and the psychological corollary of drone attacks.[45] The common denominators, he argues, are the prolonged exposure to 'uncontrollable' and 'unpredictable' stressors that threaten the physical and/or psychological wellbeing of individuals, while trapped in an inescapable environment, and leading to intense fear-induced helplessness responses.[46] These psychological detriments, he concludes, 'essentially [amount] to mass torture from a learning theory perspective ... [and] cannot be easily dismissed as "collateral damage" by any moral standard.'[47] The psychological reality for these victims of U.S. drone attacks in Pakistan, Yemen and Somalia, resemble, to some extent, the conditions the people of Gaza suffered from before the latest war on Gaza. The incessant threats from the *zananas* (drones) were a constant threat not only during the major Israeli operations, but also during the alleged periods of ceasefire in between the wars.[48] However, as I argue above, the level and scope of the Israeli attacks on Gaza, in the recent operation, indicate a paradigm shift taking shape in the colonial management of the Gaza Strip. In this recent war, the life-threatening fear, unpredictability, uncontrollability, and helplessness were greatly amplified, through the intensity and reach of the bombings, sustained over a long period of time. Gaza is transforming yet again, this time from a zoo to a torture chamber.

Sumud in the Face of Torture

The purpose of this paper, first and foremost, was to call attention to the experiences of the people of Gaza during the recent 50-day war, and to provide some context and meaning to the inhumane and cruel acts inflicted on them. From a psychological perspective, these acts seem to embody a policy of mass torture that was enacted on an entire population of 1.8 million Palestinians. The full scope of this policy is yet to be revealed and analyzed. But if history is any indication, then we should expect this war to have been a 'trial run' that was tested to be repeated (in Gaza), and generalized elsewhere in the occupied territories.[49] The Israeli colonial regime seems to have graduated from collective punishment to mass torture, which if left unchecked, would pose an existential threat to Palestinians as a whole. Such cruel and inhumane practices risk creating long-term psychological disturbances to a large segment of the population, if not its entirety. This I assume might be the hidden agenda of the regime after all: to weaken the Palestinian society from the inside, by breaking the psyche of its most vulnerable segment, mainly its children. The perpetrators of such mass torture may believe that severely traumatized children, conditioned on learned helplessness, would not be able to continue the long tradition of colonial resistance and the Palestinians' struggle for freedom. Following the Zionists' failed prophecy of 'the old will die and the young will forget,'[50] the new generation of Israeli generals seem to believe that if the young refuse to forget their just cause, then they will break their little minds and make their memories too painful to remember.

However, what the Israeli war machine did not take into account, and continues to undermine, is the resilience of Palestinian people, epitomized by the *sumud* of Gaza. Despite the deep physical and psychological scars, we did not witness the mass mental breakdown, which I believe the current Israeli regime was hoping for. This heroic resilience is not to be taken for granted, and deserves a thorough examination to identify the sources of Palestinians' psychological strengths, which afford them the capacity to withstand the cumulative effects of trauma upon trauma for four generations now. This capacity for resilience is conceivably rooted in the strong sense of community, faith, social support, capacity to preserve positive emotions during hardship, as well as the unwavering belief in their just struggle for freedom. *Ghazeh el sumud,* then, should not merely be a solidarity chant we repeat hollowly. It is a model for steadfastness and resistance against violent colonial occupation, which Gaza imparts to us, after paying the ultimate price in bloodshed, pain and suffering. It would behoove us, then, to learn from Gazans how to be resilient and protect our communities from extreme political trauma, however meticulously engineered by the Israeli war generals.

GAZA AS A METAPHOR FOR UNSUSTAINABILITY[1]

Pierre Krähenbühl

When I was awoken by a call from our Gaza director at 6:20 in the morning on 30 July 2014, it was instantly clear the news wouldn't be good. And it wasn't. A UN Relief and Works Agency (UNRWA) school sheltering 3,000 displaced people from the raging conflict had just been hit by artillery fire, and many people were reported dead or injured. Children seeking refuge in classrooms had been killed in their sleep. It was an outrage, a disgrace.

The Israeli military operation that began on 8 July was the most extensive in Gaza in many years. The deaths, injuries, and destruction it caused will remain with us for years to come.

Having worked in conflict zones for twenty-five years, I have often been confronted with the deep polarization that characterizes such environments. The Israeli-Palestinian conflict is a prime example: everything related to the occupation of the Palestinian territory and the blockade of Gaza generates particularly high levels of passion and hostility. UNRWA has not been spared in the past, and it was not spared in the latest conflict. I will therefore address how we responded to this acute crisis and some of the questions and criticisms we have received.

At the heart of the situation in Gaza are people. At present, 1.8 million live in the Gaza Strip. In its urban areas, the population density is above 20,000 people per square kilometer — one of the highest in the world. Over 70 percent of Gaza's residents are Palestinian refugees who fled or were forced to leave their homes during the war of 1948. UNRWA's activities in Gaza focus on providing education, health care, and social services to this community, which numbers approximately 1.2 million people, or emergency aid in times of war.

* * * * *

When I first visited Gaza as the newly appointed commissioner-general in April 2014, I was immediately struck by the sheer unsustainability of the situation. The refugees and wider population of Gaza have no prospects, no jobs, nowhere to go, and no future. The territory suffers from over 40 percent unemployment, over 65 percent youth unemployment, and 80 percent female unemployment. I was also struck by the depleted and heavily contaminated aquifer in Gaza, which will — along with Gaza's run-down health, water, electricity, and sewage systems — make the Strip unliveable in a matter of just a few years. The staggering increase of people on UNRWA's food distribution lists is another serious concern: the number has soared from 80,000 people in 2000 to nearly 830,000 people just before the 2014 war.

UNRWA is at times challenged by people who criticize us for allegedly keeping the refugee question alive and holding refugees in a state of dependency. While I believe it is important that any humanitarian or development agency regularly and critically reviews how it operates, these questions fail to address the core underlying issues that affect the population in Gaza.

It is not UNRWA that perpetuates the Palestinian refugee crisis, but the lack of a political solution to the Israeli-Palestinian conflict. I have yet to meet anyone, anywhere in the world, who wishes to remain a refugee — and this includes Palestinian refugees. The increase in the number of people dependent on UNRWA assistance is the direct consequence of the illegal blockade imposed on Gaza since 2007.

Israel has significant security considerations and the right to take measures to protect its citizens from harm or attack. This does not include, however, what the International Committee of the Red Cross and the United Nations have determined to be forms of collective punishment imposed on the population of Gaza, such as the ban on exports.

During one of my first visits to Gaza, I talked to one refugee who described how he had gone in a few years from being a successful businessman who employed fifty people and traded with Israel and the

West Bank to a man ashamed of having lost his business, his employees, his home, and his dignity. The blockade ended his possibilities to continue as a tradesman and sustain his family. Such stories abound in Gaza.

Denial of dignity and rights

While I feel strongly that we must help people in such dire conditions, there is no pride in referring to the high numbers of people UNRWA assists. It is a measure of the denial of dignity and rights to the people of Gaza. It can be changed by lifting the blockade and ending the occupation.

With the situation for Gaza's population already so bleak, the 2014 Israeli attacks have further pushed the territory to the breaking point. While casualty figures in times of war are always contentious, the UN estimates on 21 September 2014, put the number of deaths at 1,480 Palestinian civilians, including 504 children, and five civilians in Israel. Having been to Gaza four times since the beginning of this last conflict, I have seen the destruction of entire neighborhoods and the broken bodies of children in the emergency wards of Gaza's al-Shifa Hospital. The ultimate denial of dignity would be to allow the dead and injured to remain anonymous: I invite all observers tempted to minimize the war's impact on civilians to join me on my next visit to Gaza.

I do not minimize the impact of rocket fire by armed groups in Gaza, including Hamas, on Israeli cities. In fact, I have repeatedly stated — and not from the relative security of my home, but from Gaza itself at the height of the conflict — that the firing of such rockets, which the United Nations has condemned as indiscriminate, has to cease.

Yet, I find it very difficult to reconcile the destruction and death in Gaza with the notion that Israel took every possible measure to abide by its obligations under international humanitarian law. Many of the victims of this latest conflict were due to the Israeli use of excessive and at times disproportionate force.

Another dramatic aspect of this conflict was — and still is — the high number of people displaced by the fighting. UNRWA sheltered nearly 300,000 Gaza residents in some ninety of its school buildings. In other words, we had to assist between 2,500 and 3,000 people per school — or over eighty people per classroom — for weeks on end. While we were very effective in distributing food, mattresses, blankets, and hygiene products, we struggled with improving the provision of water in the early stages of the conflict and containing the spread of disease.

The number of people displaced by this war was over six times more than during the conflict in Gaza that ended in January 2009, so called Operation Cast Lead. It was as if almost twice the entire population of my hometown of Geneva, Switzerland, was forced to flee their homes and live in shelters in the middle of an active war zone.

Our feeling of indignation reached its peak when UNRWA's own facilities, where Gaza's displaced citizens were seeking refuge, came under fire. On seven separate occasions, UNRWA schools that had been used as emergency shelters and whose exact positions we had provided to the Israeli army were either hit or struck nearby by Israeli shells or other munitions. Armed forces operating in combat zones — whether regular or irregular, state or non-state — have the obligation to preserve civilian lives and civilian infrastructure. They also have the obligation under international law to respect the sanctity and inviolability of UN premises. These obligations were repeatedly violated during the war.

This is all the more serious because UNRWA improved the system of notification to the Israeli army about the location of its emergency shelters after similar incidents during the 2008–2009 war. The precise GPS coordinates of the Jabaliya school, for example, which took a direct hit on 30 July 2014, causing multiple deaths, was conveyed seventeen times by email to the Israeli army. The Rafah school, where an Israeli strike on 3 August hit just in front of the main entrance gate, killing and injuring civilians inside and outside the compound, had been similarly notified to the Israeli army on thirty-three separate occasions. We have unreservedly condemned these Israeli actions and called for investigations and accountability for these attacks.

The world knows about this story

We also explicitly condemned the abuse by armed groups in Gaza of the sanctity of our premises when weapons were found in UNRWA schools. The world knows about this story because UNRWA found out about the incidents during its inspections and proactively informed all parties and the world through our public statements on the matter. While we do not know which Palestinian groups placed these weapons in the schools, we have said repeatedly that it was unacceptable and endangered staff, civilians, and the security of the premises themselves.

In this context, it is important to set the record straight on a couple of points. First, I categorically refute that UNRWA ever handed the weapons over to any group. Second, the weapons were found in empty schools, closed for the summer break, not in schools sheltering displaced people. That being said, the suggestion that UNRWA's discovery of weapons in some of its schools provides an explanation for why other UNRWA schools housing civilians were shelled would fail basic scrutiny under international law, and is also morally unacceptable.

Many observers argue that Hamas and other Palestinian groups endanger civilians by operating in close proximity to homes and civilian installations, including UNRWA schools. We are currently exposed to a series of pictures released by official Israeli sources on their Twitter accounts trying to make that case. It is not disputed that the recent war took place in the heart of Gaza's heavily urbanized environment and consequently exposed the civilian population. This would apply also to operations carried out by Israeli ground forces. But this fact does not release any of the armed forces from their obligations under international humanitarian law — rather, it should force them to take even greater measures of precaution.

Pictures are an inescapable part of modern war — but they can also be misleading. One particularly interesting photograph shows a square-shaped hole in the ground, which we all instantly take to be the entrance of a tunnel in Gaza. Beside that entrance we also see two bags marked with the UNRWA logo. These images were posted on official Israeli social media sites, and the narrative reinforced by subsequent briefings to journalists has suggested that UNRWA cement was being redirected away from humanitarian purposes. The fact that there is no such thing as a UNRWA cement bag, and that we have never brought a single such bag into Gaza, seems not to matter to those who relay the picture on social media.

Similarly, the Israeli army disseminated a story about three Israeli soldiers allegedly killed in a booby-trapped UNRWA clinic. As is often the case, there was less media exposure of the Israeli army's unequivocal admission — which was communicated by the army to us by phone and in subsequent face-to-face meetings — that the incident had not in fact occurred at a UNRWA clinic. This is how much false mythology about UNRWA has taken root.

As the population of Gaza emerges from the devastation of this conflict, its needs are greater than ever. As many as 60,000 homes have been damaged or destroyed in this conflict, of which 20,000 are totally uninhabitable, rendering around 110,000 people effectively homeless. Even those with homes find themselves in neighborhoods where the water, sewage, and electricity systems are demolished. In addition to food and other requirements, people need materials to repair and rebuild. The United Nations estimates that 80,000 projectiles fell on Gaza, of which as many as 8,000 may have failed to explode. These will have to be cleared before recovery and reconstruction can take place in earnest. Beyond the physical destruction are also the mental scars — the multiple traumas to which Gaza's population has been exposed for the third time in five years.

In this context, the big question hanging over Gaza is the conditions under which the reconstruction will take place. I welcome the recent agreement on a mechanism to import building materials into Gaza.[2] But if it fails to be properly implemented and if the process of rebuilding homes does not begin very soon, the levels of despair and anger in the Strip will grow very rapidly.

Only trade and employment will allow Gaza's inhabitants to rise from dispossession and dependency to self-reliance and self-sufficiency. Humanitarian aid alone, after all, cannot make up for the denial of rights and dignity. It doesn't elsewhere in the world, and one should not expect it to do so in Gaza.

For Palestinians, this has become an existential matter. As the population emerges from the most severe conflict in decades, many have so little hope in the future that they are prepared for any eventuality — including taking the appalling risk of crossing the Mediterranean in rickety boats, which has already cost many their lives.

The challenge of unsustainability and indignity of life

Ultimately, the unsustainability and indignity of life in Gaza represents a major challenge for all, including Israel.

To date, no one has expressed this better than a Gaza businessman I met in June. 'I am a good man,' he said. 'But my children are not as good as I am.'

Seeing from the expression on my face that this needed some more explanation, he added: 'I am almost sixty; I have worked most of my life with Israelis, in their factories; I have traded with them. I think I can say that I know how they think and understand some of the things that worry them. But my children have no understanding of that, as they have never met an Israeli. They know only the barrier, the blockade, the tanks, the drones, and the fear. This is a major concern for any future coexistence.'

After this latest conflict in Gaza, we have to move beyond the realm of humanitarian action alone. The planned mechanism that will help rebuild Gaza under a consensus Palestinian government is an essential step in the right direction. However, more political action is required to solve the underlying causes of this crisis. While it is not UNRWA's role to determine what those solutions should be, we do not accept that it is taken for granted that this dismal state of affairs will continue year after year, conflict after conflict. It is time to address the human cost of these repeated and avoidable tragedies — including the cost to our own colleagues, eleven of whom have been killed between 8 July 2014 and 27 August 2014. It is time for a change of paradigm in Gaza, one that recognizes that the population of the Strip, and all Palestinians, have the same aspirations for freedom as any other people in the world.

ISRAEL MOWS THE LAWN[1]

Mouin Rabbani

Among all the sanctimonious howls about Israel's right to self-defense, and in the face of the categorical rejection of the Palestinians' equivalent right, the fundamental point that the latest Israeli assault against Gaza in July and August 2014 is an illegitimate attack is often lost.

As Noura Erakat has cogently argued, 'Israel does not have the right to self-defence in international law against occupied Palestinian territory.'[2] Its argument that it no longer occupies the Gaza Strip has been dismissed by Lisa Hajjar of the University of California as a self-generated 'licence to kill.'[3] Once again, Israel is 'mowing the lawn' with impunity, targeting civilian non-combatants and civilian infrastructure.

Given its continual insistence that it uses the most precise weapons available and chooses its targets carefully, it is impossible to conclude that the targeting is not deliberate. According to UN agencies, more than three-quarters of the more than 260 Palestinians killed so far have been civilians, and more than a quarter of them children.[4] Most were targeted in their own homes: these victims cannot be described as collateral damage under any definition of the term. Of course Palestinian militants have also been recklessly targeting Israeli population centers though their attacks have resulted in just a single death: a man handing out sweets to the soldiers pulverizing the Gaza Strip. Human Rights Watch has criticized both sides but, true to form, has accused only the Palestinians of war crimes.

* * * * *

61

GAZA AS METAPHOR

In 2004, a year before Israel's unilateral disengagement from the Gaza Strip, Dov Weissglass, éminence grise to Ariel Sharon, explained the initiative's purpose to an interviewer from *Ha'aretz*:

> The significance of the disengagement plan is the freezing of the peace process [...] And when you freeze that process, you prevent the establishment of a Palestinian state, and you prevent a discussion on the refugees, the borders and Jerusalem. Effectively, this whole package called the Palestinian state, with all that it entails, has been removed indefinitely from our agenda. And all this with [...] a [US] presidential blessing and the ratification of both houses of Congress [...] The disengagement is actually formaldehyde. It supplies the amount of formaldehyde that is necessary so there will not be a political process with the Palestinians.

In 2006 Weissglass was just as frank about Israel's policy towards Gaza's 1.8 million inhabitants: 'The idea is to put the Palestinians on a diet, but not to make them die of hunger.'[5] He was not speaking metaphorically: it later emerged that the Israeli defense ministry had conducted detailed research on how to translate his vision into reality, and arrived at a figure of 2,279 calories per person per day — some eight percent less than a previous calculation because the research team had originally neglected to account for 'culture and experience' in determining nutritional 'red lines'.

This wasn't an academic exercise. After pursuing a policy of enforced integration between 1967 and the late 1980s, Israeli policy shifted towards separation during the 1987–93 uprising, and then fragmentation during the Oslo years. For the Gaza Strip, an area about the size of Greater Glasgow, these changes entailed a gradual severance from the outside world, with the movement of persons and goods into and out of the territory increasingly restricted. The screws were turned tighter during the 2000–5 uprising, and in 2007 the Gaza Strip was effectively sealed shut. All exports were banned, and just 131 truckloads of foodstuffs and other essential products were permitted entry per day. Israel also strictly controlled which products could and could not be imported. Prohibited items have included A4 paper, chocolate, coriander, crayons, jam, pasta, shampoo, shoes and wheelchairs.

In 2010, commenting on this premeditated and systematic degradation of the humanity of an entire population, UK Prime Minister David Cameron characterized the Gaza Strip as a 'prison camp' and — for once — did not neuter this assessment by subordinating his criticism to proclamations about the jailers' right of self-defense against their inmates.

It is often claimed that Israel's reason for escalating this punitive regime to a new level of severity was to cause the overthrow of Hamas after its 2007 seizure of power in Gaza. The claim doesn't stand up to serious scrutiny. Removing Hamas from power has indeed been a policy objective for the US and the EU ever since the Islamist movement won the 2006 parliamentary elections, and their combined efforts to undermine it helped set the stage for the ensuing Palestinian schism.

Israel's agenda has been different. Had it been determined to end Hamas rule it could easily have done so, particularly while Hamas was still consolidating its control over Gaza in 2007, and without necessarily reversing the 2005 disengagement. Instead, it saw the schism between Hamas and the Palestinian Authority as an opportunity to further its policies of separation and fragmentation, and to deflect growing international pressure for an end to an occupation that has lasted nearly half a century. Its massive assaults on the Gaza Strip in 2008–9 (Operation Cast Lead) and 2012 (Operation Pillar of Defense), as well as countless individual attacks between and since, were in this context exercises in what the Israeli military called 'mowing the lawn': weakening Hamas and enhancing Israel's powers of deterrence. As the 2009 Goldstone Report and other investigations have demonstrated, often in excruciating detail, the grass consists overwhelmingly of non-combatant Palestinian civilians, indiscriminately targeted by Israel's precision weaponry.

* * * * *

Israel's 2014 assault on the Gaza Strip, which began on 6 July with ground forces moving in some ten days later, was intended to serve the same agenda. The conditions for it were set in late April. Negotiations that had been going on for nine months had stalled after the Israeli government reneged on its commitment to release a number of Palestinian prisoners incarcerated since before the 1993 Oslo Accords, and ended when Israeli Prime Minister Benjamin Netanyahu announced he would no longer deal with Palestinian President Mahmoud Abbas because Abbas had just signed a new reconciliation agreement with Hamas. On this occasion, in a sharp departure from other occasions, US Secretary of State John Kerry explicitly blamed Israel for the breakdown in talks. His special envoy Martin Indyk, a career Israel lobbyist, blamed Israel's insatiable appetite for Palestinian land and continued expansion of the settlements, and handed in his resignation.

The challenge this posed to Netanyahu was clear. If even the Americans were telling the world that Israel was not interested in peace, those more directly invested in a two-state settlement — such as the EU, which had started to exclude any Israeli entities active in occupied Palestinian territory from participation in bilateral agreements — could start considering other ways to nudge Israel towards the 1967 boundaries. Negotiations about nothing are designed to provide political cover for Israel's policy of creeping annexation. Now that they've collapsed yet again, the strategic asset that is American public opinion may start asking why Congress is more loyal to Netanyahu than the Israeli Knesset is. Kerry had been serious about reaching a comprehensive agreement: he adopted almost all of Israel's core positions and successfully rammed most of them down Abbas's throat — yet Netanyahu still balked. Refusing even to specify future Israeli-Palestinian borders during nine months of negotiations, Israeli leaders instead levelled a series of accusations at Washington so outlandish — encouraging extremism, giving succour to terrorists — that one could be forgiven for concluding Congress was funding Hamas, rather than Israel, to the tune of $3 billion a year.

Israel received another blow on 2 June 2014, when a new Palestinian Authority government was inaugurated, following the April reconciliation agreement between Hamas and Fatah. Hamas endorsed the new government even though it was given no cabinet posts and the government's composition and political programme were virtually indistinguishable from its predecessor's. With barely a protest from the Islamists, Abbas repeatedly and loudly proclaimed that the government accepted the Middle East Quartet's demands: that it recognize Israel, renounce violence and adhere to past agreements. He also announced that Palestinian security forces in the West Bank would continue their security collaboration with Israel. When both Washington and Brussels signalled their intention to co-operate with the new government, alarm bells went off in Israel. Its usual assertions that Palestinian negotiators spoke only for themselves — and would therefore prove incapable of implementing any agreement — had begun to look shaky: the Palestinian leadership could now claim not only to represent both the West Bank and the Gaza Strip but also to have co-opted Hamas into supporting a negotiated two-state settlement, if not the Oslo framework as a whole. There might soon be increased international pressure on Israel to negotiate seriously with Abbas. The formaldehyde was beginning to evaporate.

At this point Netanyahu seized on the disappearance on 12 June 2014 of three young Israelis in the West Bank like a drowning man thrown a lifebelt. Despite clear evidence presented to him by the Israeli security forces that the three teenagers were already dead, and no evidence to date that Hamas was involved, he held Hamas directly responsible and launched a 'hostage rescue operation' throughout the West Bank. It was really an organized military rampage. It included the killing of at least six Palestinians, none of whom was accused of involvement in the disappearances; mass arrests, including the arrest of Hamas parliamentarians and the re-arrest of detainees released in 2011; the demolition of a number of houses and the looting of others; and a variety of other depredations of the kind Israel's finest have honed to perfection during decades of occupation. Netanyahu whipped up a demagogic firestorm against the Palestinians, and the subsequent abduction and burning alive of a Palestinian teenager in Jerusalem cannot and should not be separated from this incitement.

For his part, Abbas failed to stand up to the Israeli operation and ordered his security forces to continue to co-operate with Israel against Hamas. The reconciliation agreement was being put under serious pressure. On the night of 6 July, an Israeli air raid resulted in the death of seven Hamas militants. Hamas responded with sustained missile attacks deep into Israel, escalating further as Israel launched its full-scale onslaught. For a year Hamas had been in a precarious position: it had lost its headquarters in Damascus and preferential status in Iran as a result of its refusal to give open support to the Syrian regime, and faced unprecedented levels of hostility from Egypt's new military ruler. The underground tunnel economy between Egypt and Gaza had been systematically dismantled by the Egyptians, and for the first time since seizing control of the territory in 2007 it was no longer able regularly to pay the salaries of tens of thousands of government employees. The reconciliation agreement with Fatah was its way of bartering its political programme in exchange for its own survival: in return for conceding the political arena to Abbas, Hamas would retain control of the Gaza Strip indefinitely, have its public sector placed on the PA payroll and see the border crossing with Egypt reopened.

In the event, the quid pro quo Hamas hoped for was not permitted to materialize and, according to Nathan Thrall of the International Crisis Group, 'life in Gaza became worse': 'The current escalation,' he wrote, 'is a direct result of the choice by Israel and the West to obstruct the implementation of the April 2014 Palestinian reconciliation agreement.'[6] To put it differently, those within Hamas who saw the crisis as an opportunity to put an end to Weissglass' regime gained the upper hand. So far, they appear to have the majority of the population with them, because they seem to prefer death by F-16 to death by formaldehyde.

ON WAR AND SHIT[1]

Naim Al Khatib

Dear World,

My name is Naim Al Khatib. I am a Palestinian man who lives in the neighborhood of Tal al-Hawa (or Hill of the Wind) in Gaza City. I get so exasperated when people mistakenly spell my address by replacing the extended alif (ا) with the shortened alif (ى); making it Hill of Passion, which, I presume, has provoked some to change the name of the area to Great Islam Hill. What annoys me is the term 'Great': if it refers to Islam, it confirms what is already certain without adding anything to the meaning. If the adjective refers to the hill, it is not consistent with reality.

The night, or the day, as my young daughter would say, that the war tightened its grip around the neck of our ('great') neighborhood, Dina asked me, 'Baba, why did they make it all daytime?' The truth is that my intelligence got in the way of understanding her question, and when I asked for an explanation she clarified, 'because they didn't let us sleep.'

We were close to thirty people, brought together by coincidence, or by some unannounced collusion, at the home of our Christian neighbor, who happens to be the only Christian in the building or maybe in the whole area. None of us expressed any objection, especially later when we all clustered around the remaining sweets from the holiday of Saint Barbara.

When my eyes met those of the Virgin Mary hanging on the wall, I reassured her and stressed that the misunderstanding was mutual.

We gathered in a corner of the dark kitchen after a rapid security sweep of the area. Under missile strikes, the whizzing of bullets, and the shaking building, the summation of our existence transpired as two connected ideas: the fear of death and the need to go to the bathroom. Many of us know that water makes up three quarters of the human body, but few of us are aware that the entirety of these quarters flows into the bladder at times like these.

The suicide missions of taking our children back and forth to the bathroom did not cease, even though the trip required crossing an area in the line of fire that faced the big glass balcony overlooking the street. A person would stand and hold their little one, taking cover and waiting for an opportunity to dart forward like an arrow. In the bathroom, the army was only a half-opened glass window away and the sound of their machinery was enough to shorten all protocols. As for the return, it was a reverse trip not without anticipation and euphoria for those waiting their turn.

Why, in situations like these, do the principles of architecture, the fundamentals of interior design, the rules of public health, and the recommendations of environmental health all fail us when we have a basic functional need as simple as having a bathroom in the kitchen? The call of nature did not stop; rather it became a continuous scream. I then decided to take initiative and accept my new responsibility as the group's shit engineer. I searched the kitchen cupboards for an appropriate receptacle; I emptied a bucket and placed it behind the kitchen table. I then lowered the tablecloth to the ground as a cover, proudly announcing to the group the official opening of the new kitchen bathroom. Children under ten expressed their happiness about the idea and began practicing their tasks standing, sitting, and even without a chaperon.

Of course the new bathroom did not solve everyone's problem, mine included. The need to go to the bathroom was heightened by the degree of risk taking. For my turn, I traversed the miles separating the kitchen and the bathroom, and did what I had to do in a speed that baffled me. I do not know whether it was because of fear, the flow of adrenaline, or the mind's superior ability to control our limbs at a given moment.

After hours of the army's control over the neighborhood, the raging war calmed and shit was no longer the master of the situation. The women enjoyed staying in the master bedroom that had its own bathroom. We men were left with a separate bathroom but the trip there was no longer as dangerous. We were deliberating over matters of non-interest such as providing food and blankets and determining the locations and hours of sleep. Some began designing white flags in case we were asked to leave. We argued over the need to keep the door open for fear of getting it blown up should the army enter. Some even went as far as to joke about looking for a prayer rug in our friend's home.

In the evening of the next day, horror visited us again with the sounds of feet behind the door followed by intense banging. We gathered immediately and reviewed the plan we had prepared in advance. One woman went ahead and opened the door amid everybody's trepidation. After a tense, long wait, our elderly neighbor peered in, jokingly saying: 'People, why are you so afraid? We are now under the protection of the army.' He was accompanied by a group of women we did not know and who had come halfway through the neighborhood in the darkness of night in order to help one of them who was looking for diapers for her young children.

'Diapers!!!' What a reaction! I do not think that the woman had faced such reprimands or need for justification or terror from the army as much as she did from the women in our group. 'You are crazy! Who leaves their home for diapers?' 'People, the lady is only asking if you can help her.' 'I don't understand why you are treating me like this.' 'Wipe him with a cloth or with your clothes' … 'Are you willing to die because of your child's shit?' … 'No one here uses diapers' … 'For God's sake, O Jamal, do not leave us' … 'That's it, I don't want anyone to open their mouth' … 'Enough, enough, I am sorry' … 'People, I tell you that the army's tanks entrenched themselves in the sand.'

The situation became surrealistically analogous with the conclusion of Orwell's *Animal Farm*. My eyes met once again with those of the Virgin Mary, and I thought this time she was smiling from her place on the wall. The mutual misunderstanding still stands. And, as for shit, it has returned to chasing us like a ghost of or a refrain for a war that has not finished yet.

Sincerely Yours,

Naim Al Khatib

PLACING GAZA

TUNNELS: LOVE, LIONS AND … ABSURDITIES

Khaled Hroub

Love

There was a magical will for life and love, against all the gods of death and destruction looming in the skies. The Egyptian Security did not allow Imad's fiancée, Manal, to travel from Egypt to Gaza via the Rafah Crossing — legally and above the ground — to marry him. All attempts by both families, in Gaza and in Egypt, to convince the guardians of Egypt's sovereignty that the young bride Manal, 18 years old, presents no threat to Egypt's national security failed completely. Imad came up with another idea: he would bring his future wife in via the tunnels, against all odds, including the stupidity of those security men. Arrangements were put in place, and the bride in her white dress entered a full-height tunnel (secretly) from the Egyptian side. The bridegroom in full suit and tie met her halfway in the middle of the tunnel. Their smiles lit the entire tunnel and made Eros himself envious! He embraced her and both processed their way down along the Palestinian side. They could envision, feel and hear the songs of the souls of all the men and women who had passed through those tunnels. Their spirits were standing in ovation, row after row, singing, clapping and welcoming the couple. Once they emerged from the mouth of the tunnel, the air exploded with living shouts of joy, ululating, singing and happiness. Imad and Manal's wedding — their joyous procession among the celebrating spirits in the tunnel, Manal's family's farewell to her at one end, and Imad's family waiting for them at the other — was somehow unreal, belonging to the world of mythology. It is the story of Gaza's Orpheus here inscribing his devotion on the fleeting souls around him, carrying out his bride — a love story like those many tales of human passion and heroism, against misery and oppression.

Stories of Gaza's Orpheus are endless. The grim reality of the tunnels was trumped by the lust for life and love. Poor and desperate young Palestinians would 'take a tunnel trip' travelling up into the Sinai desert. They would search for forbidden love in the desert: beautiful and pure … and without exorbitant expense! They would come back through the tunnels again, happy but alone. Or, sometimes, with their Bedouin 'brides', dressed modestly, but smiling playfully. Perhaps these desert brides did not know about all the love stories that had passed through the tunnels before them: the story of Alexandra, the Russian girl who fell in love in a 'chat room' with a bullish, conservative but romantic Palestinian young man. He was clear and blunt: he loved her deeply, but she had to come to Gaza as he would never think of leaving it. Not only this, but she had also to convert to Islam and cover her hair! Willingly, she accepted and travelled all the way to Egypt from Russia, then through the tunnel to marry Mr Right, then and there.

Or, perhaps those desert brides had not heard of Mousa, the Chinese young man who fell in love with Eiman, from Deir Al-Balah. They met while Mousa, who had mastered Arabic, was accompanying some journalists as a translator in Gaza. Working together for a short period of time was enough for Cupid to softly release his arrows into the two young hearts. They stayed in touch after Mousa's departure. The love story heated up, leading the couple to vow to meet again and marry. Months later, the Chinese lover travelled back to Egypt but he was denied entry via the Rafah Crossing. He spent some days lingering around, then managed to arrange a tunnel journey for himself. All the way from Xinjiang in north China to this obscure spot on the world's map called the Gaza Strip, and finally, against all odds Mousa stood tall in front of Eiman's father asking for her hand! A Palestinian father who never thought of accepting a non-Palestinian man to marry his daughter now yielded before the brave demand of this determined man, and the boldness of his daughter. He gave them a big yes. Mousa and Eiman became a couple. Later on, Eiman officially declared that after weeks of training she was able to use chopsticks to eat the tasty Chinese food made for her by Mousa.

Lions

The drugged lion started to wake up in the middle of the tunnel earlier than 'planned'. Stretching his body all around, the impact of the primitive dose of anesthesia seemed to have faded away. The young men who where 'smuggling' him on a plastic slide through the tunnel from Egypt to Gaza shot looks into each other's horrified eyes; instinctively, they dropped everything and ran frantically in both directions for the longest run of their life! What an irony to be 'accidently eaten' by a lion in this tunnel when they had succeeded for years in escaping all the death dropped on them by Israeli fighters! The young men had a bit of luck — the lion needed some extra time to fully come around before roaring loudly and angrily now on his own in the tunnel.

The lion then loped to one end of the tunnel following the tiny source of light–in the direction of the Gaza end. For a hungry lion this was the wrong direction to choose! No meat there but hungry people and angry men with guns. Why the lion did not run to Egypt's end instead of Gaza's is part of the many existential absurdities that will be left to future philosophers to contemplate. Did the lion decide instantly that striking his paws into human flesh in Gaza would be easier and/or more accepted? Nobody knows! The original plan was to transfer the lion to the 'Beesan Recreation City' in Bait Lahiya in northern Gaza to become the centerpiece of a local 'zoo' — and generate money.

Unintentional luck was on the boys' side because the tunnel they chose for this mission was one of the 'dumb-waiter tunnels', where 'people and goods' had to use a makeshift elevator at either of the end: a strong metal base with cables that was lowered and lifted vertically by a wheel and motor down the fifteen-meter-deep hole at each end of the tunnel. If the 'elevator' is in the 'pulled up' position no one can get out of the tunnel — including the roaring lion, luckily. Other tunnels are designed in ways that the ground of the tunnel slides gradually at both ends so that 'people and goods' can walk or be slid on their way up and out of the tunnel without the need of any mechanical help. In the end, to fix the problem of the wandering lion in the tunnel, the decision was made to injure him with a non-deadly shot then carry on with the 'transfer operation'. The bleeding animal was finally moved into Gaza in order to enjoy being imprisoned there — along with the rest of Gaza's inhabitants.

Later in his new home, our lion — along with another comrade and a lioness — escaped death during the two wars waged by Israel against Gaza in 2009 and 2012. Their zoo was hit badly and many other animals were killed. Not only did the lions stay alive, although frail and starved, but they also responded to the call of life, as the lioness got pregnant then produced two beautiful cubs. It should be reported here that we still don't know which of the two male lions was the father who triumphed in this leonine love story — yet another existential question to be left to future inquiry!

'The Palestinians do not exist'

Gaza tunnels summed up the Palestinian saga in a snapshot, in a word. Push them and the cause for them out of sight, and then have a toast! Once out of sight, no misery can be seen, no guilt is felt. The tunnels had superbly symbolized and maintained this. There was no trace of 'them' above the ground along the border; or in anyone's line of sight. It was a strange action of conscious self-betrayal — ignoring what existed, and knowingly making it unknown. The world knew and still knows about them (the tunnels and the Palestinians who were driven to dig them), but did not and still doesn't want to see them. An open secret!

The Gaza tunnels were political surrealism and post-modernist politics at its best illogicality: everyone was aware of 'these' tunnels (a thousand tunnels or so!) and everyone wanted to deny their existence or even any knowledge about them. Israel, the US, and Egypt, the three main concerned parties, knew that there was a 'vibrant' Palestinian life that went on daily in these tunnels! This irony made these parties and others very nervous: Palestinians were allowed to move freely underground but not so under the sun. It is as if 'the Palestinians do not exist' — a reminder of Jean Baudrillard's maxim 'The Gulf War did not take place'.

Gaza's tunnels also intensely exposed the contrast between a profound longing for the return to their homeland deep inside diasporic Palestinians, and a deep desire to leave the same homeland inside those who were locked within its inhuman conditions. The latter desire was (and remains) profoundly bitter and paradoxical. Leaving Palestine meant that Israel's policy — in creating unbearable living conditions to force voluntary migration on the Palestinians — was working. Dry statistics and polls clashed continually with emotional attachment and declarations. Many Palestinians in Gaza strongly wished to migrate outside Palestine, as shown in surveys and figures. But when confronted with the fact that any such departure would serve ulterior Israeli interests, they backtracked, expressed anger, and cursed the nearest thing that came to mind. Tired and torn apart they stayed — or as captured by the title of Atef Abu Saif's marvelous new fiction set in Gaza, they remain, imprisoned in *A Suspended Life*.

If only these tunnels could speak

They could tell thousands of stories. Gaza's tunnels were called 'lines', each designated with a name or by reputation according to the specific function it served. A 'Passenger Tunnel or Line' would tell of those people who crossed into Gaza full of energy and enthusiasm, to support the impoverished Palestinians from one season to the next. In the middle of the excitement of a tunnel-journey, they would meet with people coming from the other side, departing the Strip, pale, destroyed and disillusioned, wanting to find a place where they could simply breathe ordinary life. In the near-darkness of the tunnels, the departing and arriving individuals would momentarily meet face to face, then pass each other. They would curiously sneak quick glances in each other's faces then keep moving in the opposite direction. Those who managed to sustain more composure murmur *As-Salam 'Alaikum* to the passing silent and hurrying ones.

'Trade and Business Lines' could tell their own stories too. Constructed purposefully, they come in various shapes, width, height and length depending on the type of 'goods' they are designed to bring in: from milk, sugar, wheat, medicine and other basics, to cars, computers, hotel marble and ... lions! They have moving conveyor belts with two little motors at each end, with containers stacked on the belt and tied to each other. The tools may have been primitive, but the execution and ideas were genius. These 'lines' were the most controversial. Inside them, around them and about them all kinds of stories abound, a mixture of good and bad. They brought food and life to Gaza's two million Palestinians, but they also brought shady businesses, corruption, war-profiteers and their crookedness. These lines were built to break the blockade on Gaza, but they also built monopolies and fat bank accounts for the few. These were the tunnels that compelled Hamas to shelve some of its religious strictness in return for immediate and pragmatic gain. Before the blockade, Hamas — both the organization and its government — hated cigarettes and discouraged the habit of smoking and harassed smokers across the Strip, coming very close to imposing a legal ban on it. It was a religious drive clothed in health considerations. After the blockade, however, cigarettes proved to be a source of great income. Hamas's government set up a specialized 'Tunnels Department' that was in charge of collecting tax on all goods entering the Strip through the tunnels. The well-organized and vigilant monitoring system became the main source of generating revenue for a beleaguered government that was left cut-off from any external help or ordinary taxation. Cigarettes, as one of the 'top entertainment' commodities in the Strip, were taxed heavily — and allowed to be sold everywhere. What once had been a modest product in the Strip, regulated by the government and only sold in big supermarkets, became available in every scruffy alley in cities, villages, and refugee camps.

The 'Resistance Lines' would tell other stories. Masked resistance men and gunmen were running in both directions vowing to fight until their very last drop of blood. In the eyes of many Palestinians, these were the men that made miracles possible: manufacturing weapons from raw materials, digging out mazes of underground networks, and defying all the sophistication of Israeli military might and its powerful Intelligence. Part of the sustained and astonishing determination of these men was unearthed during and after the 2012 war. They were using networks of tunnels and concealed pathways that ran underground for tens of kilometers in all directions. It was said that thousands of dedicated and highly disciplined members of Hamas had worked in the construction of these tunnels for years. How Israel did not know about the magnitude and spread of these resistance tunnels burrowed under its borderlines, with Gaza thus enabling Palestinian fighters to come above the ground on the Israeli side during the war, is yet another astonishing question. Given the great number of people who worked in the construction of these 'lines' without allowing any piece of information to slip to Israel's informers, those tunnels were the biggest kept secret in Palestine in recent years. An admiring but somewhat dismayed Fatah leader in the West Bank whispered to me recently how ashamed he felt when he saw how Hamas was investing its hard-raised money in building resistance fortresses compared with how the Palestinian Authority was squandering its money.

Building, or rather digging, a tunnel is a secretive and highly complicated operation that requires exceptional skills and months of relentless work. It must, first of all, be done away from the eyes of Israeli and Egyptian spies. A typical Israeli air strike on the ends of tunnels 'under-construction' buried scores of young poor workers alive. Hamas also had to approve any new tunnel, particularly during the prosperous period of the tunnels industry under the Hamas government, and before Egypt's decision to demolish them entirely in 2014. At the beginning of the siege of Gaza from 2007, the tunnels had something of an innocent or heroic image as they were truly lifelines for the people there. Later on, though, fat cats jumped in and dirty business, monopolies and exploitation marched hand in hand with the continuation of the tunnels' original noble function.

A passing woman in a tunnel

I saw her emerging from the far dusky light, walking as quickly as her heavy burden would allow her. She was overstrained with a child resting on her arm and neck, a rucksack thrown on her back and a tight grip on the hand of another child walking fast in front of her. Thick darkness would fill the narrow and low spaces of the tunnel behind and surrounding her body, giving her face and the faces of her children brighter contrast. They looked luminescently white, and I thought I must look white as well. Our tunnel was classified as a 'VIP' line because people could walk through it at full height — without bending, let alone crawling. Gaza tunnels used to have a scale of prices, moving up in cost in accordance to the 'length', 'height' and 'walkability' of each of them. 'Crawling', long-distanced and low-ceiling tunnels were the cheapest option. 'Sliding' tunnels had a middle-scale price, as you would be put onto a big piece of hard rubber (usually a second-hand tire), and somebody would pull you to the other end. In height and distance they were relatively better than the 'crawling' type. The 'VIP' tunnels are the really 'luxurious' ones: you could walk heads-up and enjoy a shorter distance.

She and I passed across each other: fleetingly and uninterestedly on her side, but slowly and curiously on my side. With a rucksack on my back, I was dragging a heavy suitcase in one hand and in the other hand videoing my journey with a smart-phone. I seemed like a tourist in the wrong place, but she was 'real' — dragging the world on her shoulders. In that unique moment of human contact I could barely murmur: *As-Salam 'Alaikum.* There was no reply. I only heard the muffled sound of our shoes hitting the dampened ground, along with the suffocated squealing of my suitcase wheels. In fact, I am not sure if I uttered any greeting to her at all! I had a quick glimpse of her face, but I could read nothing in its stony features, especially as her eyes avoided mine.

There, in the midst of the thick darkness that blocked sight beyond a few steps, encountering another human being became quite an experience. The child on her arm was looking backward so I did not see his face. The strap of the bag on her back was clearly cutting deep into the middle of her shoulder, pulling her scarf aside and revealing part of her hair. Her second child, around three years old, was actively marching in front of her, but firmly attached to her other extended arm. Obliviously he was outpacing her; she was trying to slow him down. His speedy, hyper childish walk was tiring his mother. Maybe no harm would happen even if he slipped from her hand — there was little chance to get lost. When I finally reached the Gazan eye of the tunnel and came out into the sun, I admittedly took a deep sigh of relief. But my heart stayed with that unknown woman with two kids as if she was on a journey to nowhere. I looked back and waved goodbye to my 'VIP' tunnel that I had slipped into from a little barren garden of a scruffy, dusty house on the Egyptian side of Rafah.

Jihan dead-locked

Perhaps there is nothing relating to the Gaza tunnels that sums up the Palestinian saga more than the story of Jihan and her five children. The impoverished family travelled to Egypt legally, via the Rafah Crossing with all passports stamped, a couple of years ago. Their plan was to continue their migration journey to Europe seeking a better life. Jihan and the kids stayed in Egypt while the husband travelled first to explore and prepare the new destination for his family. He took longer than expected and Jihan was left with no choice but to go back to Gaza because school days were approaching, and she did not want her children to miss a school year. Back she went to Rafah; the Crossing had been closed for months and no one could enter or leave Gaza, except for very exceptional cases. She decided to 'tunnel' her way back to Gaza — and so she did. Her passport and those of her kids, therefore, were not fixed with an exit stamp from Egypt. While waiting for news from her husband, the Egyptians decided to destroy all the tunnels (after Abdel Fattah El-Sisi came to power). Jihan's *de facto* existence was in Gaza but her *de jure* existence was in Egypt! Now even if she were lucky enough to get permission to use the Rafah Crossing in the very few days allowed by the

Egyptian authorities, she would be arrested right away. 'Legally speaking', she and her children were still in Egypt. 'Illegally' speaking, she had travelled through the tunnels and was in Gaza. 'Illogically' speaking, since the tunnels were now destroyed, she could not go back to Egypt. 'Absurdly' speaking, this is only one story out of thousands of people's whose *de jure* is above ground but their *de facto* is underground!

FROM FENCE TO FENCE:
GAZA'S STORY IN ITS OWN WORDS

Jehad Abu Salim

> Beyond the Horizon
> I have a Homeland
> Soon I shall return to Her
>
> There I will meet my Brothers
> And the Promise will be Fulfilled[1]

Summer days are long, but in Gaza, they are longer than one might think. They get even longer when the electricity and the internet are shut off, which is most of the time. This had been my daytime nightmare ever since Israel imposed its siege on the Gaza Strip in 2007. To escape it, you could read or visit a friend to talk to; but when the weather was hot and humid, the energy to do any of these activities would evaporate. On one such hot and humid day, I went to the roof of my house out of boredom. Although this was not the first time I had looked at the landscape from my family's rooftop in Deir Al-Balah, some thoughts and reflections made this day unforgettable. I looked east and there were the borders between the Gaza Strip and Israel, and I looked west and there was the sea. From that same spot, both borders were visible, and between them, the familiar scene of innumerable drab houses stretching towards both horizons.

At that moment I recalled one of the famous common sayings used by Palestinians in Gaza to refer to the Strip: we're trapped '*min el-silik ila al-silik'* (from the fence to the fence). This simple phrase sums up Gaza's current reality: A fenced place, surrounded by dead-ends and, within it, a caged human sea with almost no hope or future. Such thoughts never abandoned me. They chased me most of the time I spent in Gaza, where I observed how the Strip grew ever more overcrowded. Indeed, phrases such as 'urban population density,' 'lack of space,' and many other metaphors relating to overcrowding populations, have become synonymous with Gaza. These descriptors have taken on a life of their own, straddling the line between disparate nomenclatures. Ostensibly, they cast Gaza in terms of a hackneyed humanitarian discourse, referring to Gaza's deteriorating economic and social conditions. Perhaps, and more importantly, the significance of looking at Gaza's current state beyond such humanitarian frameworks cannot be overstated.[2] As with most people who live in Gaza, my understanding of its reality could never be detached from politics and history. This is not the framework most commonly used to understand the Gaza Strip. Instead, humanitarian frameworks that use the language of crisis, aid, and emergency dominate discourse on the Strip. Regardless of intent — and it should be noted that much of this discourse is well-meaning — humanitarianism has reshaped Gaza; politics and history have been stripped away, and what remains is a de-politicized rendition of life in the Strip.

This rendition has led to a number of problems. First and foremost, because the current Gaza Strip is a product of political history, humanitarian discourse contributes to normalizing Gaza's current reality, transforming it into another case, albeit one without history, of hunger or poverty that the international community has to deal with through aid and expertise. Second, Gaza's current fate was not a result of a natural pull factor that attracted almost 200,000 refugees between 1947 and 1950. On the contrary, the movement of large numbers of Palestinian refugees was a direct result of the 1948 Zionist conquest of Palestine, the root cause of Palestinian refugees' plight. Therefore, it is crucial to refer to Gaza's current problems in light of the history of the Zionist settler-colonial project and the conflicts it generated. Third, and most importantly, the tendency to view Gaza's problem through a merely humanitarian lens, of employing scientific rhetoric without referring to the direct political factors that created the humanitarian crisis, deprives Palestinians of the Gaza Strip — both refugees and original residents — of their agency. It functions to silence their voices and undermine their individual and collective perception of the events that led to Gaza's current situation.

In lieu of historical contextualization, an examination of Gazans' everyday sayings can help us reassert and uncover the historical and political roots of their oppression. More importantly, it helps us understand them on their own terms, an essential first step in surpassing the humanitarian discourse that has so far been dominant. Although it is impossible to show how frequent a common saying is used, 'from fence to fence' does appear in articles published by the local press in the Gaza Strip.[3] The phrase can be thought of as part of everyday politics. Consider, for example, Laleh Khalili's *Heroes and Martyrs of Palestine: The Politics of National Commemoration*, an examination of Palestinian practices of national commemoration and the role of memory. Khalili argues against considering memory as 'absolute, emotional, magical, and as such insusceptible to reason, dynamism, or change'.[4] On the contrary, she examines memory's 'effect and appearance in practice.'[5] Whereas Khalili's focus is on physical practices and acts of commemoration, I would argue that phrases, metaphors and expressions, although intangible, also represent people's positions towards social and political realities. In other words, they are not merely proverbs or part of a folkloric cultural repertoire; they make up a profoundly political statement.

'From fence to fence' is a simple enough expression, and yet it reflects the geographic space Palestinians inhabit. For them, 'the fence' is the most pernicious manifestation of the Zionist conquest in 1948, and its continuity into the present. The fence is a physical barrier that was imposed by an external force which divides what the Palestinians in Gaza consider their historic land and which prevented them from returning to their original towns and villages. The fence is a constant reminder of the rupture caused by the 1948 war, which pushed many Palestinians out of their towns and villages in what is today the state of Israel. Even when some Gazans refer to the armistice line of 1949, the line that was drawn in the aftermath of the 1948 war, few people refer to it as a border. It is mostly referred to in Arabic as '*al-silik*' — literally, 'the wire,' or 'the fence.' In short, for the Palestinians in Gaza, the fence evokes the *Nakba*, the refugee struggle, and the occupation. The fence, as a physical barrier to refugee return, was the beginning of the tragedy. The fence today is its continuation. And since the fence caused the problem, the solution must include its removal. The fence is the history that Palestinians in Gaza never want to forget, and no amount of aid can induce them to do so.

Gaza: Between the Humanitarian, the Political, and the Historical

A relatively small area in the south-western region of historic Palestine, the Gaza Strip is bounded by Israel from the north and east, Egypt from the south, and the Mediterranean Sea to its west. The Strip is forty kilometers long and ten kilometers wide[6], with a population of approximately 1.8 million,[7] 1.3 million of whom are refugees. The Gaza Strip is an overcrowded place. It is sometimes referred to as a slum, or, as described by the United Nations Relief and Work Agency (UNRWA), a place with 'one of the highest population densities in the world.'[8] Such characterizations lead to the conclusion that the Gaza Strip faces a 'demographic crisis', and we are left with the sense that population density is the root of Gaza's problems. In 2012, a UN report titled 'Gaza in 2020: A livable place?' was issued, sounding the alarm over the Strip's deteriorating situation.[9] According to the report, Gaza's livability is at stake given the 'substantial population growth' from a population of 1.6 million, when the report was issued, to an estimated population of 2.1 million by 2020. This demographic pressure comes in conjunction with a deteriorating infrastructure and severe gaps in basic social services. The report described Gaza as 'a heavily urbanized environment with little room for further growth.' Of course, the report's premise is humanitarian, pleading for more intervention and support by the international community and concerned bodies to save Gaza from becoming unlivable. No one can deny the importance, indeed necessity, of such effort, especially in light of the grave living conditions that Gaza's residents do in fact face. Nevertheless, Gaza's demographic and urban crisis is part of a larger picture of a complicated history, and not simply a humanitarian issue.

Certain metaphors and descriptors contribute to creating a de-politicized discourse when attention is limited to humanitarian aspects. Gaza is a clear example of the effects of this discourse.[10] In one such work that discusses this issue, Toine van Teeffelen examines Israeli press coverage of Gaza in the 1980s. He refers to two main discourses in the Israeli media: a semi-literary discourse which talks about pain, emotions and tragedy, and a discourse based on a rhetoric of science that is concerned with crises — such as the demographic one — their size, and potential impact.[11] Both discourses, as van Teeffelen shows, contribute to de-politicizing the problems of Palestinians in general, and Gaza in particular, and make 'other conditions than the occupation constitute the central matter of concern'.[12] Ilana Feldman, in her article 'Gaza's Humanitarian Problem,' also acknowledges that in addition to responding to Palestinians' needs, humanitarianism has a negative side. She argues that a mere humanitarian context may be 'deployed as a strategy for frustrating Palestinian aspirations and the often unintended political effects of the most well-intentioned humanitarian interventions.'[13]

While the humanitarian context and the simplified discourses in the Israeli press differ in their functions and the audience they seek, both are examples of de-politicized discourses vis-à-vis the situation in Gaza — discourses that historian Avi Shlaim has warned against. On the eve of Operation Cast Lead (the Israeli military operation against the Gaza Strip in 2008–9), Shlaim argued that the 'undeclared aim [of the war] is to ensure that the Palestinians in Gaza are seen by the world simply as a humanitarian problem and thus to derail their struggle for independence and statehood.'[14] Calling for a change in these approaches, he argued that 'the only way to make sense of Israel's senseless war in Gaza is through understanding the historical context.'[15]

History Matters

Understanding the historical context in which the Gaza Strip with its problems and crises emerged is the key to making sense of Gaza's present reality. The central element of this historical context is the *Nakba* (catastrophe) of 1948, as this was the moment of spatial and territorial rupture experienced by most of those who became refugees in Gaza. In this sense, the *Nakba* is not history relegated to the past, but history lived in the present: in the narrow alleys of the crowded refugee camps, in the women who leave their humble houses in the camps every morning to receive their food packages, in the barefoot children who play soccer on Gaza's beach, and in the lands of depopulated villages just beyond the fence still visible from the rooftops of Gaza's refugee camps. The *Nakba* is still present in Gaza, not only by the continuation of the state of refuge, but also by the continuity of the rupture that it caused.

The year 1948 was a turning point in Palestinian history. The war was the culmination of decades of Zionist colonization activities and Palestinian resistance to British occupation and its support for this colonial project. The spark for the war was the British Empire's decision to withdraw from the territory under its Mandate, and the issuance of the imprudent UN plan to partition the territory into a Jewish majority state and an Arab majority state. Arab states and Palestinian leaders rejected the blatantly unfair partition deal, while Zionist leaders took it as a source of international legitimacy to launch their 'war of independence,' a war that led to the uprooting of over 750,000 Palestinians from the areas controlled by the fledgling state of Israel, and seized 78 percent of the Mandate territory of Palestine. The remaining 22 percent of historic Palestine included the tiny Gaza Strip, which fell under an Egyptian administration, and the West Bank, which was annexed by the Kingdom of Jordan. Over 750,000 Palestinian refugees sought refuge in these two regions and the surrounding Arab states. For the most part, that is where they and their descendants have remained ever since.

From Qada' to Qita': the Nakba as Rupture

Undoubtedly, the *Nakba* had a catastrophic outcome for the Palestinians. In addition to disrupting Palestinian social formation and identity-development,[16] it prevented the Palestinians from enjoying territorial independence and sovereignty over the land where they embraced their heritage and culture, and witnessed their earlier national development. Palestinian nationalism crystallized with a clear agenda: to establish independence over all of historic Palestine. One of the general motives behind the crystallization of such a vision was that there already existed cultural, social, economic, and political practices and connections within the space of historic Palestine in general, and within each of the bigger regions inside Palestine itself.

The Gaza Strip was born out of the *Nakba*. Before 1948, the 'Strip' (*Qita'* in Arabic) as a geographic unit did not exist. Before 1948, Gaza was a 'district,' (*Qada'*) an administrative region of Mandate Palestine, as it was during the four centuries of Ottoman rule.[17] By the end of the British Mandate, the 1948 Gaza sub-district's area was 1196.5 square kilometers, which included three major cities: Gaza, al-Majdal (now Ashkelon), and

Khan Younis, in addition to fifty-three towns and villages.[18] Throughout history, the area of the Gaza district changed in size, but for centuries it had maintained most of the area that was officially part of the Gaza sub-district on the eve of 1948. The long historical consistency of Gaza's position as a political, economic and cultural center for the surrounding area placed it at the heart of this district. These dynamics, relations, and interactions within the Gaza space were the result of centuries of consistent connection between the city and its surroundings that were barely disrupted except in short periods of political turmoil. The 1948 war radically disrupted this state of affairs, effecting dramatic changes on all levels: political, demographic, economic, and social.

In 1949 when the war was almost over, a number of armistice agreements were signed between Israel and its neighboring Arab countries. The armistice agreement stated that:

> The Armistice Demarcation Line is not to be construed in any sense as a political or territorial boundary, and is delineated without prejudice to rights, claims and positions of either Party to the Armistice as regards ultimate settlement of the Palestine question.[19]

During the war, Israel occupied areas beyond those allocated to the Jewish majority state according to the 1947 United Nations partition plan. The Israeli forces conquered 78 percent of Mandate Palestine, which included 70 percent of the Gaza sub-district. The remaining 365 square kilometers of the Gaza district was to come under Egyptian administration, which was the first to use the term 'Strip'.[20] The phrase 'Gaza Strip' was attached to Gaza by a decree from the Egyptian president Muhammad Najib in 1954 in which he 'assigned Amir-Alay Abdullah Refa'at as an administrative governor of the Gaza Strip in its new borders which start from the town of Rafah in the south, to Beit Hanoun in the North.'[21]

By the time the armistice agreement was signed, around 200,000 refugees had already arrived in the Strip and gathered in eight refugee camps. Unlike many of the refugees that fled to neighboring Arab countries, Gaza's new arrivals were never far from their original homes.[22] Across the armistice lines, they could see their old villages. After the Six-Day War in 1967 and the beginning of Israel's occupation and military administration, these refugees were allowed to travel into Israel with special permits where they were able to finally see their towns and villages — but of course, were never allowed to return. Some of Gaza's original residents, many of whom were landlords with several holdings, even continued to hold title to lands beyond the lines of demarcation. Indeed, most of Gaza's refugees came from peasant societies that had historically worked the land of the Gazan landlords. Since 1948, those same peasants have lived in refugee camps near the old landowning families and clans within what became the Gaza Strip.

In 1950, the Israeli Knesset passed the 'Law of Return,' which allows only Jews to 'return' to Israel proper, whereas its policy towards the Palestinian refugees who were spirited across the borders and the demarcation line was clear: they shall not return. Around the Gaza Strip the demarcation line become impassable. In *Gaza: A History*, historian Jean-Pierre Filiu describes the situation:

> The grave difficulty of overcoming the trauma of dispossession was exacer-bated by the artificial nature of the lines of demarcation when the former dwellings and family lands of the refugees were so close at hand. The despair of enclosure was even worse for the Bedouin, who were accustomed to roam-ing in the southern desert but were now stuck in the outskirts of Khan Yunis. In June 1950, an Israeli intelligence report noted that the refugees in Gaza were 'condemned to utter extinction as the goods they brought with them are being used up bit by bit.'[23]

The post-*Nakba* history shows that Palestinian refugees in Gaza resisted the demarcation line. For them, in Filiu's words, the land beyond the demarcation line was perceived as a lost paradise to which generations of refugees yearned to return. As for the early refugees, it took them time to understand that the demarcation line had become practically impassable. In his book, Filiu reports a number of attempts by refugees to cross to their towns and villages, including 'farmers who tried to cultivate their land.' Such attempts were brutally confronted by kibbutz residents and Israeli military outposts located near the demarcation line, and led to the deaths of many of those who attempted to cross.[24] During this period, the armistice line began to develop into a frontier of confrontation and resistance, despite its artificial nature. Later on, the demarcation line would take the physical shape of a fence, to be engraved in the Palestinian collective memory and awareness as both a material and a symbolic monument of rupture and territorial and emotional disconnection.

The 1950s witnessed what Israeli historian Benny Morris calls the 'border war,' referring to conflicts aroused around the Gaza Strip-Israel frontier and across the demarcation line or Israel's borders with surrounding Arab states where refugees were pushed. Attempts by refugees to return to their towns and villages after the end of the 1948 war were labeled as 'infiltrations' by Israel and received with brutal acts of retaliation.[25] In 1954, Israel issued the Prevention of Infiltration Law, in which the definition of infiltrators included 'a Palestinian citizen or a Palestinian resident without nationality or citizenship or whose nationality or citizenship was doubtful and who, during the said period, left his ordinary place of residence in an area which has become a part of Israel for a place outside Israel.'[26] One of the most violent examples of Israel's attempts to crush the so-called infiltration was the Khan Younis massacre of 1956, when 275 Palestinians lost their lives — including 140 refugees.[27] In fact, the persistence of Palestinian refugees attempting to return to their lands beyond the demarcation lines belied earlier expectations by Israeli government specialists, who predicted that Palestinian refugees 'would die and most of them would turn into human dust and the waste of society, and join the most impoverished classes in the Arab countries.'[28] On the contrary, the inability of Palestinian refugees to return to their land supplied them with the will and determination to return to their homes and resist normalizing their condition of dispossession by persevering in their memory and attachment to their land beyond the fences.

Beyond the Fence: Rediscovering Gaza's History

The persistence of Palestinian attempts to return to their land, marked by the portentous tenacity of refugees throughout the decades that followed the *Nakba*, challenges one of the core arguments of Zionism that Palestine was an empty land, or 'a land without a people.' Of course, the Zionists saw the Palestinians, but emptiness here is an abstract concept. This is what Gabriel Piterberg calls the 'empty land' concept in *The Returns of Zionism: Myths, Politics and Scholarship in Israel*. He argues that for the settler colonial narrative, the colonized land is empty, even though it had physical presence of a community other than the colonizers.[29] The Zionist denial of any sort of Palestinian presence or connection to be worthy of recognition would lead to the assumption that Palestinian refugees would 'turn into human dust and waste of society.' Contrary to such expectations, Palestinians' connection to their land, which springs from a deeply rooted history, produced a collective memory that inspired decades of resistance and patriotism.

The Gaza district, as a geographic region, like other regions and districts of Palestine, had its share of such long histories. In fact, there is an unfolding history of Gaza City and its district that is stocked with accounts of life prior to the *Nakba*'s rupture and the fences it brought. Such accounts of Gaza can be found in works written by Palestinian historians before and after the *Nakba*. Some of these works include *Ithaf al-A'izza fi Tarikh Ghazza*, or 'Delighting the Beloved with the History of Gaza' by Shaykh 'Uthman al-Taba' (1882–1950), a religious and legal figure originally from Gaza City. The second work is *Tarikh Ghazzah* or 'The History of Gaza' by Arif al-Arif (1892–1973) who served as the District Officer of Gaza district as part of his administrative career when Palestine was under the British Mandate. In these works, one can find compelling accounts of the city's history, where it is clear that Gaza as a region had been an eternal stage for interactions since early history. There, one can find stories of a place where history was never static, and where a local identity was forged throughout time.

The Gaza in the accounts of al-Taba' and al-Arif bears some resemblance to the current Strip. For millennia, Gaza has never experienced long periods of peace. In many of the conflicts and invasions in the Middle East, Gaza was destined to suffer either directly or indirectly. Most of the armies moving from Africa and Europe to Asia, and vice versa, passed through Gaza, thus making it part of long-lasting conflicts in the region. However, one can notice, while reading the pre-*Nakba* history of Gaza, that it never suffered as serious a rupture as the one of 1948. According to al-Taba', people used to identify the borders of Gaza as located 'between al-Dayr and al-Dayr,' referring to the towns Dayr Sunayd, a village approximately eight miles to the northeast of Gaza City, and Dayr al-Daroum, which lies almost ten miles to the south of Gaza City.[30] Within this space, in which Gaza city served as one of its main arteries, a set of practices, activities, norms, festivals, and other economic, social, and political interactions, took place for centuries. For example, al-Arif writes in detail about the religious festivals that Gazans used to celebrate. One of these festivals was called 'the Valley of Ants' which was located, according to al-Arif, close to Ashkelon. Al-Arif writes:

> On that Wednesday people head in droves to a place located near Ashkelon called the Valley of Ants; it is said that this was the spot when Prophet Solo-

mon heard the ants talking as mentioned in the Quran. In this sport gathers the people of al-Majdal [Ashkelon] and its villages, and the majority of the people of Gaza and its villages: carrying their flags, riding their horses, wearing their most beautiful clothes, bringing the best food, and singing the best songs until sunset. [31]

Al-Arif traces the roots of this festival, and many other similar festivals and events, as being many centuries old. In 1948, the residents of the Gaza region would be unable to celebrate their 'Valley of Ants' festival. In that year also, what was 'between al-Dayr and al-Dayr,' became trapped 'from the fence to the fence.' Forty years after this rupture, Saleem al-Mubayed, a historian from the post-*Nakba* generation, published a book titled *Gaza and its Strip*, where he writes in its introduction:

the Strip with the villages and towns it includes, is not the son of the natural geography which does not believe in manmade architecture, lines, and borders. In fact, Gaza city and its villages were never separated at any stage of their history from their landscape, which extends to the north and to the south and to the east, across a fertile coastal plain that is far larger in its limits and size from the current Strip, which was forcibly stripped of the land of Palestine — also a part of Greater Syria and separated from the larger Arab homeland. [32]

In what I have presented, I hope, is an apparent significance of reading Gaza's past and present in its people's words, terms and metaphors. This is not merely a call to understanding the oppressed 'in their own words' for its own sake, but a recognition of the fact that their description of their reality actually holds true to their situation. Metaphors such as 'from fence to fence,' remind Palestinians in Gaza — both as refugees and natives — of their loss, their tragedy, and the abnormality of the fence that divides their land and prevents their return. Not only are these borders artificially drawn and reinforced with the use of brutal force, but they highlight the utter insanity of fencing an entire population in the world's largest open-air prison simply because of Israel's need to maintain a Jewish demographic majority. The fact that Gaza's crisis could be solved tomorrow if the majority-refugee population were granted its right of return is completely ignored by the humanitarian discourse. The tragedy of Gaza needs to be understood through the intensity of loss, especially since in Gaza's situation, what was lost is only a stone's throw away for many refugees, who can still see their former towns and villages beyond the fence.

GAZA: ISOLATION

Ilana Feldman

During the Israeli assault on Gaza in summer 2014 considerable media coverage was given to the Israeli tactic of calling people a few minutes before their homes were bombed. Some observers appeared to accept the Israeli contention that this was a humanitarian gesture. Others raised the question of where, in this landscape of violence, in a tiny, densely populated strip of land with no free points of egress, the inhabitants were supposed to go. As Jon Stewart put it: 'Evacuate to where? Have you seen Gaza?'[1] Palestinians living in Gaza's 'open air prison'[2] are not only targeted for attack, but also victimized by enforced immobility. Through years of policies of increasing control, closure and blockade, Israel has created this vulnerability and then deployed immobility as a lethal weapon. There is frequent reference in the media to the blockade imposed on Gaza in 2006 after Hamas won parliamentary elections, but the process of isolating Gaza began long before that. Understanding how immobility was imposed and then weaponized requires looking at the history of borders, movements and constraints on motion that have defined this place since 1948.

The creation of the Gaza Strip as a distinct space was itself part of this isolation process. Before 1948 Gaza was part of Palestine — distinguished as a district, like other districts, but inseparable from the rest of the country. Its residents, like residents of other parts of the country, could travel freely throughout Palestine. To be sure, during the years of the British Mandate many Palestinians (women especially) did not travel frequently or far from their home villages, but their capacity to move was not hindered by borders,

95

checkpoints, or permits. When I conducted interviews with Palestinians in Gaza in the late 1990s, the freedom of movement was one of the losses they lamented. A number of the older generation among them remembered travels around the country. As one person described, naming the places that are now off-limits: 'We used to go to Jaffa, Haifa, Jerusalem, etc. I used to go for a change of air. If I did not like Jaffa, I could go to Haifa, Tel Aviv, or Jerusalem. If I did not like Jerusalem I could go to Nazareth or Safad. I used to go wherever I wanted. It was allowed.'³ The names of these cities were recited like talismans of lost connections. And part of what was lost was possibility: the possibility that one could move, and could move just for 'a change of air.' 1948 changed all of that.

Today more than two-thirds of Gaza's residents are refugees, displaced from their villages before they were confined in Gaza. When Palestinians became refugees in Gaza in 1948 they did not cross an international border into displacement. They headed south or west, moving away from fighting, expelled by Israeli military forces. Only after the fact was a boundary marked between their homes and their place of refuge. These borders were 'provisional,' defined in the armistice agreement signed between Israel and Egypt (which governed the new Gaza Strip) in 1949. The armistice line was 'not to be construed in any sense as a political or territorial boundary, and is delineated without prejudice to rights, claims and positions of either Party to the Armistice as regards ultimate settlement of the Palestine question.'⁴ But of course this boundary has functioned as a political boundary. It has prejudiced the rights and claims of Palestinians. This border has determined much of the fate of Gazans. They have lived, generations now, in displacement just a few miles from their homes and villages. And their movement, within and beyond Gaza's borders, has been subject to the whims of occupying and neighboring powers.

Displacement is a process; it takes time for people to fully understand that their homes and previous lives have been lost. And so, too, are isolation and confinement. The official creation of a border and the on-the-ground work of border-making often proceed at different rhythms. As happened in other border zones with 1948 Palestine, for several years refugees in Gaza tried to cross back to retrieve possessions from their homes: they were shot at by Israeli forces and sometimes imprisoned by Egyptians.

Even as access to the rest of Palestine was increasingly impossible for Gazans, during the twenty years of Egyptian rule movement was possible with a permit across the southern border into the Sinai. Palestinians went to university in Egypt, they got jobs in the Gulf, they traveled; they were connected to the larger community of displaced Palestinians. Other people traveled to Gaza, not just humanitarian workers and peacekeeping soldiers, but also tourists from other Arab countries, encouraged by the duty-free zone that Egypt established in Gaza. And Palestinians also came to have a relationship with the new space of the Gaza Strip, to feel at home there even as they longed for their homes on the other side of the armistice line.

Occupation and Isolation

With the Israeli occupation of the Gaza Strip (along with the West Bank) in 1967, people were able to visit — though not to reclaim — these homes. The Israeli government's interest in incorporating the Occupied Territories, though not their populations, into Israel required that it keep the borders relatively porous. The territories became frequent shopping destinations for Israelis. Gaza, in particular, became known for its cheap car mechanics. And even if Israel did not want the Palestinian inhabitants of the territories (granting them citizenship would have immediately threatened the Jewish majority in Israel), it wanted their labor. So, Palestinian movement was relatively unimpeded for the first twenty-five years of the occupation. Along with the workers who came from the territories for jobs, Palestinians were able to travel for leisure, study, and to visit family members.

But a few years into the first *intifada*, which began in December 1987, Israel began to impose restrictions on Palestinian movement from the territories (while simultaneously bringing in foreign laborers to take the place of Palestinian workers). The first steps in developing a comprehensive 'pass system'[5] were imposed in Gaza in the late 1980s, as residents who wished to move were required to get a security-services approved magnetic card (in addition to the ID card required of everyone). The Israeli closure policy, wherein any Palestinian movement required a permit, was fully developed after 1991 (the first Gulf War provided the occasion for the first comprehensive closure of the territories). With these restrictions in place, the number of Palestinians working in Israel decreased dramatically and people's capacity to move between Gaza and the West Bank severely diminished.

Rather than easing these conditions, the Oslo Accords, signed between Israel and the Palestinians in 1993, consolidated them. Gaza was fenced off, many years before the wall was built in the West Bank. An immediate consequence of Oslo was that movement between the West Bank and Gaza became impossible for most Palestinians (those not qualifying for VIP status). Goods could still enter — and Gaza was a major market for Israeli products — but people could no longer reach the other parts and people of Palestine.

The Oslo process had many consequences for Palestinians. Among them was the further entrenchment of the process that began during the *intifada* of transforming Gaza from a labor reserve for Israeli industry and a captive market for Israeli goods to it being seen only as the latter. As is the case in so many places around the world where capital flows easily, but people's movements are constrained, the 'separation' from the Occupied Territories that Israel pursued in those years was a separation of populations (Israeli citizens were also barred from entering Gaza and all 'Area A' spaces), but not of markets.

When I was researching and living in Gaza in the late 1990s, late in the 'peaceful' days of Oslo, movement in and out of Gaza for foreigners like me was nearly unimpeded. Not so for Palestinians. A friend, another foreign researcher, visited me in Gaza to add a different comparative perspective to her research in the West Bank. She was exploring how young people experienced the landscapes of restriction and circuitous movement that characterized the Oslo-period occupation. Her opening question to me — how far does Jerusalem feel to you? — was a non-starter in a context where people had no chance of reaching that destination. Rather than offering stories about the convoluted space and time of occupation — off-roading around checkpoints, never being able to predict how long a journey might take — the young Gazans she met usually said that they had never left Gaza. And most did not seem to think it likely that they would anytime soon.

Israel's restrictions on Palestinian movement have multiplied extraordinarily in recent years. The resulting isolation has not only harmed individuals — impeding their ability to live full lives — it has also impaired the Palestinian political community, increasing distance, distrust, and ultimately division between the West Bank and Gaza. During the second *intifada* Israel began to restrict internationals' entrance into the Strip, too. Having already essentially prohibited Palestinian travel through the Erez crossing, Israel's response to Hamas' victory in parliamentary elections in 2006 and takeover of Gaza in 2007, was to impose a blockade on the entrance of many goods into Gaza, along with the export of Gazan products.

The tunnel economy that emerged at this time, and which enabled the movement of goods and people underground across the Gaza-Egypt border, was one Palestinian response to these restrictions. And this reference to the Egyptian border provides a reminder that it has never been Israel alone that has enforced isolation. Egypt has supported Israeli policy by largely shutting the border (the Rafah crossing is opened periodically and somewhat unpredictably). And, beginning under the regime of Muhammad Morsi and intensifying under Abdel Fattah el-Sisi's rule, Egypt has now destroyed most of the tunnels.

The cycles of destruction in Gaza have sped up over the last decade. In addition to the constraining closure regime of the past twenty-five years and the devastating siege and blockade of the past eight years, in the last seven years Israeli forces have launched three assaults on the Strip, two involving a significant ground invasion, all involving massive destruction. Humanitarian agencies confront this cycle of destruction on the ground. When the smoke clears from the latest round of catastrophic violence, they make the rounds to see what remains: of lives people were living and of the projects which their agencies have supported. One consequence of the repeated assaults on Gaza for humanitarian organizations is the necessity of repeatedly rebuilding the same projects.

Israeli military strategists refer to the practice of the periodic targeting of Gaza as 'mowing the lawn.' As Efraim Inbar described it in the *Jerusalem Post*, 'Israel simply needs to "mow the grass" once in a while to degrade the enemy's capabilities. . . . Keeping the enemy off balance and reducing its capabilities requires Israeli military readiness and a willingness to use force intermittently….'[6] Israel's rationale for this strategy focuses on Hamas as the target, with the effects on Palestinian society relegated to 'collateral damage.' But, as Mouin Rabbani and others have pointed out, the real target of these assaults are the Palestinian population and Palestinian society. So the reference to 'mowing the lawn' — which perhaps suggests that the grass is allowed to grow in-between mowings — doesn't fully capture the nature of this policy. These regular assaults not only result in catastrophic losses of life and damage to infrastructure, they produce a degradation of the underling 'normal.' When each round of attack concludes, conditions of life in Gaza return to an everyday that is worse than before. This process, as it is intended to do, interrupts political engagement, economic activity, and social life. And it transforms people's expectations for the future, as everyone assumes (knows?) that another attack will come.

In the aftermath of the assault against Gaza in the summer of 2014, Gaza's new condition appeared marked by the desire to escape. Palestinians in Gaza have always wanted to be able to move freely — inside and outside Palestine — but have not generally been driven by an imperative to escape Gaza. As Khalil Shaheen of the Palestinian Center for Human Rights said, 'Life before the war was already miserable,' and in the onslaught 'families lost their properties, their memories, and their families. They lost everything and now they face a loss of human dignity with limited access to water, food, shelter, and healthcare.'[7]

The consequences of trying to escape under conditions of isolation were made tragically clear in the September 2014 sinking of a boat filled with many fleeing Gazans. A migrant-smuggling boat filled with approximately 500 people was rammed by smugglers when the captain refused an order to transfer the passengers into a much smaller boat that he said would sink under their weight. Most of those on board, including the captain, drowned when the boat sank. According to a report by the *Guardian,* as many as 200 of them were from Gaza (also on-board were Palestinians from the Yarmouk camp in Syria).[8]

The fact that impoverished people pay large sums of money to smugglers and take significant risks with their lives in the hope of reaching a place with more opportunity is, horribly, a regular feature of our unequal world. And the language in which this event was reported — as the sinking of a 'migrant' boat — locates this event in the realm of global precarity. But it is a relatively new part of the Gazan experience. The tunnels that for many years of the blockade on Gaza helped sustain its economic life are now being put to use in ferrying people (mostly young men) out of Gaza and into a network of smugglers. This phenomenon is a product of both the continuing degradation of the quality of life in Gaza — squeezed by economic blockade and suffering repeated material destruction — and the increasing immobility of its population (in earlier periods of economic difficulty 'at home,' more Gazans had outlets for legal travel for work abroad). Grinding poverty, a sense of futility about the future, and the promise that things could (and could only) be better elsewhere, are global conditions of chronic suffering. In Gaza they are direct outcomes of Israeli policy, Egyptian complicity, and international indifference.

So Gazans are immobilized in every sense: cut off from other members of their community, isolated from the 'international community,' deprived of economic opportunity, basic goods, and access to advanced medical care. Imposed immobility is itself a form of violence against people, and it cruelly magnifies the violence of military assault. The 2014 catastrophe in Gaza was a product of years of preparation. Restriction of Palestinians' movement goes back to their displacement in 1948. And mobility management has been a central tactic of Israeli occupation since 1967. The phone call ahead of the bomb, the 'roof knock' (a small bomb) ahead of the lethal strike, are twists in this long trajectory. That sometimes the phone call is not followed by a strike underscores its potency in psychological warfare. These tactics are yet another weapon in the massive arsenal deployed against Palestinians.

GAZA STRIP: THE LESSONS OF HISTORY

Salman Abu Sitta

Gaza is Palestine. The Gaza Strip is a symbol of Palestine's geography and history. It has the distinction that it has never willingly raised a flag other than Palestine's.

The most recent July 2014 Israeli war on Gaza was one of the bloodiest and most deadly in a long series of Israeli attacks. During the attacks, my calls to family and friends to give condolences and support were invariably met by a reply which became their motto: 'Under blockade we were dying slowly. Now we are dying instantly. Let us die standing. This is the only piece of Palestine left.'

There is no region within the geography of historic Palestine that is called the 'Gaza Strip'. This term, and its ramifications, were created by Israel in 1948. To contextualize the Strip's turbulent history, we go back to 1947 when the southern district of Palestine under the British Mandate was divided into two sub-districts: the Gaza sub-district (an area of 1,111.5 square kilometers, with a population of 137,180 of which 98 percent were Arabs) and Beer Sheba sub-district (an area of 12,577 square km with a population of 87,000 of which 99.5 percent was Arab). These two sub-districts were almost purely populated by Arabs; there were a few Jews scattered in about fourteen Zionist colonies (*kibbutzim*) with a population of 3,200. In anticipation of partitioning Palestine, the Zionists planted eleven *kibbutzim* overnight in October 1946. A typical Zionist colony would consist of thirty soldiers assumed to be farmers, housed in prefab units and fortified by machine gun nests and barbed wire with trenches.

The intention was to occupy and conquer large areas of Palestine when conditions were favourable.

The planting of such Zionist colonies in the Arab south turned out to be crucial for the Zionists' future plans. On 29 November 1947, the United Nations passed a resolution partitioning Palestine into Arab and Jewish states. There are anomalies in this process and its terms that need to be clarified. The first is the phrase 'partition plan'. The UN had no jurisdiction to divide countries and made this clear in its proceedings. In fact, the partition plan was a mere suggestion, passed by a narrow vote, under pressure from the US, to establish a separate government in areas of presumed majority of population in each part of Palestine. Any such plan has no binding legal value; it is only valid if both parties agree to it. It allocated 55.5 percent of Palestine to the Jewish state and 43.8 percent to the Arab state with 0.7 percent for Jerusalem and surrounding villages as *corpus separatum*.

The second anomaly was that the number of Jews in the Arab state was negligible, while the number of Jews was almost equal to the number of Arabs in the proposed Jewish state. Neither state was intended to be founded on an ethnic, racial or religious basis, as such a structure would be something the UN would never propose. A third anomaly is in the naming of these states. The words 'Arab' and 'Jewish' were at that time the terms used in official papers during the British Mandate, which referred to 'Arabs' as the natural inhabitants of the country and 'Jews' as the Jewish immigrants who came from Europe under the protection of the British Mandate.

This background is necessary to understand that southern Palestine, of which the Gaza Strip was the surviving remnant, was largely Arab and that the partition plan had no legal right to bestow it on Jewish immigrants. The Zionists knew this; they decided to take it by force.

The conflict between the majority inhabitants of the country and the new European colonists flared up in early April 1948 when Plan Dalet, the Zionist strategy to conquer Palestine, was put into effect. The Haganah forces, which formed the backbone of the Jewish army, were well armed; their forces numbered 60,000 at the beginning of 1948 and increased to 120,000 by the end of the year. The Palestinian population, in comparison, was defenseless, particularly due to the decimation of Palestinian resistance by the British Army in 1939, which quelled the Great Arab Revolt (1936–1939). Under this unequal situation and moved to action by the massacres committed by the Zionists, such as the infamous Deir Yassin, volunteer fighters from Egypt, Sudan, Libya and Saudi Arabia came to southern Palestine to join the Palestinian defenders. They were highly motivated by their sense of duty, but they were small in number and had little military experience or organization.

At the end of the British Mandate on 15 May 1948, Arab regular forces entered Palestine to save what was left of it. The Haganah had already depopulated 220 villages, mainly along the coast, and expelled their populations, which made up half of all Palestinian refugees — all this before the British Mandate ended, before the State of Israel was declared, and before Arab soldiers arrived. Similarly, 48 hours before David Ben Gurion declared the state of Israel on 14 May 1948, the Palmach — the strike force of the Haganah — committed a massacre in Burayr village, 15 kilometers north-east of Gaza, killing 120 people and burning the village down.

Three days later, the Egyptian forces entered Palestine and took control of the Arab area in the south, stretching from Isdud on the Mediterranean Sea in the west to Bethlehem and southern Jerusalem in the east. The Egyptian forces were led by General Mawawi. Apart from a few successful operations against Zionist colonies, General Mawawi was inept and caused the collapse of the Egyptian forces, losing about 14,000 square kilometers of southern Palestine (almost half of Palestine). He was removed and a new General, Ahmad Fouad Sadeq, was appointed instead.

The Haganah army, which became the Israeli Defence Forces, was bold enough to advance into Egypt itself until the coastal town of El Arish. It withdrew under pressure from Britain, which had a base in Egypt. The Egyptian government ordered General Sadeq to evacuate the area and return to Egypt. He refused, writing in a memorable telegram to Cairo: 'My military honour doesn't allow me to leave my Arab brothers and sisters, defenceless women and children, to be slaughtered by Jews like chicken.'[1]

He gathered his remaining forces along with all the Palestinian and Arab volunteers and they made a determined stand against a massive Israeli attack, intended to destroy what was left of Palestine. On Christmas Day 1948, a battle took place at Hill 86, or Sheikh Hammouda: the massive Israeli force led by a Russian Red Army general was soundly defeated and the general killed. The Gaza Strip was saved. But the relentless Israeli attacks on Palestinian refugees never stopped.

The population of the Gaza Strip at the time was 80,000, living in four small towns: Gaza, Deir Al-Balah, Khan Younis, and Rafah. Added to them were 200,000 refugees who were depopulated from 247 villages in southern Palestine, making the strip, a mere 1.3 percent of the land, even at the time one of the most crowded areas in Palestine. This 'ethnic cleansing' of southern Palestine is unique in that it was completely depopulated, unlike any other area occupied by Israel, for example in the north where many villages remained. In the south not a single village remained. This was an act of total ethnic cleansing, propelled by several massacres which took place in Al Dawayma, Bayt Daras, Isdud, and Burayr, among others.

Refugees now corralled into Gaza were not immune from Israeli attacks even after their expulsion. A new element hitherto unknown to them in the Israeli warfare methods was bombardment by air. The Majdal hospital was bombed in November 1948, as was al-Joura village, which stands on the site of ancient Ashkelon and from which many future Hamas leaders would emerge. A family of eleven was killed while having supper. Even when the land war subsided in January 1949, the Israelis bombed food distribution centers in Deir Al-Balah and Khan Younis at peak hours, leaving over 200 bodies strewn in the streets by air raids. One of them was my uncle. These raids led the usually restrained Red Cross to describe it as a 'scene of horror'.[2]

Enduring al Nakba

The failure of the Egyptian army to save the Southern District from Zionist expansion left under its control a sliver of land called the Gaza Strip. Unlike Jordan's absorption of the West Bank, Egypt had no desire to annex the Gaza Strip. Pending a new Palestinian state, Egypt was obliged to administer the Strip. The Egyptian administration issued travel documents for the refugees and Gaza citizens, but the flag of Palestine continued to fly high across the skies of Gaza. Naturally, refugees started to return home to their villages to fetch their remaining family members, to water their gardens, to feed their cattle and to bring back some of their belongings, in anticipation of final return. The Israelis were not yet in total control of this vast territory in southern Palestine, so they laid mines at water sources and cross roads. According to the Israeli historian Benny Morris, in the period between 1949 and 1956, Israel killed between 2,700 and 5,000 people trying to cross the imaginary line back to their homes.[3]

The area of the Gaza Strip, according to the Armistice Agreement signed between Egypt and Israel on 24 February 1949, was 555 square kilometers.

In the joint Egyptian-Israeli Mixed Armistice Commission, the Israelis complained that many people were crossing the imaginary line to their homes. They called them 'infiltrators' and suggested the creation of a buffer zone in order to deter refugees from crossing the line. One year after the Armistice Agreement was signed in February 1949, a secret agreement to serve as a *modus vivendi* was agreed in February 1950 between Egyptian and Israeli officers, under which a new 'temporary' line advancing into the Gaza strip by two to three kilometers was agreed. This reduced the area of the Gaza Strip to 365 square kilometers. This new line, which is reproduced in practically all the published maps, is not the actual Armistice line according to the agreement. In the *modus vivendi* agreement, it is clearly stated that the original Armistice Agreement of February 1949 is the only official binding agreement. It is curious to note that neither the Egyptians nor the Palestinians have ever demanded the return to the original Armistice line which would add an area of 200 square kilometers to the Strip. Instead, Israel introduced a new buffer zone in stages which reduced the Strip's area by a further 20 percent.[4]

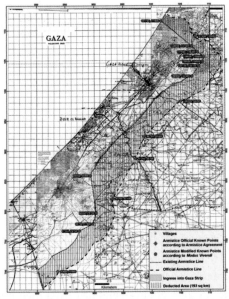

The receding Armistice line of 1949 shrinking the area of the Gaza Strip by 200 km² to its present size. Israel unilaterally imposed another buffer zone reducing the area of the Strip by a further 20 percent. Source: Salman Abu Sitta, *Atlas of Palestine 1917–1966*, Palestine Land Society, London, 2010.

Succession of disasters

The occupation of Palestinian land and the expulsion of its population gave rise to a resistance movement known then as the *fedayeen*. These resistance fighters crossed the Armistice line to attack the occupiers of their land. They were a small group, courageous and dedicated, but they were not much of a threat to the Israeli army. In order to stop the attacks and attempt to eliminate even the idea of resistance, Israel continuously attacked the Gaza Strip. In August 1953, Unit 101, led by Ariel Sharon, attacked Bureij refugee camp and killed forty-three people in their beds. In August 1955, the Israeli army, again led by Ariel Sharon, blew up the Khan Younis police station and killed seventy-four policemen. In the same year the Israelis killed thirty-seven Egyptian soldiers in a Gaza railway station and twenty-eight others who were on their way to defend the others. This prompted Egyptian President Gamal Abdel-Nasser, who assumed power in Egypt in July 1952, to seek new sources for arms denied to him by the British.

The Israeli attacks against Gaza and its people were not the only problem Palestinians had to deal with. The United Nations Relief and Works Agency (UNRWA) started a plan to resettle the refugees on the Sinai coast between Port Said and El Arish, ostensibly to ease the crowded Gaza Strip. The refugees would not accept any place to live other than Palestine; they revolted against this plan and an uprising began in March 1954, continuing until March 1955 when UNRWA abandoned the plan. Many arrests were made by the Egyptian authorities. One of those arrested was the famous Palestinian poet Mouin Bseiso, who spent eight years in an Egyptian jail in the western desert and wrote poems which later were popularized into songs.

Disaster struck the Gaza Strip again. On 29 October 1956 Israel invaded Sinai in collusion with Britain and France. The invasion, called the Suez Campaign or the Tripartite Aggression, was aimed at toppling Nasser. Then Israeli Prime Minister Ben Gurion had the added objective of converting the Armistice line into recognized borders for the occupied part of Palestine, now called Israel. The Israeli military occupied all of Sinai and turned backward to occupy the Gaza Strip for the first time. The advancing Israeli soldiers entered Khan Younis on 3 November 1956, and collecting all males between the ages of fifteen and fifty from their homes shot them in cold blood at their doorstep, or against a wall in the town's main square. The killing spree lasted until 7 November in Khan Younis town and the adjacent villages. The bodies of the dead were left in the streets for days before people were allowed to bury them. A local university teacher and Khan Younis resident, Ihsan Khalil Al Agha, listed the names of the 520 people killed in his book *Khan Younis Martyrs*.[5] Two of the victims were my sister-in-law's brothers. In the same week another massacre took place in Rafah. Joe Sacco, the well-known artist, graphically documented these massacres in his 2009 book, *Footnotes in Gaza*.[6]

With their expulsion from their homes only a few months previously and with continued Israeli attacks inflicted on them, the refugees struggled to form political parties to represent themselves and to recover their rights in their homeland. In 1950, the Executive Committee of the Refugees' Conference was elected to represent the Palestinian refugees, the first of its kind. It continued to assume that role until the PLO was formed in May 1964. Secret political parties were also formed in the Gaza Strip, including those of the Muslim Brotherhood, the Communists, and to a lesser degree, the Arab Nationalists.

Nasser's stature as a third world leader grew internationally, especially after the Bandung Conference which formed the Non-Aligned Movement. As a result of this positive political development, Jawaharlal Nehru, Prime Minister of India, and Che Guevara, the Latin American revolutionary, both came to visit the Gaza Strip at Nasser's invitation. Nasser told several Gazan Palestinian delegations to Cairo that he had no practical plan to liberate Palestine. He nonetheless encouraged Palestinian expression and democratic representation. In 1961 he arranged for the first Palestinian delegation to go to the United Nations to present their case of the right to return to their homes. That was the first time that Palestinians themselves spoke with their own voice before the world. At all previous international conferences one Arab delegation or another spoke on their behalf. Moreover, in 1961, a legislative council was elected in Gaza; it was the first ever democratically elected council in Palestine. It is not surprising therefore that the Gaza Palestinians were prominent in the formation and the composition of the first executive of the PLO, under the leadership of the veteran Palestinian diplomat Ahmad Shukairi.

Disaster struck Gaza again in June 1967 when Israel re-occupied Sinai and crossed the Suez Canal. Israeli forces moved back from El Arish to blockade the Gaza Strip and occupied it again, eleven years after the first occupation. The occupation persists until today. Immediately after 1967 Israel created travel plans for refugees to be sent to Europe and Latin America with financial and work incentives. Although some people took advantage of the offer, they were a minority. In 1971, as the IDF Operational Commander of Southern Command, Ariel Sharon destroyed rows of refugee camps in order to disperse them. Israel deported prominent Gazan leaders in order to quell any attempt at resistance.

In March 1979, Gaza had to cope with a blow from another direction. Anwar Sadat of Egypt entered into a peace agreement with Israel, effectively forfeiting both the battle for Palestine and full sovereignty for Sinai, in return for a non-aggression pact with Israel. This peace treaty has had profound effects on the Arab-Israeli conflict over Palestine. For the first time in history, the 1906 administrative line between Egypt and Palestine was converted into an international border, after which Egypt recognized the land east of the line to be Israeli, rather than Palestinian. Sinai was divided into sectors A, B, C and a narrow sector D in Israel. The crucial sector C with an east-west width from Rafah to El Arish, extending south to Sharm El Sheikh on the Gulf of Aqaba, was allowed to have a tiny Egyptian police force and was monitored by a US-dominated international force. This in effect created a new barrier between Egypt and Palestine, the gate of which into Palestine was the Rafah crossing. And thus, the Gaza strip became once again a concentration camp, stripped of its sovereignty, blocked from three sides by Israel, and by Egypt on the fourth side. Yet, or because of this, Gaza remained the center of resistance. In 1987 the first *intifada* erupted in Gaza and spread to the West Bank.

In 1993 the Oslo Accords between Israel and the PLO were signed amid much euphoria in the hope that the 1967 Israeli occupation would be removed. However, by 2000 with the outbreak of the second *intifada*, it became clear that Oslo was a hoax, intended to entrench the occupation, not to remove it. The second *intifada* was followed by the Israeli destruction of all physical symbols of the Palestinian National Authority created by the Oslo Accords, including Gaza's airport and port, thus dashing the hopes that the West Bank and Gaza would become an independent state, free from Israeli occupation.

In 2004, Palestinian leader Yasser Arafat died and Mahmoud Abbas, the architect of the ill-fated Oslo Accords, took over. Since then the situation of Palestinians in the 1967 Occupied Territories has deteriorated even more. Palestinians had remained without democratic representation after the last recognized Palestine National Council (PNC) meeting in Algiers in 1988. Although all political parties agreed in Cairo in March 2005 to hold elections for a new PNC, Abbas and his cohort refused to implement that agreement on various dubious grounds. When the 2006 local elections were held in the West Bank and Gaza under the scrutiny of international observers and recognized as fair and accurate, Hamas was the winner of these elections. As *Vanity Fair* reported in April 2008, plans to remove Hamas from office were hatched by the US/Israel through their agent Muhammad Dahlan, but the plot failed.

In its sustained campaign to destroy the Gaza Strip, Israel waged three wars in the space of six years (2008–2014) causing tremendous loss of life: over 5,000 killed, mostly civilians, and 30,000 wounded, in addition to the destruction of tens of thousands of houses, hospitals, places of worship and infrastructure. The amount of explosives dropped on Gaza in the 2014 war alone was estimated to be equal to that dropped on Hiroshima. The 2014 war is just one chapter of Israel's decades-long campaign to eliminate Palestinians by any means possible. The reason is clear: as long as there are refugees demanding their right to return to their homes occupied by Israel, Israel's legitimacy remains dubious. The refugees remain the evidence of Israel's crime of ethnic cleansing which it is determined to remove.

Lessons of history

What we learn from this short history of the Gaza strip, particularly during the last wars on Gaza, is the following:

Gaza is the remaining symbol of Palestine, its dispossessed people, and its occupied land. If Gaza falls it will be difficult to raise the case of Palestine again anywhere, especially where Palestinians are ruled by a non-Palestinian government.

Israel lives by the sword alone. It is supported in this policy in every way by the same colonial powers of the twentieth century who created it. Its institutions practice racism and apartheid and its army commits war crimes. Western support protects it from facing action under international law. As history shows, this situation cannot be sustained for long. When the crash comes it will be sudden.

The people's armed resistance, even though it is modest and with limited military means, has shown that Israel is fragile and its victories over Arab armies were caused by Arab incompetence rather than by Israel's superior fighting skills.

Arab governments are weak, meek and undemocratic; they do not tolerate the burning desire of their people to stand by and defend Palestine.

Israel's horrendous massacres have become known internationally thanks to new communications technologies which brought the images of Israeli war crimes to the homes of millions of people around the world, dealing a crushing blow to the self-image Israel had cultivated as a peaceful democratic nation caring for human rights. This has also created new tactics of peaceful resistance against Israeli crimes, such as the Boycott, Divestment and Sanctions (BDS) campaign.

Finally, the continued resistance of the people in Gaza, a population of 1.8 million, equivalent to the whole population of Palestine in 1948, together with another ten million Palestinians worldwide, shows that Palestinians will not vanish, will not be destroyed and will not be subjugated. The stalemate between the military power of occupation and the Palestinian quest for freedom from occupation will one day be broken. And the people will be set free in their homeland. Let us hope that this will come sooner rather than later.

GAZA: ENCYSTATION

Glenn Bowman

Cyst: 1. *Biol.* a thin walled hollow organ or cavity in an animal body (or plant) ...2. *Path.* a closed cavity or sac of a morbid or abnormal character...3. *Biol or Cryptogamic.* A cell or cavity containing reproductive bodies, embryos etc...

(*Oxford English Dictionary*)

A cyst is a closed sac, having a distinct membrane and division compared to the nearby tissue. Basically, a cyst is a cluster of cells that have grouped together to form a sac (not unlike the manner in which water molecules group together, forming a bubble); however, the distinguishing aspect of a cyst is the cells forming the "shell" of such a sac, being distinctly abnormal (in both appearance and behaviour) when compared to all surrounding cells for that given location. It may contain air, fluids, or semi-solid material. Once formed, a cyst may sometimes resolve on its own. Whether a cyst that fails to resolve may need to be removed by surgery will depend on what type of cyst it is and where in the body it has formed.[1]

As I write in January 2015 the Egyptian government under Abdel Fattah el-Sisi is completing the extension from 500 to 1000 meters of a free-fire buffer zone at the Egyptian-Gazan border. This 'construction' (which involves the destruction of at least 1200 houses in Rafah) consolidates the process of closure of Gaza which the military regime inaugurated soon after coming to power, canceling the policy of his predecessor's government of permanently opening the Rafah Crossing to movement in and out of Gaza.

El-Sisi's buffer zone links up with the 'shell' Israel has — since its early efforts at walling Gaza in 1991 — built up around the whole of Gaza incorporating palisades, fences, 300-meter buffer zones (these expropriating Gazan land unlike that of the Egyptians which is on Egyptian territory), naval blockades, air space closure and sealed gates. Israel has, with the connivance of Egypt, literally closed the population of Gaza within a sac; this short essay will examine the metaphorical implications of that 'encystation' — metaphorical implications with deep historical roots and very literal consequences.

Encystation as the process of enclosing within a cyst and the encirclement of Palestinian communities within the territories over which Israel claims sovereignty is indisputably an act of quarantining 'matter' held to put the surrounding social body at risk. Although Israel, as now Egypt, claims that walling is a matter of security (used, as the former claims, for the prevention of Palestinian attacks on Israeli civilians[2] and, as the latter claims, for the prevention of Salafist entries into Egyptian territory from Gaza), 'encystation' is — at least in the Israeli instance — a long standing practice which works to very different ends on both the Palestinian and Israeli populations. In this short paper, I will stress that 'encystation' differs from the term 'encapsulation' as used by Frederick Boal[3] and 'enclavement' by Mary Douglas[4] in that it emphasizes a bodily metaphorics of disease and generation that resonates with a biopolitics deeply embedded in Israeli conceptions of nation and statehood.

The Question of Borders

The use of the metaphor 'encystation' to describe Israeli practices draws on the idea that the 'shell' surrounding encysted materials is analogous to the walls[5] Israel erects to divide Israeli and Palestinian populations. 'Walling' is an act of asserting and enforcing borders, and, as such, an examination of the concept of border in Israeli discourse enables us to assess differences in the practices of 'walling' as they are applied to Gaza, the West Bank, Palestinians in Israel[6], and both Israel proper and Israeli settlements.

The concept of 'border' has been both central to, and multivalent in, Israeli practice and discourse since the early days of the state, as Adriana Kemp has shown in her study of the role of the border and of military border violations in the shaping of Israeli identity. Kemp contends:

the territorialist idiom of settlement, which presented the boundary as the ultimate symbol of state sovereignty, did not take root in the Israeli mind. The army gradually initiated practices which transferred activity to the other side of the border... [so that] the breaching of the border became a symbolic practice, a genuine territorial ritual, which had the effect of both trivialising the border and instilling a sense of lordship over the territories across the lines.[7]

Kemp details cross-border violations in the period when the West Bank was in Jordanian hands (although a favourite Israeli destination for the incursions of that period was Petra, well to the east of the Jordan River). In the period she discusses (1949–1957), border crossings by the Israeli military were designed to punish Palestinian communities for allowing attempts to access Israel by refugees (who, for the most part, were attempting to return to houses and properties from which they'd been forced in the course of the 1948 war and subsequent 'mopping up' operations):

crossing of the lines by the Palestinians was portrayed as a 'gross violation of the armistice agreements' and was called 'infiltration'. However, when border-crossing became a habit of the Israeli army, even if unacknowledged, it was known as 'routine security measures' and depicted as part of the attempt to achieve 'border discipline'.[8]

Michel Warschawski, in his excellent book, *On the Border*, writes that 'in May 1966, while out hiking with some friends, I wound up in Jordan without knowing it, and it was an Israeli patrol that brought us back to the railway zone, an extraterritorial zone, and made us get on the next train. None of us even questioned then what an Israeli patrol was doing inside Jordanian territory.'[9]

The 'frontierist' conception of borders Kemp claims then characterized Israeli attitudes towards state and sovereignty is still in play in Israeli state policies not only towards Lebanon and Syria but also with regard to the illegally occupied territories of the West Bank, the Golan Heights and (until recently) the Gaza Strip where the state establishes settlements, builds roadways and other infrastructural 'facts on the ground', and maintains the citizenship of 'extraterritorial' settlers. Settlements are simultaneously 'walled in' to protect them from surrounding Palestinian communities, and connected — by Jewish-only bypass roads — to Israeli territory so as to in effect superimpose a continuous Israel over West Bank Palestine.[10] At the same time Palestinians are always susceptible to being 'walled off' from their surroundings. This is strikingly manifest in the operations of the 'Border Police', a 'police' unit under the command of the Israeli military which is supposed to patrol borders as well as ports and airports. In practice, the Border Police go into operation wherever Palestinians confront Israelis in what the authorities perceive as a political manner.

When Ariel Sharon's 28 September 2000 'visit' to the Haram ash-Sharif (which provoked the Second Intifada) sparked demonstrations in Arab towns and cities within Israel's 1949 borders, it was the Border Police which was sent into the Galilee to suppress these, at the cost of thirteen 'Israeli Arabs' shot dead. Borders, whether those drawn by the Wall or those of 'Closed Military Areas' which any officer can declare at whim, pertain to Palestinians, and are erected wherever and whenever a Palestinian is seen to impinge upon or question Israeli sovereignty over 'the land'. As is evident in Israeli incursions into Gaza and the West Bank to assassinate activists or arrest government ministers, in Israel's numerous invasions of Lebanon, and in its 18 January 2015 air strike on the Syrian Golan Heights, a similar logic operates; 'Arabs' must remain passive and in place while the Israeli military can go anywhere it wants to ensure that quiescent immobility.

If borders for Israelis exist in large part for what Kemp calls the 'symbolic practice' of breaching them, how does one discern the limits of 'the land of Israel'? This question concerns not only the legal rights of settlers to benefits accruing from Israeli citizenship, which are refused their 'Arab neighbors' in the Occupied Territories. It also has 'extraterritorial' applications. Israel's 'Law of Return 5710-1950' promises that 'every Jew has the right to come to this country as an *oleh* [an immigrant]'[11] which in practice has come to mean that any person claiming to be a Jew, either by descent or conversion, is granted automatic citizenship as well as guaranteed housing, full tuition for language and university education and significant discounts on cars, appliances and other aids to settlement.[12] Beyond, however, easing *aliyah* [immigration], the Law of Return implies that, by virtue of being Jewish, Jews outside of Israel are in effect always already Israeli citizens (a parallel instance from the former Yugoslavia is analysed by Dimitrijević).[13]

In line with the effective extension of Israeli state sovereignty that, this guarantee of automatic citizenship entails, Israel has, in the past few years, intervened in cases in which Jews were on trial for crimes committed outside of Israel, as though these were cases in which its own citizens were being tried by a foreign state. It has also organized massive 'rescue missions' in Iraq, Iran and Ethiopia to take Jewish citizens of other countries out of those countries and 'resettle' them in Israel. If Israeli sovereignty is extensible to anywhere Jews exist, then there are in effect no borders constraining its population.

Gaza and the West Bank are clearly delineated by borders, marked by the aforementioned 8-meter tall walls and buffered and ditched fences (effectively sealing the territories to Palestinians but leaving them permeable to military assault from Israel and, in the case of the West Bank, the free movement of settlers). The logics of encystation operate differently in the two cases however and I will investigate the operative and conceptual differences between the two applications through examining the relevance of Giorgio Agamben's concept of the 'sovereign exception' to both Gaza and the West Bank.

Sovereign Exception

Agamben, in *Homo Sacer: Sovereign Power and Bare Life,* speculates on the 'extra-territoriality' of persons excluded from the conceptual and legal domain of the nation state within which they nonetheless live. Unlike the diasporic extra-territoriality of persons or communities belonging to a national collectivity, but located outside national territory (such as Israeli settlers or Jews outside of Israel), the 'outside inside' that Agamben examines is exemplified by the situation of detainees in Guantanamo Bay: 'the detainees of Guantanamo do not have the status of Prisoners of War, they have absolutely no legal status. They are subject now only to raw power; they have no legal existence.'[14] These detainees, whom Agamben explicitly compares with Jews in the Nazi camps, are held within the embrace of the state but without the protection that state affords its citizens:

The exception that defines the structure of sovereignty is... complex. Here what is outside is included not simply by means of an interdiction or an internment, but rather by means of the suspension of the juridical order's validity — by letting the juridical order, that is, withdraw from the exception and abandon it. The exception does not subtract itself from the rule; rather, the rule, suspending itself, gives rise to the exception and, maintaining itself in relation to the exception, first constitutes itself as a rule. The particular "force" of law consists in this capacity of law to maintain itself in relation to an exteriority. We shall give the name relation of exception to the extreme form of relation by which something is included solely through its exclusion.[15]

As was the case for those imprisoned in the concentration camps at the core of Agamben's argument, the withdrawal of the juridical order from the Palestinians 'behind the wall' is not a matter of disregard but one of dehumanization (the production of what Agamben terms 'bare life', which can be defined as 'life exposed to death' at the hands of sovereign violence).[16] The 'enclosed' populations are carefully regarded — profiled, branded with identity cards, confined to specified areas, tracked — while simultaneously being denied the rights or legal status accruing to citizens of the incorporating state. The encysted are brought far more under the control of the state than its citizens but, rather than enjoying protection by the state correlative to that control, stand in constant risk of extermination by it.

For Agamben this construction of an 'inside' (the sovereign juridical order of the state) by the inclusion of an excluded population (the threatening 'other') is a central rhetorical (and practical) move by modern sovereign powers. This interiorisation of a national exteriority not only provides its citizenry with evidence of the protective power of the state but simultaneously grounds — on the threat that incorporated other presents — that state's demands to increase its power over, and reduce the rights of, that citizenry.[17]

Yehouda Shenhav and Yael Berda commend the analytic grip of the concept of sovereign exception, but query its apparent lack of a genealogy (its a-historicism) and, in rectifying that, show how it evolved in British colonial practice under Lord Evelyn Cromer in Egypt and Lord George Curzon in India and how its application by the British and later the Israelis changed from the Mandate Period to the wake of the second *intifada*. Constant to the sovereign exception's colonial application is the assumption of the potentially violent irrationality of the colonial subject and the consequent necessity of revealing colonial sovereignty to that subject as 'a phantom organ that manufactures miraculous decisions, but that conceals the locus of the decision making process, the inner working of its machinery, and its criteria of judgement.'[18] That sovereignty, in other words, manifests itself as a simultaneously illegible and irresistible power. In the contemporary Israeli instance, racialized profiling of 'the Palestinian' is 'based on an all-powerful instant *classification as security threat...* rel[ying] on the belief that inside every Palestinian — regardless of age, residence or profession — hides the ghost or demon of a Palestinian terrorist.'[19] Earlier profilings acknowledged that inherent violent irrationality, but were accompanied by different strategies for bringing it under control.

Historically, the face that the sovereign exception shows to the subject population will very much depend on that population's perceived 'use value'. As Neve Gordon shows, Israeli policy between the 1967 occupation and the first *intifada* was that of employing 'numerous forms of control to craft an economically useful Palestinian society while reducing the inhabitants' political aptitude'.[20] With the first *intifada* Israel radically curtailed its dependence on Palestinian labor and simultaneously withdrew from managing Palestinian civil life, shifting 'the governing paradigm... to control of the Palestinian population seen from the single vantage point of "Israel's security"'.[21] Although orders were given to the military to avoid killing civilians, Israel emphasized its sovereignty over the Palestinians through 'the implementation of the entry-permit regime and the pervasive practice of incarceration, torture and beatings in order to repress the population's political aspirations'.[22] However with the second *intifada*,

> Israel adopted a new approach toward the Palestinians which rendered them, in many respects, expendable....In place of the politics of life that had characterized the OT until the second intifada, a politics of death slowly emerged. The paradigmatic practice of this new politics is the extrajudicial execution which in contrast to incarcerations or even torture does not intend to shape or alter Palestinian behavior, but to do away with 'recalcitrant' individuals.[23]

Gordon notes the escalation of killings of Palestinians after September 2000 (the number of Palestinian fatalities during each year of the second, or al Aqsa, *intifada* was more than all of those killed during the first twenty years of the occupation), an escalation highlighted by its savage attacks on Gaza in 2008–2009, 2012 and 2014. Concurrent with the institutionalisation of assassinations and other forms of extermination of Palestinian militants was that of a policy of weakening the general population so as to sap its will to resistance. Dov Weissglass, in 2006, announced a policy, grounded on research by the defence ministry into minimal daily caloric needs, of taking the Gazan population to the edge of, but not into, starvation: 'the idea is to put the Palestinians on a diet, but not to make them die of hunger'.[24]

The path mapped here between valuing a subject population as a labor pool and judging it expendable and collateral to the extermination of resistance activities traces the development of Israeli policy towards Gazans from surveilled incorporation to the isolated 'bare life' of the camp.

A Matter of Degree

I initially assumed that there was a qualitative difference between the walling of Gaza and that of the West Bank insofar as the encystation of Gaza seemed much more brutal and all-encompassing than that of the West Bank.[25] Gaza's wall tightly encysts a population which is exclusively Palestinian and the area is, aside from military incursions, closed to Israelis. Israeli policies, not to mention invasions and bombardments, have effectively destroyed the economy, radically restricting the provision of water, electricity and, as mentioned above, food. The 'expendability' of the Gazan population was made very clear in Operations Cast Lead, Pillar of Defense and Protective Edge through Israeli willingness to destroy occupied apartment blocks in putative pursuit of Hamas or Islamic Jihad militants as well as, on 1 August 2014, to raze an entire neighborhood, killing its inhabitants, so as to prevent the incarceration of a single Israeli soldier. The West Bank wall appears to operate according to a different logic in drawing a border between Israel and the West Bank (a border which massively violates the 1949 armistice line but only so as to expropriate Palestinian territory) and allowing, within that border, a significant degree of mobility as well as supply of goods and services to West Bank Palestinians. What Gordon refers to as the 'politics of death' is not there endemic; although assassinations and targeted killings — both at the hands of the IDF and militant settlers — are far from infrequent, collateral damage is nowhere near as extensive as it is in Gaza. However, further investigation of the implications of post-Oslo developments has shown that Israeli policies are fundamentally the same for both areas but that Gaza is further along the road to encystation and bare life than the West Bank. The difference is temporal rather than qualitative.

Oslo II (1995) divided the West Bank (excluding East Jerusalem) into three administrative divisions: Areas A, B and C. Area A was designated as being under full civil and security control by the Palestinian National Authority and closed to Israelis other than Israeli security forces on raids against militants. Joint Israeli and Palestinian policing would take care of security concerns in Area B, although all civil issues (water, electricity, sewage, health provision, education, etc.) pertaining to Palestinians living in Area B would be the exclusive concern of the PNA. Area C was placed under full Israeli security and civil control. The 'Interim Agreement', signed by Yitzhak Rabin and Yasser Arafat under the aegis of American president Clinton, stated that Areas B and C would, aside for concessions to be negotiated, be handed to full Palestinian control in the wake of the permanent status agreements. In the subsequent two decades no moves towards any agreement over permanent status have been reached and, insofar as it is evident that Israeli state policy is to ensure that no such moves can occur, it is important to investigate the status quo established by Areas A, B, and C.[26]

Area A, that under full civil and security control of the PNA, makes up no more than 3 percent of the West Bank, and is effectively the territories occupied by the major cities: Bethlehem, Jericho, Ramallah, Qalqilya, Tulkarm, Jenin, Nablus and 80 percent of Hebron (the remainder of which is designated settler property).[27] East Jerusalem, annexed by the Israelis in 1980, is not included; although the agreement referred to the cities and their 'surrounding areas', the latter are continually being encroached on and expropriated by settlement expansion, road building, and the declaration of closed military zones. In the Bethlehem District, the wall has voraciously bitten off olive groves and agricultural lands right up to the edges of the inhabited areas. The aquifers underlying the region have been tapped by the Israelis for supplying water to Jerusalem and the surrounding settlements, and Palestinians are not allowed to draw from them. Although Israeli civilians are legally forbidden from entering Area A (which impedes not only contacts between Israeli peace activists and Palestinians but also economic interaction — supply and services — between the two populations), settlers and soldiers make frequent incursions into the regions.

Area B makes up 24 percent of the West Bank and contains some 450 Palestinian villages and their surrounding lands. In this region civil affairs are purely the concern of the PNA while 'security' is the 'joint concern' of the Palestinian Authority and the Israeli military. The protocols, however, point out that 'the [Palestinian] Council will assure responsibility for public order for the Palestinians. Israel shall have the overriding responsibility for security for the purpose of protecting Israelis and confronting the threat of terrorism.'[28]

The PNA, in other words, polices the Palestinian population but steps aside to make way for IDF intervention when Palestinian activities are seen to threaten Israelis or Israel's security concerns; such activities include responses by Palestinians to attacks by settlers on individuals or communities and civilian resistance to settlement expansion onto Palestinian lands. Settlements, nominally restricted to Area C, frequently expand into Area B expropriating private lands for building or cultivation and sparking local resistance which is then suppressed by the Israeli military.[29]

Area C is by far the largest portion of the West Bank, making up approximately 73 percent of the whole. 68 percent of this is allotted to settlements and their lands, 21 percent is designated as closed military zones, and 8 percent is dedicated as nature reserves. The entire region is under Israeli civil and security control, but the civil administration applies solely to the resident 341,000 settlers leaving a substantial majority of the 300,000 Palestinians who live there without connection to the water network, blocked from building by restrictions on Palestinian construction, and deprived of basic amenities such as schooling and medical facilities.[30] Palestinian movement through Area C is fiercely monitored and restricted by a permit system, permanent and 'flying' checkpoints, roadblocks and settler-only roads.

In effect, despite the impression that the West Bank is 'encysted' as a unit within the 'Apartheid Wall' or 'Separation Barrier', the facts on the ground reveal that the region is itself shattered into a multitude of discontinuous Palestinian 'cysts' encompassed by Israeli territory under the sovereignty of a combination of Israeli state military and armed settlers. As the UN Office for the Coordination of Humanitarian Affairs argued strongly in May 2006, it is difficult to any longer speak of the West Bank as an entity:

> a combination of checkpoints, physical obstacles and a permit system has effectively cut the West Bank into three distinct areas....Within these areas further enclaves have been created — also bordered by checkpoints and road-blocks — that has led to one Palestinian community being isolated from its neighbor.[31]

Here the vast majority of the 2,267,000 resident Palestinians live amidst 464,000 settlers on 27 percent of the land with only 3 percent of that territory under 'full' civil and security governance by the PNA.[32] The speed and efficiency with which Israeli troops are able to impose full closure on the cities and towns of the West Bank was first demonstrated during the 'reconquest' of the West Bank during the Al-Aqsa *intifada* of 2000, while the militarization of Areas B and C by a combination of the IDF and the settlers renders the villages in those regions highly susceptible to expulsions in the event of Israeli perceptions of their, or Palestinians in general, posing heightened 'security threats'. The current state of affairs, in which right wing nationalist provocations by Israel threaten to spark a third *intifada*, could well bring about such actions at any time, especially in the light of Israeli sabre rattling towards Iran and the general tumult of the Middle East. Were that to happen, the situation of Gaza could easily be reproduced in the urban areas of the West Bank with open warfare on an encysted population swollen by refugees flooding into the cities from the villages of Areas B and C.

What I've sketched above might be seen as an apocalyptic scenario, and there are forces at play — even though they appear to be fairly muted in the current Israeli climate — which are working against its possibility. It is important however to stress that the groundwork is very much in place to allow its enactment when Israeli politicians judge that the time is right. Gaza, like the Gazan population, has been judged expendable by Israel; its groundwater is salinated and heavy with pollutants and it does not have the biblical aura that makes 'Judea' so desirable to religious ethno-nationalists. It would be difficult — politically, practically and ideologically — to do with the people of the West Bank what has been done with those of Gaza (so many of whom are themselves refugees, or descendants of refugees, from the ethnic cleansing of the territory that became 1949 Israel) but this may simply be a matter of waiting for the opportune moment. At present escalating emigration, particularly of those with the potential to build a viable Palestinian entity to counter Israel's project,[33] is quietly carrying out the labor of politicide while encirclement and etiolation of those that remain works to fragment the sense of national community and substitute a simple will to survive for aspirations for self determination and national sovereignty. The question of whether and when Israel will opt for surgical intervention depends on many factors, but the equipment for removing the cyst is already at hand.

Imperial Sovereignty

I return, in closing, to the concept of 'encystation'. Like the term 'border' in Israeli discourse and that of 'extra-territorial' in this paper, 'cyst' has a double meaning; it is both a closed sac in which morbid matter is quarantined so as to protect the surrounding body and a 'cell containing an embryo' which provides a defensive membrane within which that foetal entity can develop until it has grown sufficiently strong to emerge into the world outside. It is in the latter sense that Israel, as a homeland for the Jewish people, was conceptualized by Herzl and the late nineteenth century Zionist pioneers who saw the land as a place distant from Europe and its anti-Semitism where Jews, weakened by centuries of discrimination, could shelter while developing into what Herzl termed 'real men.'[34]

Unsurprisingly, as a protected space within which a people could shelter and grow strong without encountering debilitating competition and challenges, Israel's founders envisaged not only the need for strong defences against an 'outside' but also means for ensuring that any internal challenge to the development of sovereignty would be contained, expelled or destroyed.[35]

Modern day Israel, which — with its massive army, its nuclear capabilities, and its high technology economy — certainly has entered forcefully into the global community of mature states, nonetheless still wants to pose itself as a protective womb for a foetal people. As a result it encysts non-Jewish populations within the territory over which it imposes *de facto* sovereignty, refusing them even the semblance of self-determination while simultaneously extending its protective wall outwards so as to encompass and protect all the members of a globally distributed ethno-religious population it sees as its 'concern.'[36] Like the United States which, with the demise of the Soviet Union, assumes its right to celebrate its power to defend its citizens and its interests everywhere, Israel has, with its victories over the antagonisms against which it established itself, become unrestrained in its will to sovereign power both within and beyond its borders. It is hardly surprising that this sovereign power becomes, in effect, genocidal against populations such as those within the 'cyst' of Gaza that Israel's religio-nationalist ideology increasingly defines as inferior, threatening and expendable.

124

NARRATING GAZA

INVENTING GAZA

Selma Dabbagh

Fictive Gaza (1)

In 2003, I wrote a short story that was never published as a short story. I called it all kinds of things; at one point it was called 'Walks With Two Legs.' It had a complex café scene in it: a girl with wild hair and a young boy getting stoned on a roof. There was an F-16 overhead and bombing in the background. I did not want to set it in a named country and I did not want the characters to have names, so I called them X's and Y's instead. Some readers loved it. One writer friend said it engrossed him so much on a flight that he did not realize that the plane had taken off. Others got confused and wanted to know where the hell it was set.

In the winter of that year, the first F-16 attacks on Gaza took place. I was still agitating over the mass killings in Jenin in 2002 when they happened. I lived in Bahrain at the time where black and Palestinian flags were hoisted above rooftops in solidarity, in commiseration and in grief for the West Bank onslaught. It felt, as I now realize we are coming to feel each time, as if we had never witnessed such brutality before. In 2003, post-9/11, Islamophobia was rising at an exponential rate and we still had no idea where it would take us. Shocked and outraged over what had happened, stunned and disgusted over what was being planned for Iraq, there was very little that could be done, from the anti-political expatriate place where

I lived. Appalled, inspired, powerless, I watched global demonstrations of protest on my screen.

Starting to write fiction, having trained and worked in law and human rights, I found the same themes of impotence coming up again and again in my stories: characters who felt they had failed the revolution or that the revolution had failed them. The narrator of my first story, 'Aubergine,' was a Palestinian fighter who had lost his leg during the Lebanese civil war and now, slightly overweight and rather affluent, drove a Lexus in the Gulf. 'That's you isn't it?' a Palestinian film-maker friend asked me, 'the fat man in the expensive car. That's how you feel, right?'

At the time I had a crush on a Chilean writer, Roberto Bolaño. He had just died and I had not even known that he existed when he was alive. He developed a cult following for his borderline bonkers 2,000-page novels that were mainly published posthumously. It was his short stories that I loved and sought out in the *New Yorker* magazine. I ordered all the collections that came tumbling out in translation from a small publishing house in New York. *Last Evenings on Earth* was the story that inspired the step to X's and Y's as the names in the stoned-rooftop-boy short story I wrote. Written like a crime report, *Last Evenings* delves into the interior world of an aspiring revolutionary as he mulls over the lives of surrealistic poets while his father gets into bar fights.

What excited me was the idea that this may be the way of denying English language readers the distance and disdain that Arab names give rise to. If I could remove that prejudice, then the reader on the outside would find it easier to slip into the skin of fictional characters and experience their emotions. War zone horror could be humanized and universalized through the power of imagination and language at a time when an inherited religion and a given name seemed enough to reduce the complexity of a personality into the perishable nature of a target. Literature, I believed, could transcend these prejudices.

I discovered, however, that I could not carry off the X and Y nomenclature with the stylistic sharpness of Bolaño. Although inspired, I did not want to mimic. But there was something about the boy on the roof, the girl with wild hair and the café scene that I wanted to expand on. This, I decided, was the novel that I wanted to write, but I sensed that my personal ability to write works of heightened reality was limited to the short form. If this idea was the theme for my novel, then I needed to bring my characters down from high reality and decide where on earth this would be.

INVENTING GAZA

Non-fictive Gaza (1) 1999

By 2003, I had visited Gaza a couple of times. The last time had been on New Year's Day in 1999. The Erez checkpoint was sinister beyond expectation, although I am assured that it was a picnic then compared to the extreme experience it offers today. Our Gazan friends, who were due to meet us early that morning, did not turn up at the Gaza City hotel that was our rendezvous point. We waited. There were huge shiny bronze pots at the entrance and boys sadder and more resigned than any other boys I had ever encountered. The hotel conveyed a sense of cheap grandeur and erroneous ambition. I, freaked out by Erez and an overnight flight, decided the reason our friends had not arrived was that they had all been arrested by the Palestinian Authority (PA). It was, to my political-reason-seeking mind in this besieged land, the only possible explanation. But no, they had simply partied too much the night before. Remembered, rescued and fed with food and offers of Chivas Regal at their flat, I had the distinct impression that not one, but two women emerged from the bedroom of one of our friends. Party tales abounded. My puritanical sensibilities rattled in my core.

This was meant to be a time of transition. We, as diaspora Palestinians with qualifications, could return and assist this movement for change. I, as a lawyer, could come and help sue the police (my speciality at the time) in Gaza; my then-husband, also a lawyer, could become legal advisor to the UN. There were UN visa provisions to allow qualified diaspora Palestinians, like us, to 'return' and work. Our host fussed over his plant pots; his son peddled SIM cards; another friend reminisced about burning toilet rolls in prison to heat food, of being taught to cook by the fishermen he was imprisoned with, or of stringing out a day with a description of one particular spice used on one particular fish. There was laughter and an urgency in conversation and movement that could not be dismissed. We mattered, our actions and views mattered. We could be part of it. Gaza was where it was all at, where it all could happen. Palestinians were coming back, our international peer group of buddies could all live in the same place for once. We could be part of a nation building project. It seemed like a terrific plan.

It didn't work out. We ended up in Bahrain, employed by the corporates and sedated by the comforts and consumerism that that conservative, but not altogether unsatisfactory, world entailed: a different fork in the road, an alternative outcome.

Fictive Gaza (2)

In Bahrain, in around 2004 I started expanding my short story into a novel and bringing it down to ground. It took years to steer it down to earth in Gaza. In as much as the boy leaping on the roof had been a subconscious vision, the choice of Gaza was a conscious decision. It had to be Gaza; Gaza encapsulated the extremity of the Palestinian situation: the youth of the population, the proportion of refugees, the land, sea and air blockade, the mass incarceration, the heavy security presence, the aerial bombardments, the poverty, the wealth, the corruption, the resistance, the energy, the conversations, the defiance, the despair and the hope.

In the splitting of worlds into centers and peripheries, Gaza is a periphery that has to be vilified in order to be marginalized and attacked. Occupations and wars are now carried out not by individual soldiers who settle and colonize, but remotely using skies heavy with drones. The type of occupation depicted by John Steinbeck in *The Moon Is Down*, is a complete form of command and control design, compared with the anonymous war games being played out now. Gaza has become District 12 of *The Hunger Games*, a place where children are routinely sacrificed in the public gaze to punish their parents for resisting the oppression forced upon them.

I invented a fake, constructed Gaza. I decided that was okay. Nabokov had said he invented Russia and went on to invent America. I drew maps in notebooks — sea, camp, fence, house, flat. I sketched floor plans and crime scenes.

Gaza was the place that Palestinians were forced to inhabit: closed in, forbidden, forgotten, besieged; a place of watching your neighbors and then dying for them in the next breath; a place of manic parties and the unveiling of hypocrites, sell outs, and informers. This was where the tightness of living conditions was palpable, as was the wealth and co-option of leadership, the repressed desires of girls and boys, the strictures of religion, and the unemployability of youth.

Gaza also represented our refusal to accept to be that place. The Gaza I created conflated the Palestinian experience. I brought in cafes that could exist in Ramallah, but not in Gaza, a bombing of a hospital that had not, at the time I wrote, ever happened in Gaza, but had in Jenin.

INVENTING GAZA

Non-fictive Gaza (2) 2002, Amman

At a pre-wedding party in 2002 in Amman I heard a throwaway comment of the type I had heard many times before. It was a marriage of diaspora Gazans to internal Gazans. The bride's brother, from inside Gaza, wealthy, handsome, and trapped, collapsed in the kitchen crying. In the main living room the talk was of drones outside children's bedroom windows. A pallor of spooky ill health descended on all the guests and the heavy drinking and smoking sorted nothing out. The young man cried against the fridge, 'What is it?' asked friends, handing him alcohol and joints, 'What?'

'It's my girlfriend. She's Christian, I'm Muslim. We can't marry.' At that point, his sister strode in,

'What is it that you are crying about? The Palestinian nation?' And then she was out, with a clattering of heels.

I see two sides to this sibling discord and am still unsure where my sympathy lies.

Fictive Gaza (3) Themes

What space for the personal is left when there is an expectation that all that is personal should be political? The peer pressure to politically engage when the necessity of social and political engagement is so stark is not limited to Gaza, but Gaza is an extreme example of it. The difficulty in finding a meaningful political movement to place your energies is also increasingly becoming a challenge for the kind of secular characters I depicted in my novel. My novel has been noted for its depiction of Palestinians who wish to live 'ordinary' lives. I wished to explore what happened to the emotional and the personal when a situation of crisis is so abnormal, besieged and crisis-ridden, that the ordinary is no longer an option and the possibility of change is not in your hands.

I ended up travelling extensively with my novel, *Out of It*. I spoke to packed halls of sympathetic, concerned people in British towns as diverse as Glasgow, Guildford, Marlborough and Frome, as well as to the energetic student-dominated international Festivals of Jaipur and Lahore. It was in Pakistan that I felt the strongest sense of commonality of themes with my audience: youth trapped between a corrupt, weakened pro-Western government and a religious alternative that they did not identify with. There I found parallels: Western-backed bombing, drones, social inequality, religious militancy and diasporic families were all there. There was a lot of Gaza in Pakistan, including the energy for partying.

Although much of Gaza is about being trapped, it is also about the space to move, thoughts of movement, of leaving, of family members on the outside. Dispersed families are part of the Palestinian experience. Having every family member in the same country is a rarity. One of the reasons I set the novel between Gaza, London and the Gulf, was to show that Gaza, as a sense of political consciousness of injustice, does not leave you when you are out of it as a physical space.

After considering how divided Palestinians have become, split apart by wars, expulsion programmes, settler roads, walls, borders, national terrains, identity documentation and languages, there was a need for positivity and for connection. E. M. Forster's maxim regarding turn of the twentieth century class relations from his novel *Howard's End*, to 'Only connect … connect without bitterness and all men are brothers', is rarely otiose in application but frequently abandoned under strain. I considered the point of connection among Palestinians now to be one of political consciousness, the continuing sense of an unresolved injustice taking the form of a phantom leg that you can feel, even if you are no longer physically attached to it. In my experience, even when I was in the Gulf, the Palestinians' desire to continue to connect was still there, even if they outwardly expressed a distance from political engagement. It would show up in body language and in a detailed knowledge of recent political developments.

There is a Gaza in all of us. By 'us', I would go beyond a Palestinian-ness of ancestry, to include a Palestinian-ness of outlook: the idea of continuing to fight for what one believes to be morally and legally compelling, even if all the odds are against you, to believe, as the Palestinian writer Fawaz Turki, author of *The Disinherited*, once put it, 'in the anti-determinist vision of the open-endedness of the future.' When the 'Freedom Flotilla' to Gaza was attacked in 2010, there were more than forty nationalities represented, all of them 'Palestinian', in the broadest sense of the term.

Broadening what it means to be Palestinian out from a particular locale, war, or set of documents is one way of ensuring the cultural diversity that any state structure fought for would be able to provide. There is no place for chauvinism. We need to be as sensitive to representing those who have suffered the most, while being alert to the potentially divisive nature of a hierarchy of suffering. Our aim should be to broaden and include, when everything encourages us to split apart. And here again, a note of credit to the people of Gaza for staving off the proximity of civil warfare in 2007 and for holding on to a PA-Hamas agreement in 2014. Disasters avoided are rarely reported, but the determination to maintain cohesion, however shaky, is commendable.

Non-fictive Gaza (3) 2012, Gaza

In 2012, I returned to Gaza for the Palestinian Festival of Literature. I was nervous that I had somehow got it wrong. All the friends I had known there had since left. I had written and published a book about a place I hadn't seen for over ten years. In 2012, I kept a mental checklist that I kept ticking off on all the points I could not research over the internet (for example, 'Were there any men with ponytails?' There were.) Mainly I felt I had got it right as a physical environment, but from conversation to conversation, experience to experience, my sense of the tonality of the place changed. The darkness of Gaza and the electricity blackouts were a shock to me, along with the dastardly nature of some of the ramifications of CIA-Israeli-PA collusion and PA-Hamas tensions, the brutality of Hamas crackdowns on internal opposition, and the Salafi strictures. Then, within a moment there would be such lightness and extraordinary generosity from hugely energetic, defiant, Bolshie students that I would feel I had got it wrong. The atmosphere was better than I had thought: lighter, brighter, more brilliant and hopeful.

I had feared more than anything that I would meet Gazans who would ask me how I dared to write about their place, being who I was: a privileged Anglo-Palestinian who had hardly ever been there and spoke bizarre Arabic. I got none of that. There were some students who construed the book in an overly allegorical way, and others who felt uncomfortable with the infighting depicted. However, one journalist said that I wrote of Gaza as though I had lived there all my life; he didn't understand how I had done it. I feared I would be raged at, blasted out, ridiculed; but instead there was a curiosity, an acceptance and a gratitude for expanding Gaza's place on the literary map, and for doing my bit to make sure it was not forgotten.

FIGHTING ANOTHER DAY:
GAZA'S UNRELENTING RESISTANCE

Ramzy Baroud

My last visit to Gaza came in 2012, shortly after Egypt celebrated its first democratically elected president. It was a short-lived event in a history dotted with dictators. For Gaza, however, it was respite. However limited; however brief. For me, it meant the chance to visit home after many years away.

The faces in the refugee camp looked familiar but distant as a band of kids followed me through the heaving streets, happy for the opportunity to practice their English. 'Welcome. How are you?' shouted one with a distinct Gazan accent. It sounded cute and funny. I smiled. They had mistaken me for an *ajnabi* — a foreigner. Despite my insistence that I was from this very refugee camp, I increasingly felt I was a stranger.

My old house stood still and unbending, while everything else had been altered. Neighbors' homes had grown into strange dimensions in my aging refugee camp because they had to make use of every inch of available space out of desperation. The houses felt enormous, contorted and mostly unfinished. What had been my home dwarfed in comparison, but it was no longer mine. My father had sold it shortly before he passed away. He had become very poor and obsessively worried about the future. The Israeli-Egyptian siege on Gaza was intense and was coupled with sporadic bombardments and occasional war. Although people were not afraid, they seemed exhausted and deeply nervous. The tangible standard anxiety seemed to be a built-in defence mechanism innately used as a survival technique.

Abu Nidal was still alive. He was old when I had last seen him twenty years ago, but now, he was full of stories that would take another twenty years to tell. He habitually sat underneath the washed white wall of my old home where my father would sit. My father, Mohammed Baroud, also known as 'Abu Anwar', was the leader, or *mukhtar*, of our local clan. He hailed from a school of thought of 'adaptable ideology'. At times he was a communist, at times a Nasserite or an Arab nationalist. At other times, he saw home-grown Islamic movements as an authentic response to imperialism and the decadence of Arab elites. But he was committed to being an ardent cynic, despite occasional gushes of hope.

My father's place underneath the washed white wall had been taken by some other cynical refugees. Every evening, plastic chairs stacked atop one another are brought in, unpacked, and arranged in a semi-circle. The men gather in a predictable order, with the older ones taking center stage. Lively political discussions ensue. Having me join in that political choir that had probably been assembled every single day since I had left the camp for the United States many years ago was a strange encounter. Shortly after the initial shock that 'Abu Anwar's son was back' — that being me — the conversation would go back to talk of Fatah, Hamas, disunity, Israel, border issues, the latest casualties, Arab treachery and such. My attempt at contributing to the discussion seemed irrelevant even though I could relate to much of what they said. However, I felt that I could hardly say anything worthwhile. Eventually I became muted by my old neighbors' despair, shocked at times holding my head in dismay, and chuckling at times when hearing obvious ironies. When I discovered through the flow of conversation about those losing loved ones, I tried to console them appropriately. Abu Nidal had lost his son Mohammed who had been a fighter with Hamas. My last memory of Mohammed was when he was a child. He had a pointy forehead, a runny nose, and an annoying squeal that used to drive my father crazy as he desperately tried to settle into a short nap after an exhausting day of work in Israel.

I am still yet to resolve if I or my neighbors had or hadn't changed, but my house stood still, vacant of glory, and burdened with memories. I wished the crowd farewell. Abu Nidal nostalgically cried a little as he recalled my parents and what he perceived to be better days.

A poster of Abu Nidal's son adorned the wall. He was bearded and handsome. Two automatic rifles, an olive wreath, and Quranic verses

FIGHTING ANOTHER DAY: GAZA'S UNRELENTING RESISTANCE

intermingled in the background, behind Mohammed's smiling face. He wore a military fatigue.

Mohammed was killed during the Israeli war on Gaza dubbed Operation Cast Lead, which took place from December 2008 until January 2009. Over 1,400 Palestinians were killed, mostly civilians, and many while trying to protect other civilians. Nearly 5,500 people were wounded. Many homes in Nuseirat had posters of killed members, children, women, men, and youth in military fatigues.

Cast Lead had been Gaza's worst war, at least since the *Naksa* — the Setback — when Israel defeated the Arab armies in 1967 and conquered Gaza. Many Gazans were killed then with a high ratio of civilians among the dead. But a few years after my visit, another even uglier war was waged on the besieged Strip: the fifty-day war dubbed Operation Protective Edge, which started in July 2014. The death toll was significantly higher; the number of wounded doubled. The destruction was beyond extreme.

It was through Facebook that I discovered that Abu Nidal's house was completely destroyed and that much of the neighborhood was erased by missiles. My old house stood still, despite many scars. The kitchen wall had a large hole on the side.

The 2014 summer war lasted for fifty days; it began with aerial bombardments on 8 July, followed by a land invasion on 17 July. Israeli Prime Minister Benjamin Netanyahu might have thought that the small and impoverished stretch of land that had been under a hermetic siege of seven continuous years was ready to surrender. Gaza was shelled from the air, land, and sea. But still, Gaza didn't surrender.

Sentimentalities aside, when a poor place, populated with refugees, sealed off completely by its neighbors, is subjected to an atrocious war by a power that is deemed the strongest in the Middle East, surrender may seem like an obvious probability. Gaza's fighters from Hamas, Islamic Jihad and various socialist and secular groupings are armed with improvized weapons. Some are developed locally and others are smuggled through tunnels. Comparing the military machines of both Israel and the resistance is a preposterous notion to compel much research and elaborate infographics: homemade 'resistance' rockets against the finest state of the art killing technology that US-European-Israeli weapon experts can muster.

But why is Gaza still standing? How can it be that resistance is still holding on for this long?

How often does Gaza's infrastructure need to be obliterated before the impoverished strip is to wave a white flag? Gaza's morgues were filling up beyond capacity. There was no room for Gaza's injured, especially as hospitals were themselves targets for the Israeli military. Schools were too. According to the journalist Mohammed Omer, reporting from Gaza for *Middle East Eye*, seven UNRWA schools, which served as shelters, were bombed on 24 July alone. Dozens were killed and hundreds were wounded. The final tally of destruction has been beyond extraordinary. Yet, not only did the place survive the punishment, it somehow prevailed.

This time, like every other previous military encounter, resistance would re-emerge from the ruins of Gaza and strike back. Scores of Israeli soldiers were killed as the resistance fought back, refusing to concede an inch without a fight to the death.

The destruction was overwhelming. The Massacre of Shejaiya, on 20 July, resulted in over 100 victims, all of whom were civilians. Their bodies were piled up on the streets of Gaza's impoverished neighborhood in images analogous of the Israeli-orchestrated massacre of Palestinians in the refugee camps of Sabra and Shatila in Beirut in September 1982.

Gaza: a distinctive phenomenon

Gaza's bravery is a distinctive phenomenon. It is unmatched. Yet the resistance movement in Gaza is often misrepresented intentionally, sometimes innocuously. In the heat of the information battle that has ensued since Israel unleashed its latest war, many facts and essential contexts have gone missing.

Historically, Gaza has been a hub for uninterrupted popular resistance since the ethnic cleansing of Palestine at the hands of Zionist militias, and later the Israeli army, in 1947–8. An estimated 200,000 of Palestine's then nearly 800,000 refugees were forced into Gaza, with most enduring squalid and humiliating conditions.

Despite the shock of war and the shame of defeat, Gazans fought back almost immediately. Back then, there was no Fatah, no Hamas, and no siege — in comparison to its current definition. And Gazans didn't organize around any political factions, or ideologies. Instead, they assembled in small groups known to Gazans as *fedayeen* — freedom fighters.

The prowess of those young refugee fighters was on full display in November 1956, when Israel invaded the Gaza Strip and large swathes of Sinai following the Suez Crisis. Egyptians fought the Israeli army with much courage, but the Palestinian garrison based in Khan Younis — a major target in the 2014 Israeli war — refused to surrender.

When the fighting was over, Israel moved into Khan Younis and carried out what is now etched in the Palestinian collective memory as horrific mass killings in Gaza's history: a massacre of 124 men and boys in the Rafah refugee camp known as the al-Amiriyah School Massacre.

Palestine's fiercest resistance fighters' group today, the Izz al-Din al-Qassam Brigades, was formed by a small band of school kids in the central Gaza Strip.

These were poor refugees who grew up witnessing the brutality of the occupation and the abuse it invited into their daily lives. The first young men who started al-Qassam were all killed shortly after the inception of their group. But what they started has since become a massive movement of thousands of fighters.

Resistance in Gaza, as in any historical inevitability, can never be interrupted. Successive Israeli governments have tried extreme measures for decades, but have continuously failed.

After the 1967 war, Ariel Sharon was entrusted with the bloody task of 'pacifying' the headstrong Strip. The then head of Israel's Defence Forces' southern command, Sharon was nicknamed the 'Bulldozer' for good reason. He bulldozed thousands of homes to pave the way for tanks and bulldozers to move in and topple more homes.

Modest estimates put the number of houses destroyed in August 1970 alone at 2,000. Over 16,000 Palestinians were made homeless, with thousands forced to relocate from one refugee camp to another.

Indeed, the people were the very infrastructure pounded for many days and weeks. Sharon's bloody sweep also resulted in the execution of 104 resistance fighters and the deportation of hundreds of others, some to Jordan, and others to Lebanon. The rest were simply left to rot in the Sinai desert.

It is the same so-called 'terrorist infrastructure' that Sharon's successor, Benjamin Netanyahu, was seeking to destroy by using the same tactics of collective punishment, and to which he applied the same language and media talking points.

Just by taking a quick glance at the history of this protracted battle — the refugees versus the Middle East's 'strongest army' — one can say with a great degree of conviction that Israel cannot possibly subdue Gaza. One may call that a historical inevitability as well.

To understand Gaza resistance requires an understanding of the history that compelled resistance in the first place. The discussion is much bigger than Hamas and the Islamic Jihad. Early models of resistance movements were mostly socialist and secular, yet the fight was the same one. It was, and remains, the same collective spirit that guided every uprising and *intifada,* whether kids throwing rocks or youth in military fatigues. The resistance remained the same.

Due to the lack of cement, because of the siege, Gazans smash the rubble of destroyed buildings and reconstruct it into bricks to build new homes. I have no doubt that Abu Nidal will build his home once more, with the help of his neighbor. The hole in my old kitchen is sealed. The neighborhood mosque was blown up as well, killing a few worshippers, but the neighbors continued to pray, in the vacant lot where the mosque once stood. New young faces are now on the fresh posters adorning the walls of my refugee camp, new 'martyrs' to be mourned and celebrated. And many new recruits, survivors of the latest war, are now being trained to join the resistance in its upcoming fight, because that's what Gazans have done since the days their ancestors were made refugees, some sixty-six years ago.

IN THE COMPANY OF FRANTZ FANON: THE ISRAELI WARS AND THE NATIONAL CULTURE OF GAZA

Atef Alshaer

> Try to understand this at any rate: if violence began this very evening and if exploitation and oppression had never existed on the earth, perhaps the slogans of violence might end the quarrel. But if the whole regime, even your non-violent ideas, are conditioned by a thousand-year-old oppression, your passivity serves only to place you in the ranks of the oppressors.
>
> Jean-Paul Sartre, preface to Frantz Fanon's *Wretched of the Earth* [1]

The Israeli war on Gaza that took place in the summer of 2014 and which was the third over the span of five harsh years demonstrates the extremity of domination Israel is exercising to preserve its sense of superiority. The repeated Israeli patterns of violence and Palestinian acts of resistance in response to violence bring to mind relevant narratives developed by the psychologist Sigmund Freud and psychiatrist Frantz Fanon in discussing nationalist, colonial, and postcolonial conditions and the traumas endured by the natives. Both thinkers reflect on the underpinnings of the operative mode of impulses that indulge in asserting themselves beyond any rational or moral considerations, at the expense and to the determent of other people. As far as Gaza is concerned, we see a small territory with fatigued but defiant inhabitants tortured by the impunity of Israel, a power established through and rooted in aggressive habits and stubbornly destructive intents made evident in its last war on Gaza from 8 July to 26 August 2014.[2]

Much has been said about the 360 km² that make up the Gaza Strip; its 1.8 million people; its crowded space besieged from sky, sea, land and the scarcity of every ingredient of life, including water and food supplies. Gaza's history is littered with massacres and abuses and with foreign occupations, such as the Crusaders, the Ottomans, the British and the Israelis.[3] The latter are particularly gruesome in exhibiting sustained patterns of abuse culminating in unprecedented tragedies in Gaza. The deliberate targeting of schools, hospitals, mosques and other vital areas for survival, alongside the discourse and practice of elimination Israel exercises against the Palestinians in Gaza and indeed elsewhere in the West Bank and East Jerusalem, underlining the persistence of colonial conditions, has far reaching political and psychological consequences for the Palestinians.

This essay asks how thinkers such as Fanon and Freud can help in understanding how such conditions of colonial violence are encountered with resistance that carries heroic as well as traumatic aspects in equal measure. In order to do so, I combine theoretical insights, particularly from Fanon, with Palestinian literary materials, and particularly poetry, that responded to the Israeli onslaught and exposed its severity and, as such, highlighted the inevitability and legitimacy of resistance. Then, I draw on nationalist Palestinian discourses emerging within the context of the onslaught and highlight their relevance to Fanon's exploration of violence and nationalist culture as he noted in his most well-known book, *The Wretched of the Earth*. I will show how the historical-situatedness of these narratives gives them legitimacy. Most importantly, the poems in question demonstrate the extraordinary capacity of human beings for endurance and dignity and their refusal to be victims of inhumanity. These poems are evocatively situated within a nationalist culture congruent with Fanon's understanding of the importance of a political culture that corresponds to people's aspirations to be freed from the colonial yoke. But as a corollary, the violent resonance of some of these poems is entangled within the violent conditions of Israeli aggression. As such, the creation of abject conditions under Israeli colonial practices gives way to violent consequences that become operative in the psyches of its victims, the Palestinians.[4]

* * * * *

Freud and Fanon grappled with different contexts and concerns relating to nationalism and belonging and yet reached similar conclusions, albeit with different life-histories in mind. Both understood the severe effects of a nationalism rooted in aggressive exclusion of others. While Freud rejected nationalism in favour of universalism,[5] Fanon diagnosed it in a way that accepted its importance in colonial contexts, but called for its transcendence towards humanism.[6] However, the road to humanism takes different paths depending on the conditions of the people living under colonial rule — this much both Freud and Fanon seemed to have appreciated. In fact, there are conditions and contexts that make humanism a far-fetched ideal, even if an abiding one, that no honest thinker could ignore as a vision for better human conditions. Israel's aggression against Gaza and Palestine is best understood as fascism propelled by the extreme militaristic and nationalistic culture of the occupier. Therefore, entering the realm of Gaza with the Israeli wars against it in mind impels one to mine a terrain filled with painful realities and to acknowledge that Palestinian nationalism is inevitable in the face of a colonial power hell-bent on destroying another population with living memories of attachment to their land and their political history, and above all, with unfulfilled political rights.

Here, Palestinian nationalism assumes violent, political and artistic dimensions that correspond to the extreme violence of the Israeli occupation in the first place, as was seen during the wars on Gaza. Palestinians were actively involved in responding to the Israeli violence in a manner complementary to Fanon's observation regarding the effect of colonial violence. For example, the language used by the spokesperson for Hamas' military wing (the Izz ad-din al-Qassam Brigades), Abu 'Ubaydah, to respond to the Israeli violence included phrases such as: 'We have dug the earth with our nails and built up the power we now have;' 'we will darken the faces of the occupiers [meaning, to humiliate them];' 'we are involved in the battle for complete liberation;' 'we are heading towards the grand strategic victory;' and 'we will keep attacking the enemy until it recognizes our rights and stops its aggression against our rights.'[7] Abu 'Ubaydah's discourse entails military and political references affirming the determination to fight for denied rights in a strategic and comprehensive way. In this sense, he is manifesting what Fanon highlighted as discourses and practices that respond to the occupation's violence and denial:

For the native, life can only spring up again out of the rotting corpse of the settler. This, then is the correspondence, term by term, between the two trains of reasoning [...] the practice of violence binds them together as a whole, since each individual forms a link in the great chain, a part of the great organism of violence, which has surged upwards in reaction to the settler's violence in the beginning.[8]

Such aspects of violence can be explored through poetic references that shed light on the Palestinian resistance in its holistic embrace of struggle as the most effective means of liberation. Thus, while the political discourse, aspects of which will be explored below, sheds light on the legal, historical and political dimensions, the poetic discourse unveils the emotional content of attachment that justifies these rights and the methods employed to regain them.

The poetic output during and following the summer 2014 attacks highlights themes such as resistance, including its evolution from one based on stones and rifles to rockets, planes and ambushes and naval confrontations. In this context, the poetry of resistance emerging from Gaza is embedded within the ideological constructs of the resistance itself and its discourse. But it is also a poetry that mediates and justifies its projection of resistance, the suffering of the Palestinians in Gaza, their steadfastness, creativity in survival and living under impossible conditions of siege, violence and internal and external political and economic pressures and strangulations. To this end, this essay will conduct a discursive reading of some of this poetic output using Fanon's insights on nationalist discourses and resistance to demonstrate the condition of Gaza as a space of heroism and defiance as well as trauma and tragedy. To do this, however, it would help to briefly digress by shedding light on the nationalism of Israel, as it bears the ultimate blame for the Palestinian predicament in general, and the tragedies it has inflicted on Gaza.

Gaza in the Fray

In *Understanding and Politics*, Hannah Arendt acutely observes: 'The trouble with the wisdom of the past is that it dies, so to speak, in our hands as soon as we try to apply it honestly to the central political experiences of our time. Everything we know of totalitarianism demonstrates a horrible originality which no far-fetched historical parallels can alleviate.'[9] It is not difficult to notice the grain of originality in Israel's conduct in Gaza, an originality that

IN THE COMPANY OF FRANTZ FANON

thrives on sustained destructiveness. It is in a league of its own with the seedlings of fascism advocated by Zionists such as Ze'ev Jabotinsky, only to be practised with frightening deception and power, as Laleh Khalili explains in her article 'A Habit of Destruction.'[10] Indeed, the entire project of Israel is rooted in maintaining the military power it established in 1948, rendering all others helpless and destitute in the face of its power. Thus, to see Israeli spokespersons given international media forums to justify on-going criminal acts is novel, even if familiar, in the scope of normalising and giving voice to criminal actors and a criminal state.

As an entity refusing to see the other, Israel shocked the consciences of many people in the world with its attacks against civilian areas and facilities, including mosques, hospitals and schools. Israel is indeed steeped in a colonial vision of controlling power which limits its ability to see the Palestinian people as human beings and as a historically-grounded political community. It is the ways in which Israel has always seen the Palestinians as 'Other' and the ways in which it essentializes their 'Otherness' that drives it to such excessive violence. It is tragically interesting that Israelis in the majority increasingly, if not often, oppose peaceful solutions with the Palestinians, whereas the majority of Israelis approved of the war against Gaza, as various reports showed.[11] Interestingly, the fact that the Israelis supported the 2014 assault on Gaza illustrates Freud's thought on aggressive nationalism as articulated in his book, *Civilization and its Discontents;* it is telling of an extreme nationalism, totally dependent upon aggression to maintain itself:

> It is always possible to bind quite large numbers of people together in love, provided that others are left out as targets for aggression[...] the Jews of the diaspora have made valuable contributions to the cultures of the countries in which they have settled, but unfortunately all the massacres of Jews that took place in the Middle Ages failed to make the age safer and more peaceful for the Christians.[12]

Bearing in mind the first part of the quote, a similar observation can be made for Israel and its crimes: 'all the massacres of Palestinians that took place since 1948 and even before failed to make the age safer and more peaceful for the Israelis.' Israel started by denying that the Palestinians existed, then reluctantly acknowledged them but subjected such acknowledgment to racist qualifications that make the Palestinians unworthy of their homeland, and it finally accepted them verbally but denied them in reality through processes that emaciate their existence of agency or sovereignty. In Israel's eyes, the Palestinians are not to have any sovereign voice or will of any kind. The Palestinian will to resist is essentially to exist. Had it not been for Palestinian resistance since the 1960s, with all its shortcomings and at times tragedies, the name Palestine would have likely been consigned to history and memory, and would not have been traded internationally in news and the corridors of the United Nations on a constant basis. Hence the crushing violence Israel has unleashed on any organized Palestinian entity attempting to assert its national right in Palestine as a country and people with a rich history and with ties to a larger Arab community.[13] Its military and technological power is not supposed to be challenged in any serious form in a manner that confirms its militaristic character. Israel is a classic colonialist country where its army is made sacred not only among the military sectors but also spreads as an ethos inculcated into the very fabric of the society. In the course of his latest novel *To the End of the Land*, the Israeli novelist David Grossman mentioned how a sort of sacred silence permeated the space in one of the events of the novel when the soldier involved in a military campaign in Gaza was mentioned:

> Ora said boldly, 'His son is in the army, in that campaign that's going on now'. A coo of understanding and sympathy spread through the room, and blessings rolled off tongues, for this particular soldier and for our Defence Forces in general, and there were declarations, and God curse the Arabs, with everything we gave them they still want more…[14]

The absence of Gaza, the Palestinians absently swallowed by the general category of 'Arab' and their depiction as irrational, 'with everything we give them they still want more', turn the Palestinians into abstract objects. The campaign is justified and the soldier is to be glorified for taking part in it: he is the only one who evokes such respect and solemnity; the Palestinian stands for an 'other' that could not even be mentioned. This colonial logic, as made clear in the paragraph in question, summarizes a history of Israeli denial of responsibility for the Palestinian tragedies, of which Gaza is the latest manifestation.

Though it is beyond the scope of this paper, it is worth noting that whenever Israeli sympathizers express solidarity with Gaza, as a few did in poetry, they often do so in the abstract, reflecting on the beauty of Gaza before it was made ugly by Israel's destruction. While they empathize, and some genuinely do, this comes from a place of detached reflection and guilt.[15] For example, Amos Oz, one of the most important Israeli writers, ignores the Palestinian history of oppression by Israel, equating it in a moralistic language with that of the Jews and their suffering. He uses terms that apply to the Palestinian refugee conditions to refer to Israel and the Israelis. Such sophistry only serves to render the specific historical experience of Palestinian dispossession irrelevant. In *Help Us to Divorce - Israel & Palestine: Between Right and Right,* he writes:

> Israel is indeed one large Jewish refugee camp. Half of us are actually Jewish refugees from Arab countries, but Arabs don't see us this way; they see us as an extension of colonialism. By the same token we, Israeli Jews, do not see the Arabs, particularly the Palestinians, as what they are: victims of centuries of oppression, exploitation, colonialism and humiliation[...] In this respect there is a deep ignorance on both sides: not political ignorance about the purposes and the goals, but about the backgrounds, about the deep traumas of the two victims.[16]

While the discourse in question seems sound at an idealistic level, it is devoid of the unacknowledged history pertaining to each community that drives today's conflict. In his book, John Gee redresses the inveterate logic of Oz and indeed Zionism and its followers more broadly:

> If the Palestinian Arab presence could be denied, then it followed that no one could be seriously wronged by the creation of the Jewish state; if it had to be admitted that other people did exist in Palestine, then their claims to constitute any form of coherent society, especially one which asserted its right to national self-determination, had to be belittled and denied[...] Zionism might exist as a theory, but as a practical project it would be still stillborn[...] The readiness of the dominant trends in Zionism to pursue their objections irrespective of Palestinian Arab wishes was undoubtedly a strength, whatever its ethical ramifications. The desire to have both the moral high ground and a Jewish state in a land whose people rejected it has resulted in the creation of a vast array of justificatory arguments unparalleled in subtlety and imagination by the ideological products of any other colonialist movement.[17]

Against this backdrop, the Palestinian and indeed Arab poetic output concerning Gaza is situated within a longer history, bearing out Fanon's insight that 'the mobilization of the masses, when it arises out of the war of liberation, introduces into each man's consciousness the ideas of a common cause, of a national destiny and of a collective history.'[18] In this respect, poetry is congruent with the political discourse of the resistance and is an integral part of a nationalist culture. Fanon's prophetic relevance stems from his understanding of the native's sources of redemption and power in the face of an abusive military power. The poets who responded to the wars on Gaza highlight its heroism as a site of principled and steadfast resistance, testifying to the importance of an active and inclusive national culture that engages all the members of society in the struggle for liberation. Here, the dialectic of survival entails the will to resist and historically exist despite the sources of denial. As Fanon argues:

> Colonialism is not satisfied merely with holding a people in its grip and emp-
> tying the native's brain of all form and content. By a kind of perverted logic, it
> figures and destroys it. This kind of devaluing pre-colonial history takes on a
> dialectical significance today.[19]

While Israeli spokespersons were adept at reducing the Palestinian resistance to one group, namely Hamas, the Palestinians reacted with solidarity with the people of Gaza and with each other, notwithstanding the ideological and political divisions amongst them. Understanding the dialectic of colonial violence and native resistance as explained above, the Palestinians embraced the resistance of Hamas and other factions in Gaza. They did so as they once adopted the resistance of Fatah and other factions in Beirut 1982, Jenin 2002 and other sites of Palestinian resistance. In this context, Gaza served as a magnet for solidarity and unity at an acute moment of nationalist survival. During the 2014 attacks, several Palestinian newspapers and outlets such as *al-Quds*, *al-Ayyam*, the Palestinian Information Center and Ma'an news agency published poems, caricatures, images and articles valorising the resistance of Gaza.[20] Al-Jazeera's Arabic website put out an invitation for the submission of poetic compositions in solidarity with Gaza which saw forty-five Arab entries all sympathizing with Gaza and lauding its resistance.[21]

Alongside its poverty and destitution, Gaza has a long history of cultural production that reflects its reputation as a site of resistance that many illustrious Arab poets emphasized and reiterated, invoking its history of resistance. In fact, it has been Gaza's resistance and its development that had evoked solidarity with Gaza from Arab and Palestinian poets. In addition to depicting the serious suffering of the Palestinians and their losses in Gaza, many poets evoked the means of Palestinian resistance, including rockets and tunnels as legitimate weapons in the face of Israeli warplanes, naval ships, cluster bombs and other destructive weapons.

Historical examples were recalled, giving credence to Fanon's insight regarding the entrenchment of the colonized's national culture in history. One cannot forget that it was the great Syrian poet of love Nizar Qabbani (1923–1998) who once addressed the people of Gaza, the initiating site of the first Palestinian *intifada* (1987–1993):

O the young students of Gaza, teach us

from whatever you have, we have forgotten…

Teach us how to be men

Some men had become like powder

Teach us how stones in the hands of children

Become precious diamonds…

How a child's bike becomes a bomb

And cassettes made of silk become tools for an ambush

How the bottle of milk in the hands of a prisoner

Becomes a knife,

O the children of Gaza, do not pay attention to our media

And do not hear us…

Hit hard with all your powers

Settle your scores and do not consult us…[22]

Liberation is a primary concern for the colonized and in this sense it is also a question of survival and continuity. Fanon's observation that resistance to colonialism gives way to comprehensive creativity that engulfs the entire society is borne out clearly in the poem above; and it tallies with the discourse of the resistance. In his speech referred to above, Abu 'Ubaydah promised two hundred and fifty thousand hand grenades to Gazans instead of stones. He meant for these to be thrown at the occupiers to demonstrate their concrete involvement in the struggle against the occupation alongside the resistance leaders and personnel in Gaza.[23] In this respect, he brings to mind Fanon's observation: 'For the native, this violence represents the absolute line of action […] the group requires that each individual performs an irrevocable action.'[24]

In addition, in the most famous poem about Gaza by the iconic Palestinian poet Mahmoud Darwish (1941–2008), the latter confirms how Gaza derives its living spirit through its resistance:

> Gaza is far from its relatives and close to its enemies, because whenever Gaza explodes, it becomes an island and it never stops exploding. It scratched the enemy's face, broke his dreams and stopped his satisfaction with time [...]

> The only value for the occupied is the extent of his resistance to occupation [...]²⁵

But if Gaza is invested in resistance, it is also battered with suffering. The poems responding to this war, as in the previous wars, emphasized the heroism and the suffering at the same time. Highlighting the titles of some poems demonstrates their suffering and heroic content. These include: 'In commemoration of the martyr Ahmad Ja'bari',²⁶ 'standing over luminous body shreds', 'hail the people of Gaza', 'the *shoah* of Gaza', 'the questionings of a child displaced by the war'.²⁷ There is such rawness to war and violence engendering heroism and tragedy at the same time. The poems in question manifest several tropes among which are commemoration, courage, heroism, and tragedy. Almost all the poems entail these aspects, they commemorate the victims of Israel, they praise the courage of the Palestinians and their resistance and they highlight the tragic consequences of Israeli violence, while communicating hope that such violence will be stopped through liberationist strategies. One poem published in English and Arabic by a poet who casually registers his name as Mu'ath expresses the above themes and the contradictions involved in such a heavily charged, violent site of resistance as follows:

'The city of Antinomies'

Hello, welcome to Gaza city

Where the ugliness is beauty

Where the hopefulness cries

There is neither light nor sunrise

Just those alight corpses

We hear kids call voices

We see women shedding tears

Where is who sees and hears?

Congratulations! Feelings died

And the enemies rose let's hide

We are weaker than the fight

the life is better than the right

if that is what we think

So let's wait life is a wink[28]

Gaza is haunting in its contradictions, its resistance and suffering. Fanon most aptly captures the dimensions involved in this situation:

> This stated belief in a national culture is in fact an ardent, despairing turning towards anything that will afford him secure anchorage…because he (the native) feels he is becoming estranged, that is to say because he feels that he is the living haunt of contradictions which run the risk of becoming insurmountable, the native tears himself away from the swamp that may suck him down and accepts everything, decides to take all for granted and confirms everything even though he might lose body and soul.[29]

With Hamas and Islamic Jihad seen to be leading the resistance, many poems employed Islamic references and allusions. These included battles in which Muslims triumphed despite seemingly insurmountable odds, including the early battles of Islam when the Muslims were small in numbers. The Kuwaiti poet Ahmad al-Kindiri, who wrote and recited a widely circulated poem accompanied with evocative imagery of Palestinian resistance in solidarity with Gaza, exemplifies the point in question. The poem's title, 'Do whatever you wish,' echoes a Quranic verse along the same line, expressing defiance to the enemy that whatever he does, it will not break the will of the resistance.[30] To echo Fanon, the soul and the body have resigned themselves to resistance. The poem illustrates the content of a national culture as defined by Fanon: 'the fact that in a colonized country the most elementary, most savage and the most undifferentiated nationalism is the most fervent and efficient means of defending national culture':[31]

GAZA AS METAPHOR

A virtuous city

Whose heroes have confidence in God's promise…

The siege with the destruction and the attack

Made them forget

That God is the most cunning…

Lo unto the treacherous heart…

Arabs, if I was besieged and became hungry they approve,

And if I was attacked, they applaud

And if I was killed, they give their blessings to the killing

Are they Muslims?

If you searched, you will find that they are conspiring

They turn their humiliation into sophistry (logicizing)…

They pay with their own money for us to be killed

Hypocrites

But they do not know that

God has soldiers who stand by His guidance; they are the triumphant,

This is Gaza

The war concealed the point:

Here we will be

Our bodies are the stones of the fortress

This is my Gaza

My heaven

And your share (the enemy and its supporters) is the hellfire

The entire earth is a secret…[32]

The poem registers several points that Fanon highlighted as traits of national culture, including the uncompromising resistance as explained above, the use of the Islamic past, the confidence in victory against the enemy and the sense of redemption violence brings to the natives.[33] The poem also refers to Arab apathy in the face of the Israeli aggression as the majority of Arab leaders benefit and, therefore, collude with the capitalist and imperial system by which Israel functions. The poem includes other themes, such as the collusion of Arab governments with the Israeli occupation; themes that are central to Fanon's observation regarding the fractures that tend to exist in the national culture of the colonized. These are treated as stumbling blocks in the road towards a genuine liberation from colonialism. They are related to bourgeois elements of the culture, in this context the Palestinian authority in the West Bank that benefits from its supporters from the despotic Arab regimes, which are more on the side of colonialist Israel than the suffering Palestinians in Gaza. Fanon reflected on the importance of a coherent national culture, one that is determined and united, which came across in the unity of discordant Palestinian factions and groups during the war on Gaza. But he warned in stark terms of self-interested bourgeois elements, which sabotage the struggle for liberation and make it harder, as the poem in question shows:

> In under-developed countries, the bourgeoisie should not be allowed to find the conditions necessary for its existence and its growth. In other words, the combined effort of the masses led by a party and of intellectuals who are highly conscious and armed with revolutionary principles ought to bar the way to this useless and harmful middle class...The national bourgeoisie of under-developed countries must not be opposed because it threatens to slow down the total, harmonious development of the nation. It must simply be stoutly opposed because, literally, it is good for nothing.[34]

Several astute commentators on the Israeli/Palestinian conflict have commented on the inefficiency of the structures of authority in Palestine.[35] Palestinian-American intellectual Edward Said, inspired by Fanon, had most eloquently warned of unprincipled and shortsighted political moves that delay and indeed distort the project of liberation required for Palestine. As Said put it: 'The first step in liberating the occupied Palestinian territories is to determine that they are to be liberated.'[36]

Fanon, Freud, Sartre, Arendt and Said understood the aggressive effects of domineering nationalism on all those who espouse it with no consideration for other human beings. The Israeli wars on Gaza with their destructive effects on its people did not deter the latter from developing a national culture, along the lines described earlier, a culture that embraces the struggle and resistance as a strategic option for liberation. In this sense, Fanon's insightful diagnosis of the colonized conditions, under which the colonized fester under colonialism that demands no less than the total surrender and submission of the colonized, is important. As he writes,

> The uprising of the new nation and the breaking down of colonial structures are the result of two causes: either of a violent struggle of the people in their own right, or of action on the part of surrounding colonized peoples which acts as a brake on the colonized regime in question... [37]

Poetry and indeed art in general, when they are a product of national culture, can serve a resistance that ultimately strives towards the undermining of colonial structures. In this sense, the national culture combines aesthetic and violent elements that echo the severity of the colonial situation and the existential pressures it shackles the natives with. In this context, the violence of colonialism is met with violent resistance that responds to its scale, even if metaphorically, as the imbalance of power between Israel and Palestine is decisively in favor of the former. The fact that international powers, mainly the United States, as well as regional ones support Israel makes the Palestinian resilience and resistance an inescapable imperative. The experience of Palestinians engaging with Israel to end the occupation through peaceful negotiations has shown that peace is not on Israel's agenda, confirming Israeli peace activist Jeff Halper's assertation that 'in fact, "peace" carries a negative political connotation among most Israelis.'[38] Therefore, the Palestinians have no other choice except to keep resisting Israel until the latter understands that its occupation is unsustainable. Yet through its determination, the Palestinian resistance has asserted revolution as the principal method of liberation from colonialism, that in its very character negates the colonized and their right to live in dignity and peace. In his preface to Fanon's seminal book, jean-Paul Sartre wrote with the colonized in mind, 'for the only true culture is that of the revolution; that is to say, it is constantly in the making.'[39] Notwithstanding national fractures, the people of Gaza, the principal site of Palestinian resistance and steadfastness, constantly demonstrate that their revolution and struggle is yet to bear fruit — the specter of Israeli aggression is looming over the horizon in Gaza. In this, they are intuitively in step with Frantz Fanon's insight regarding the necessity of staying the course of struggle for the sake of liberation and freedom:

> So we must be sparing of our strength, and not throw everything into the scales once and for all. Colonialism has greater and wealthier resources than the native. The war goes on; the enemy holds his own; the final settling of accounts will not be today nor yet tomorrow, for the truth is that the settlement was begun on the very first day of the war, and it will be ended not because there are no more enemies left to kill, but quite simply because the enemy, for various reasons, will come to realise that his interest lies in ending the struggle and in recognising the sovereignty of the colonized people.[40]

It is clear that Israel as a colonial project seems hauntingly undefeated, having continuously inflicted enormous destruction on the Palestinians since its founding in 1948. This is while the Palestinians remain subject to abject conditions in Gaza and elsewhere. Fanon realizes through his powerful insight that the natives, the Palestinians in this case, have no option but to resist. Resistance is an existential necessity. In such resistance lies the important historical teaching that the colonialists' power will run out of steam as it neither has ethical legitimacy nor material basis to endlessly subject others to its perverted vision of control.

CAN THE PEN BE MIGHTIER THAN THE SWORD? PERMISSION TO NARRATE GAZA

Ilan Pappé

> True, This
> Beneath the rule of men entirely great
> The pen is mightier than the sword. Behold
> The arch-enchanters wand! Itself is nothing!
>
> But taking sorcery from the master-hand
> To paralyze the Cesar's, and to strike
> The loud earth breathless! Take away the sword —
> States can be saved without it!

'The pen is mightier than the sword' is a metonymic adage that has a long history, which first attracted popular attention when it appeared in Edward Bulwer Lytton's play *Richelieu; Or the Conspiracy*.[1] This adage is being examined here as an analytical framework for assessing the power of the pen, or the narrative, against the sword, or the mighty lethal weapons Israel has employed since 1994 in the 'killing fields' of Gaza. The phrase's trajectory — it has a long history of twists and usages — provides two junctures which are particularly relevant. It was echoed in the words of the Prophet 'the ink of the scholar is holier than the blood of the martyr', and the phrase decorates the interior wall of the Thomas Jefferson Building of the U.S. Library of Congress.

This essay moves within this adage's history and multiple meanings. It is inspired by it to ponder, yet again, the power of the narrative in the Palestinian struggle in general and that in Gaza in particular against the Israeli sword. What that sword has done in Gaza since 1994 and more forcefully so since 2006 is well recorded, analysed and explained by many. But is recording all we can do? Is there another way, such as an effective pen, that can challenge the sword successfully? In this essay, I examine how the imprint of a mighty pen can be in reality shaped by the sword of one of the world's strongest military force. Can there be a pen that can begin to stop the destruction wreaked by the pen of colonisation and genocide?

This imbalance or juxtaposition of narrative versus military force within the Palestinian context was first noted by Edward Said in 1984. In his piece 'Permission to Narrate,' he endeavored to probe the potential power of the pen partly out of despair over the international response to the well-documented Israeli carnage of Lebanon in June 1982. But probably, and equally importantly, Said used his analysis as a desperate call on scholars to use theories of knowledge as tools of solidarity even when they believed that the facts spoke for themselves.[2] The facts in 1982, like those of today, broadcast almost a finite defeat of the weak Palestinians in the face of Israel's military might. 'So much for the facts,' Said mused silently at Noam Chomsky when fusing a review of Chomsky's brilliant exposé on American involvement in the Palestine conflict in *The Fateful Triangle*[3] into the mix. Said was clearly irritated by the positivist and factual accumulative approach of Chomsky which portrayed criminality on the ground as a fact to be recorded and not, as Said saw it, as a reversible reality that demanded not only knowledge, nor only an epistemology, but also a search for a narrative that could transform that reality.

Said, thus, called upon the Palestinians to extend their struggle into the realm of representation and historical narratives. The actual balance of political, economic and military powers did not mean, he asserted, that the disempowered did not possess the ability to struggle over the production of knowledge. The call was acted upon by intellectuals who had also been thinking along these lines. The professional Palestinian historiography and the discipline of 'new history' in Israel succeeded in debunking some of Israel's more absurd claims about what happened in 1948, and, to a lesser extent, were able to refute the depiction of the PLO as a purely terrorist organization. Later on, this tour de force, with the help of many scholars around the world showing solidarity with Palestine, exposed Zionism as colonialism and the state of Israel as an apartheid regime.

The Search for an Old-New Pen

It seems that the historiographical revision and setting the record right did not have an impact on a peace process that ignored 1948 altogether. Indeed, the discourse of what passes today for the 'peace process' seems to serve the political elites of the day — on either side of the divide or in the world at large. There is no incentive whatsoever, it seems, to transform the dominant discourses from above, which on the ground translate into a consensus that perpetuates the status quo. The lack of historical context, as will be elaborated below, allows Israel to present even the worst atrocity, as happened in the summer of 2014 in Gaza, as an aberration, an isolated case, and mainly as a response to what it calls Palestinian violence.

One can continue Said's journey by challenging further the historical narrative and by questioning the hegemonic discourse on Palestine commonly employed by the powers that be. This questioning has to insist on including historical context and new terminology when discussing the 2014 attacks on Gaza and the overarching question of Palestine. The new terminology can be presented best as several pairs of antinomies: the former in each pair representing a redundant term to be replaced by the latter, a more apt one. Occupation versus Colonization; Peace Process versus Decolonization; Peace Solution versus Regime Change; Two States Solution versus One State Solution; Israeli Democracy versus Israeli Apartheid; Israeli Defence Policy versus Ethnic Cleansing (and, as we shall see, Genocide in the case of Gaza).

The fresh terminology is not necessarily new. Its main entries can be found in the anti-colonialist discourse of the Palestinian resistance fighters in the 1960s, their supporters in the West and among a small cohort of anti-Zionist activists inside and outside Israel. It was revived at the beginning of the twenty-first century by digital activism in solidarity with Palestine, and has re-emerged in some academic circles, mainly around the paradigm of settler colonialism. The terminology outside the realm of the internet became very useful for young activists at universities as well as older veteran activists operating in the public space. The activity in the real world was modeled, with the help of this terminology, on the anti-apartheid solidarity movement. This became clear in the choice of Boycott,

Divestment and Sanctions (BDS) as the main tactic, and by the organization on various campuses in the UK, the US, and elsewhere, of 'Israeli Apartheid Week', now an acceptable and common name to describe student activity on behalf of the Palestinian cause.

Settler colonialism is a conceptual fine-tuning of theories and histories of colonialism. Settler movements that were seeking a new life and identity in already inhabited countries were not unique to Palestine. In both Americas, in the southern tip of Africa, in Australia and in New Zealand, White settlers destroyed the local population by various means, foremost among them genocide, in order to position themselves as the owners of the country and reinvent themselves as its native population. The application of this definition — settler colonialism — to the case of Zionism is now quite common in the academic world. Politically, it also enabled activists to better see the resemblance between the case of Israel and Palestine with that of South Africa, and to equate the fate of the Palestinians with that of the Native Americans. Atrocities in North America and South Africa thus have much in common with the one in Gaza in the summer of 2014.[4]

This new framing has effectively challenged the peace process discourse of a two state solution that would shrink Palestine to the West Bank and the Gaza Strip and demographically exclude any Palestinian not living in these two areas from any relevance in the future of Palestine. The new movement relates to the whole of historical Palestine as the land that needs support and change. In this view, all of Palestine is an area that was, and continues to be, colonized and occupied in one way or another by Israel, within which Palestinians are subject to various legal and oppressive regimes emanating from the same ideological source: Zionism. It stresses particularly the link between the ideology and Israel's current positions on demography and race as the major obstacle for peace and reconciliation in Israel and Palestine. It is also helps to depict the assault on Gaza in the summer of 2014, and all those that preceded it since 2006, as emanating from the same ideology, strategy, and policy.

This ideology can be described as a wish to take over as much of historic Palestine as possible, leaving in it as few Palestinians as possible, so that a Jewish state could safely be democratic and belong to the 'community of civilized nations.' The strategy Israel has used since 1948 has been one of ethnic cleansing — that is, reducing the number of Palestinians by every means possible and implemented according to changing circumstances and realities: massive expulsion in 1948, and imposition of military rule first inside Israel on the Palestinian citizens there, and then over the occupied West Bank and Gaza Strip. As reality became more complex, the policy extended to include Jewish colonies in the West Bank, the Galilee and the Naqab (Negev), while limiting Palestinian living space in those very same areas. The attempt to persuade the world and the Palestinian political leadership that there will be enough Bantustans in those areas, which in the case of the West Bank can even be called a state, became the bread and butter of the peace process; it still is. In the case of Gaza, the resistance movement there and the choice of political Islam as an alternative to the disappointing secular liberation forces turned ethnic cleansing into genocidal policies. While the West Bank became an open prison ruled from the outside, the Strip became a maximum security prison frequently punished with all the military might Israel possesses when those incarcerated there try to break the siege and the ghetto that Israel, with the help of Egypt, had built for them.

It has become easier lately to disseminate the new narrative as the reality on the ground has changed. This change is evident in three areas: The first is Israel's overall Palestine policy which has obscured the green line separating Israel from the areas it occupied in 1967. All the Palestinians are now treated more or less in the same way. There are still advantages for Palestinians who are citizens of the state of Israel, but these disappear as the years go by. The green line that created different classes of Palestinians is slowly disappearing not only because the same policies of ethnic cleansing are enacted on both sides of the line, but also because the more sophisticated oppression of the Palestinian citizens inside Israel looks at times worse than life under direct or indirect military rule in the West Bank.

The second area of change is Israeli legislation in the Knesset since 2010 — demanding loyalty to a Jewish State by Palestinian citizens, reaffirming as a law hitherto informal discrimination in welfare, land and employment opportunity against the Palestinian minority, which together expose the Jewish state as an overtly racist and apartheid state.[5] The third development is the demise of the diplomatic efforts. Even those who still subscribe to the idea that underlines these efforts (the two state solution) concede the need to consider alternative ways. Whatever these alternatives are they can only be advanced if the pen erases terminologies and rewrites new ones, including those deemed in the past as counterproductive while the peace process was still alive.

The least accessible term I concede would be genocide. It is a new term, compared to the others, and one that is not easily accepted by scholars and activists alike. Nevertheless, I will suggest here it can be penned as a term accurately describing the Gaza massacres since 2006 and the fate of one group of Palestinians who are at present highest on the receiving end of the mighty military sword of Israel and who, at any given moment, can be subjected to yet another brutal swipe of the sword.

Penning the Genocide

Despite continuing efforts to pin down the quintessential nature of the crime of genocide, the search for a universally accepted definition of genocide goes on. For years, the 1948 United Nations' convention on 'the prevention and punishment of the Crime of Genocide' appeared to provide the basis for an emerging consensus. But doubts persist. The UN convention is indeed quite ambiguous in its overall definition and even more so when it refers, in its second article, to genocide as a destruction not only of a whole human society, but of part of that society. How much is a 'part'? The International Criminal Tribunal to the former Yugoslavia attempted to specify this issue by stating that the 'part' has to be substantial. But what is 'substantial'? The Tribunal suggested several criteria such as numbers, both absolute and relative to the size of the population. It also stated that the significance of the part depends on the collective identities of those targeted for the killing by the criminal agency. It seems that in general, international tribunals tend to ignore the partial genocides and relate only to cases that can be seen unequivocally as comprehensive intentional genocides. Article Two is also ambivalent in its definition of the nature of the crime. Besides massive killings of innocent human beings, it includes references to actions 'causing serious bodily and mental harm' of a kind that might affect childbirth, cause malnutrition and similar afflictions. Here, too, the international legal world preferred to deal mainly with actual massive killings as proof for genocide.

There are other ways, outside the realm of legal discourse, to expand the definition of genocide. One is to historically view the cases that were internationally recognized as such crimes and by inference apply the term to new cases. It is clear that the 1948 UN Genocide Convention, in keeping with the work of pioneering genocide scholar, Raphael Lemkin, took the Holocaust as its basic frame of reference (even though Lemkin's original work included a far broader range of case studies).[6] The relevance of the Holocaust as the touchstone for all genocides, based on a historic yet *sui generis* nature in many respects, was reaffirmed by the European Court of Human Rights in 2007 as the departure point for the definition of Genocide.[7] Historically, we can say with some confidence that this template exonerated criminal governments all around the world. The few cases that were condemned were indeed genocidal, but those which were not and yet involved intentional massive killings were neglected due, more often than not, to cynical economic, political and strategic considerations and the balances of power.

The political and public perceptions of an act as genocidal are no less important than its 'objective' definition. Widespread suspicion outside the Western world, particularly among Arabs and Muslims, that universal definitions are in fact a reflection of Western biases have opened the way for a more inclusive list of policies that are deemed genocidal. In the wake of the American and British invasion of Iraq in 2003 and against the background of Israeli policy in Palestine, the suspicion has grown that military actions in both these cases seemed to evade the harsh condemnations evoked in the West by similar acts attributed to Arab or Muslim states, guerrilla movements or terrorist organizations. Popular perceptions pay scant attention to legal and scholarly definitions. They tend towards a more inclusive, flexible view of reality, rooted in historical memory; they are affected by power relations, as is the case for any knowledge production; they are elastic enough to evade the constraints of narrow definitions. They can easily bring back memories of long forgotten, as well as incremental, policies of destruction.

The concentrated military operations of the Israeli army against the population of the Gaza Strip between 2006 and 2014 are illustrative of precisely this type of phenomenon. They do not fall into the commonly accepted — scholarly or legal — definitions of genocide. They do not fit into the framework of an act of genocide perpetrated during a war, nor do they suggest a single massive massacre, which all the historical precedents were. Legal experts are not equipped for assessing incremental policies that turn into genocidal ones, while students of genocide, and this is also true of the mainstream western media, are understandably cautious in attributing genocidal tendencies to the state that represents the ultimate victim of the ultimate genocide, the Holocaust.

As I have shown elsewhere, the Israeli attack against Gaza in 2009 produced the most explicit reference by a variety of politicians, activists and journalists to the Israeli policy as genocidal.[8] Some of them repeated the reference in 2014, and some who had not use the term in 2009, used it in 2014. The pen should not shy from using the term, but should continue to find substantial evidence for this, the worst allegation one can make against a member state of the United Nations. It is the historical contextualization of the 2009 and 2014 massacres along a continuum that begins with the case of the Gaza Strip in 1994 that will provide the strongest case yet for such an allegation. The pen has to provide the historical narrative so that the continuum of evil is recognized and so that daily limited atrocities are compared not synchronically, and dwarfed compared to other atrocities, but diachronically, so that the magnitude of the violence and suffering is better understood.

Without this context, we are left with the Israeli version that each genocidal attack is an isolated response to Palestinian 'terrorism.' The Zionist strategy of branding its brutal policies as an ad hoc response to this or that Palestinian action is as old as the Zionist presence in Palestine itself. It was used repeatedly as a justification for implementing the Zionist vision of a future Palestine that has in it very few, if any, native Palestinians. The means for achieving this goal changed with the years, but the formula has remained the same: whatever the Zionist vision of a Jewish State might be, it can only materialize without any significant number of Palestinians in it. And nowadays the vision is of an Israel stretching over almost the whole of historic Palestine where millions of Palestinians still live.

The present genocidal wave has, like all previous ones, a more immediate background. It is born out of an attempt to foil the Palestinian decision to form a unity government that even the United States could not object to. The collapse of US Secretary of State John Kerry's desperate 'peace' initiative in 2013 spurred, and provided legitimacy to, the Palestinian appeal to international organizations to stop the occupation. At the same time, Palestinians gained wide international blessing for the cautious attempt represented by the unity government between the Palestinian Authority and Hamas to strategize once again a coordinated policy among the various Palestinian groups and agendas.

Ever since June 1967, Israel searched for a way to keep the territories it occupied that year without incorporating their indigenous Palestinian population into its rights-bearing citizenry. All the while it participated in a 'peace process' charade to cover up or buy time for its unilateral colonization policies on the ground. With the decades, Israel differentiated between areas it wished to control directly and those it would manage indirectly, with the aim in the long run of downsizing the Palestinian population to a minimum with, among other means, ethnic cleansing and economic and geographic strangulation. The geopolitical location of the West Bank creates the impression in Israel, at least, that it is possible to achieve this without anticipating a third uprising or too much international condemnation. The Gaza Strip, due to its unique geopolitical location, did not lend itself that easily to such a strategy. Ever since 1994, and even more so since Ariel Sharon came to power as prime minister in the early 2000s, the strategy was to ghettoize Gaza and hope that the people there — 1.8 million as of today — would drop into eternal oblivion. But the Ghetto proved to be rebellious and unwilling to live under conditions of strangulation, isolation, starvation and economic collapse. Resending it to oblivion necessitates the continuation of genocidal policies.

It is hard to know whether the puncturing of the hegemonic discourse with the pen that writes into it terms such as Apartheid, Ethnic Cleansing and Genocide can be as mighty as the sword that is held by a powerful coalition of states, institutions and corporations all determined to perpetuate the status quo in Palestine. One can probably at this point only continue to insist on (re)drawing a 'discursive' roadmap inspired by these terms and the application of the appropriate historical context. Here, I am consciously using an old term which I want to expropriate from the hegemonic discourse by casting a different meaning into it. It is the same basic idea — a map that describes how both sides reach a solution, but our pen draws a very different map from the one Israeli and American politicians dictate to the Palestinians. This map, unlike its infamous predecessor, will hopefully reflect the reality and not add a penned insult to the military injury inflicted by the mighty sword of Israel.

Penning a New Roadmap

The cue can be taken from a new movement of Palestinians and their supporters who are not very well organized, let alone institutionalized, but, like the brave young bloggers in the Arab world who cried out for change in the name of a universal human and civil rights agenda, are able to articulate and be heard as an alternative voice by those willing to listen.

This movement, or at least alternative discourse, does not shy from pushing forward a solution which is not favored in the eyes of the Israelis, the PA and the political elites of the West: the one state solution. The activist and scholarly depiction of Zionism as a settler colonialist movement and the state of Israel as an Apartheid state also determine the mechanism of change. The new approach proposes decolonization of Israel and the substitution of the present regime with a democracy for all. It targets thus not only the policies of the state but also its ideology. From this perspective, the Israeli refusal to allow the 1948 refugees to return home is seen as a racist rather than a pragmatic position. The new activists, more clearly than some Palestinian leaders, voice their unconditional support for the Palestinian refugees' right of return. In other words, the new movement proposes a paradigm shift for the solidarity movement, which hopefully would be accepted by those in power, and, in particular, those engaged with the question of Palestine and peace. This new paradigm offers a fresh analysis for the present situation and proposes a different vision for the future. By adopting a new discourse, the activists could show the same commitment when struggling against the ideology that is behind the current Israeli abuses and violations of human and civil rights whether they take place inside Israel or the occupied territories.

The depiction of Zionism as colonialism, the analysis of Israel as an Apartheid State, and the recognition of how deeply imbedded the notion of ethnic cleansing in Israel is, produce different future entries in our dictionary: decolonization, regime change, and a one state solution. The pen is not only getting accustomed to new language — it also brushes aside common references to the Palestine reality. There is no occupation as there is no peace process. There is no war as there are no 'fences that make good neighbors.' There are no two sides to the argument that have to be constantly balanced, but an imbalance between colonizer and colonized.

Most importantly, energy in solidarity with Palestine is not directed for facilitating 'kissing cousins' industry and meetings (which so far have cost taxpayers in the West hundreds of millions of dollars in vain) nor is it based on the anticipation of the intervention of a responsible grown-up from the West that will put an end to a childish national strife, nor give rise to a Palestinian Mandela. The energy in the new roadmap is directed at turning Israel into a pariah state as long as it continues to pursue its policies of apartheid, dispossession, and occupation. In this map, the end of oppression is a precondition to peace, not vice versa.

The new terminology and roadmap may be able to put an end to a peace process that has become to be seen as a form of medical miracle pill. As a sick person, the peace process died several times, but was resuscitated for a while before it collapsed again. It holds on not because there is the slightest chance it would succeed, but because of the dividends its very existence brings to all involved. The Israeli government understands that without this 'peace process,' Israel would become a pariah state and would be exposed to international boycott and sanctions. As long as the process is alive, Israel can continue to expand its settlement project in the West Bank and the dispossession of the Palestinians there (including in the Greater Jerusalem area) and establish facts on the ground that would render any future settlement unfeasible and impossible.

The brave drawers of this map may, however, still struggle to puncture this immunity as it is sustained by the United States' dishonest brokering, Europe's international impotence, and by the cynicism of the global military industrial complex. The BDS movement with all its incredible achievements — and there are many — has still not affected the political elites in the West who are providing Israel with immunity for its impunity on the ground. But this should not dissuade us from focusing on the map drawn by such a pen — building the pressure from the outside — that has reached new peaks in 2014, or from believing that external action can one day transform Israeli society from within. The pen, or perhaps the keyboard in our case, has to find additional ways from the inside as well for dismantling the settler colonialist project of Zionism so that we have a long term project that could be called the new Palestine project if we are to stop the carnage on the ground.

There are also particular issues only a Palestinian pen can write into a future plan. The tasks of de-fragmentation and authentic representation of the five different Palestinian groups created by Israel, each with its own national agenda, is a formidable task for the Palestinian people.[9] Unity is another long-term process, probably as long as immunizing the Israeli Jewish society against the racist virus that affects it.

Without such Palestinian achievements, and as long as Israeli immunity continues to be granted, we have to brace ourselves for the map that the Israeli sword will carve in 2016. It will reinforce the racist state of Israel which will further exercise racism in its political and constitutional manifestations — in the case of the first, a systematic policy of ethnic cleansing in the Naqab, Jaffa, Acre, Nazareth, East Jerusalem, the Jordan

Valley and the south of the Hebron mountains; a racist wave of legislation in the Knesset, in the case of the latter. This new Greater State of Israel which was born out of the Oslo process has nearly completed the annexation of Area C in the West Bank and offers the Palestinians in Areas A and B either to be incarcerated in golden cages and not resist this new state or be treated as Gaza. This model is now on sale to the Palestinian people all over the new state. In the golden cage, there is no room for spatial expansion, no resources for development and progress; in the golden cage there is absolute prohibition against resistance, whether in the name of freedom or progress, and most definitely, in the name of nationalism.

This scenario unfolding in front of our eyes, still hidden today from some parts of the world by the horrific scenes from Syria and Iraq, is the one we should confront. Whoever follows the index of racism and democracy in Israel recognizes this is a creeping reality — sliding towards more racist legislation, expanded projects of Judaization, alarming increases in attacks on Palestinians under the slogan '*Tag Mehir*' (Price Tag) that daily consist of destroying Palestinian property and holy places.[10] In this new great Israel, impotent local Palestinian councils and uninterested police forces watch helplessly as organized crime takes over the more deprived Palestinian neighborhoods and villages, fed by poverty and unemployment that reach unprecedented levels between the River Jordan and the Mediterranean.[11]

This is a tough reality that could and should be challenged. It is left intact partly because of the wasted energy invested in the futile peace process, and partly because of power struggles among its victims over insignificant and small kingdoms. The penning of new entries hopes to encourage a new discourse that will inevitably lead to poignant questions Palestinians in particular will ask themselves about the strategy their leadership has employed so far, and will forcefully raise the option of ending the 'peace process' based on the two state solution. It also steers all of us to raise sensitive queries about the wisdom and continued representation of Palestinians in the Israeli parliament, the future of the Palestinian Authority, and the role of the armed struggle vis-à-vis the non-violent popular one.

But this cannot be done by me in this piece. What I can illuminate is the efficacy of the new terminology in introducing the refugee issue back into the center of the Palestine picture and connecting the social movement of change around the world to the liberation of Palestine.

Re-penning the Right of Return

The first theme this pen needs to contend with is the refugee issue. As long as this question has been discussed within the framework of the old peace orthodoxy and the two states solution discourse it has remained marginal and its solution deemed possible only as a return of refugees to the future Palestinian state. A totally different conversation about the refugee issue associates it with two subjects: the first is an analysis of Israeli refusal to allow the return of refugees as yet another manifestation of how racist this state has become, and the second is the need to consider the fate of the refugees in light of the new refugee problem in Syria (which includes large number of Palestinian refugees).

Within the framework of the diplomatic effort that was based on the two state solution, Israel's determined rejection of any return has been legitimized, as has the Israeli argument that return would not allow Israel to maintain a Jewish majority in the state. This international legitimacy indirectly licenses Israel to employ any means the Jewish state deems necessary to maintain a significant Jewish majority in the state. In this respect, there is no difference between an Israeli position that rejects the refugees' right of return and the Israeli project of ethnic cleansing: be it the proposal to annex Wadi Ara to the West Bank, uprooting the Bedouins in the Naqab or depopulating East Jerusalem and the Jordan Valley. Peace cannot be on the cards with a state that exercises such policies against its own citizens, which even the harshest countries do not implement against their immigrant communities.

The other subject associated with the refugee question is the immediate fate of the Palestinian refugees in Syria, Lebanon, Iraq, Turkey and Jordan in light of the civil war in Syria. Israel boasts its humanitarian side when it tells the world that it admitted dozens of wounded Syrian fighters to its hospitals (most of them radical jihadist fighters for some reason). Syria's four other neighbors, who have no less complicated relationships with Syria, absorbed hundreds of thousands of refugees. Even if Israel does not show any humanitarian interest in these refugees, anyone who is part of the peace camp inside and outside Palestine has to highlight the linkage between the Syrian tragedy and the Palestine issue: the need to offer the old-new Palestinian refugees a return to their original homeland has to be endorsed as both a humanitarian gesture and as a political act that can contribute to the end of the conflict in Israel and Palestine.

The right of return in general should be placed at the heart of much of the activity inside Israel (and there are early encouraging signs that the local activist agenda is orientating in this direction). The Nakba took place where Israel is today, not in the West Bank or the Gaza Strip. Any conversation about reconciliation with both communities should take this fact as a departure point. A preliminary stage is probably recognizing at least the right of internal Palestinian refugees (about 250,000 today by conservative estimates) to return to their homes, or nearby them, which is supported by all Palestinian political parties inside Israel and can help bring the Palestinian community together against Israel's discriminatory policies. The problem of internal refugees is a testimony from the past for what, and against what, the struggle is all about.

The official Israeli justification for rejecting the implementation of the right of return is that an influx of refugees into Israel will endanger the demographic balance and undermine the Jewish majority in the state. This argument cannot be used against the internal refugees as they are already part of the state's demographic balance. The objection to their return is part of the discriminatory policy of Israel that does not allow the Palestinians to build new villages and strangulates their living spaces by Judaizing the lands around them.

Social Justice for Palestine

The second theme that has to be written into the narrative that might successfully challenge the sword is that of social justice. This theme is absent in the hegemonic discourse on Palestine. Its absence is one of the main reasons the so-called peace camp in Israel (as well as J-Street in the US) has no issue with neo-liberalism. The readiness to 'concede' land for a future Palestinian state in the parlance of liberal Zionism is framed as an act that would cleanse the Jewish state from the need to directly police the Palestinian population. It does not stem from recognition of an oppressed people's desire for liberation nor is it connected to any notion of justice, including social justice. This is a pragmatic way to control the whole space of Palestine through indirect, rather than direct, means.

This worldview is not opposed to Israeli withdrawal from the occupied territories, but it does not take a position on the harsh economic and social oppression that does not distinguish between a West Bank inhabitant and an Israeli citizen. It is true that unfortunately the Jewish-oppressed classes in Israel, particularly the Arab Jews, subscribe to extreme racist views (self-hating Arabs, as some critics have put it), but their plight is another good reason not to give up on a worldview that challenges the present economic, and not just political, regime between the River Jordan and the sea.

The absence of this viewpoint has weakened our ability to understand the Oslo Accords, the creation of the PA, projects such as 'People to People,' and the maintenance of the occupation by EU and USAID money as neo-liberal projects. Economic elites lent their support to the 'peace process' because it was deemed a profitable economic bonanza. How important the insistence on such a worldview is can be gleaned from the example of post-apartheid South Africa, which maintains an economic structure that still discriminates against the African community. Those who institutionally, collectively, or individually subscribe to notions of human, civil and social rights have a responsibility to make sure the conversation about these values in relation to Palestine will not stop at the Green Line, but will encompass Palestine as a whole, and, hopefully, kick off a conversation about the future of the Middle East in its entirety.

Towards the future, we will all face a greater, racist, ultra-capitalist Israel still busy ethnically cleansing Palestine. There is however a good chance that such a state will globally become a pariah state and that international powers would be interested in knowing what alternatives exist. What they should not hear are old slogans which are no longer relevant in the struggle for a more just, democratic Palestine.

GAZA: IMAGE NORMALIZATION

Dina Matar

We begin to accept the image that the outside world has acquired of us. There are words that enter our language and become naturalized. They enter our consciousness. They are written with capital letters.[1]

The phrase 'cycle of violence' that shatters 'weeks of relative calm' repeatedly occurs in mainstream[2] Western media reporting of and commentary about the multiple Israeli attacks and consistent violence against Gaza, particularly since Hamas came to power in 2006. We, the audiences and readers, are normally inundated with news headlines, and reports, along the lines of 'Israel launches air strike in retaliation against rocket fire by Gaza militants'; or, as in the latest Israeli attacks in the summer of 2014 as part of Israel's Operation Protective Edge, the 'death toll rises in Gaza as Hamas hits new targets in Israel'; 'Israel targets Hamas rocket launchers' and 'Palestinian rockets reach farther into Israel,' thus implicitly blaming the Palestinians for breaking the truce or ceasefire and for the latest cycle of violence, while painting Israel as a liberal democracy that, if and when it uses violence, does so for 'self-defence.'[3] Such phrases, which posit an implicit violence against Palestinians, have become routine, normalized images and narratives in mainstream Western media coverage and analyses of Palestine/Israel, as, too, have the images of destruction, extreme destitution and deaths of innocent Palestinians, including women and children. We, the spectators and audiences, have come to take them for granted, as much as we have come to take for granted that there were indeed periods of relative calm, of lives returning to 'normal', of nothing extraordinary happening, particularly when no citizen of the dominant sovereign power (Israel) had been killed.

Putting aside questions of (dis)proportionate (mis)representation and questions regarding the politics of spectatorship and/or distant suffering in an over-saturated media landscape, what is overlooked in such statements is how violence, whether it is inflicted by Israel or others, has come to represent contemporary Palestinian lives. Furthermore, what is often neglected in these accounts is that even during periods of 'relative calm' when life seems to have returned to 'normal' and we, the spectators and audiences, have turned our gazes somewhere else, Palestinian lives, particularly in Gaza, are hardly calm or normal. For under occupation, 'normalcy', simply understood as living one's life in natural conditions, is not possible, nor is it possible in a state of permanent war that places entire populations as the legitimate targets of the sovereign state.

Image normalization

Writing for *Open Democracy* in September 2014, more than a month following the end of the relentless Israeli attacks against Palestinians in Gaza in the summer of the same year, Palestinian scholar Raif Zreik poignantly opens an essay titled 'Longing for Normalcy' with the question,

> What would be more normal than longing for normalcy? Waking up in the morning, for example, only to find the roof above our heads is still intact, and the number of family members has not decreased since last night. We even require normalcy in less dramatic circumstances: to find our book at the same spot we left it yesterday, to sleep on the same pillow, to be able to start the car on a rainy winter day....[4]

Longing or searching for 'normalcy' — as a negation of violence and a yearning for order or stability in daily life — has become a defining theme in the politics of the quotidian in the Palestinian/Israeli conflict, Salim Tamari writes. Normalcy, in this sense, does not reflect a longing for peace that we are told would be achieved through normalization of bi-lateral relations between Israelis and Palestinians and by living peacefully side by side. Rather, as Tamari writes, it is 'simply a desire for solace in the midst of a prolonged conflict.'[5] Among Palestinians, as the remark by Zreik shows, normalcy is a constant search for an opening to live a natural ordinary life that is not interrupted or disrupted, as it has been since 1948, by persistent violence, dispossession, and death.

Palestinians had been yearning for 'normalcy' as a way of life and as a basic human right since their dispossession and expulsion from their homes in 1948. Israelis, too, had been searching for 'normalcy' since the creation of Israel in 1948, but there are differences in perspectives and objectives. While the Palestinians yearn for living lives without constant fear of the power of the occupier and its supporters, among some Israelis, this yearning takes the form of a craving for an absent condition ('to live as Europeans do'),[6] an obsession that some have argued would give rise to considerable individual and collective neuroses[7] and that would shape Israel's story about itself, its national narrative. This search has undergone several major transformations in Israeli official and public debates, but its ultimate objective, as Tamari argues, was to 'eliminate the *exceptionalism* of the Jewish state as a settler-colonial society by using the mythology and ideology of the return of the Jews to their biblical homeland.'[8]

Such an objective could not have been achieved without the imposition of a state of permanent war against the Palestinians, in general, and Gaza, in particular. This is a practice that post-colonial critic Achille Mbembe has argued has been, and remains, a powerful practice of colonial states to perpetuate colonization and to empower the sovereign. Thus, he says,

A fact remains, though; in modern philosophical thought and European political practice and imaginary, the colony represents the site where sovereignty consists fundamentally in the exercise of power outside the law and where peace is more likely to take on the fact of a war without end.[9]

In a state of permanent war, he suggests, colonial regimes combine Michel Foucault's disciplinary and biopower with 'necropower' to maintain control over the life and death of unwanted, abandoned or enemy populations.[10] 'Necropower' is, according to Mbembe, the ultimate and most violent of all contemporary forms of power as it subjugates life to the power of death through the deployment of weapons 'in the interest of the maximum destruction of persons and the creating of death-worlds; new and unique forms of social existence in which vast populations are subjected to conditions of life conferring upon them the status of living dead.' For Mbembe, the most accomplished form of contemporary 'necropower' is the colonial occupation of Palestine.[11]

Israel, this essay suggests, derives legitimacy for its colonial practices through the use of discursive and image normalization processes intended to present an image of Israel as the Zionist ideology wants it to be presented and represented in order to deny Palestinians self-representation and agency. The use of the term 'image normalization' I am proposing here is different from the common term 'political normalization' we often hear about in international relations speak, which often refers to processes meant to bring opposed parties together. Image normalization refers to discursive practices intended to impose a hegemonic representational order that, through repetition and association, imposes particular ways of seeing or not seeing the world and the 'Other.' Image normalization, to follow a broadly Foucauldian terminology, involves the establishment of patterned processes of thinking aimed at exacting disciplinary power that are then normalized in public and media discourses, making them sound natural and unproblematic. Normalization, as a method of disciplinary control, means that powerful structures can manipulate people into obedience and acceptance of the status quo.[12]

Image normalization can also silence and make invisible what Walter Benjamin has called the 'tradition of the oppressed'[13] while positioning the colonized as the subjects of its power. Image normalization, thus, connotes a recursive power dynamic that reflects both structural and discursive relationships as well as real and symbolic struggles between the occupier and the occupied, the ruler and the rules and the colonizers and the colonized. Image normalization produces knowledge that can privilege ways of knowing the 'other' while silencing the 'other'. As such, the media — the most ubiquitous institutions and terrains through which struggles over symbols, image and discourse are played out most visibly and where knowledge is circulated — are centrally involved in image normalization.

Regimes of representation

The role of mainstream media in struggles over power has been discussed extensively as has its role in privileging the voices of the powerful over the powerless. In the US context, Noam Chomsky goes as far as to say the mainstream (elite) media in the Western world (by which he means the United States primarily) had been complicit in representing the views of the powerful and are therefore complicit in distorting the image of the other. Edward Said, too, has argued in the 1970s that the Western mainstream media had played a key role in mis-representing Muslims and in recreating exceptionalist discourses about the Orient, in general, and Islam, in particular.

In the context of Palestine/Israel, a number of studies, particularly in the field of media and cultural studies, have shown that Western mainstream media organizations, such as the BBC in the UK and CNN in the US, have played a role in normalizing (and legitimizing) Israeli narratives about itself through the repetition of phrases and language such as those mentioned at the beginning of this essay. In periods of armed hostilities, the BBC's coverage has tended to reflect the Israeli perspective, citing more Israeli sources than Palestinian ones and repeating claims that Palestinians through their acts of resistance (including the firing of rockets by Hamas into Israel) were responsible for the lack of normalcy. The quantitative bias in the BBC coverage has been established by the Glasgow University Media Group in two empirically-based books, *Bad News from Israel* and *More Bad News from Israel*, in which scholars Greg Philo and Mike Berry revealed through empirical evidence that Israeli narratives and spokespeople were often seen speaking calmly and rationally in contrast to Palestinians who were seen shouting and gesturing against a backdrop of demonstrations and violence.[14] In a different study focusing on the *New York Times* coverage of Palestine/Israel, US scholars Howard Friel and Richard Falk provide evidence that the newspaper often neglects to mention the rights of the Palestinians, including the right to basic human rights, such as normalcy. When reporting on Gaza, the Western media tends to favour Israeli rights over Palestinian rights, reflected in the recurrence of statements such as 'Israel's right to exist and its right to self-defence.'[15] There is little, if any, mention of Palestinian rights. What is more serious than questions of bias or blame is the fact that such media narratives not only reproduce power dynamics, but also dominant 'regimes of representation' that effectively legitimize the narratives of the powerful. It is in this way that media are complicit in image normalization practices. It is through these processes that we, the audience and spectators, cannot see that anybody else was ever involved in producing them: not the propagandists, not the speech writers, not the marketing people, not the public relations managers, not the slick spokespeople, such as the now familiar media presence of Israel's chief spokesperson, Mark Regev.

Renowned cultural critic Stuart Hall argued that dominant regimes of representation have been particularly effective in colonial and post-colonial contexts, constructing their subjects as colonial subjects and making them aware of themselves as such. As he notes, such representations meant that 'black people, black experiences [...] were positioned and subjected in the dominant regimes of representation' which were 'the effects of a critical exercise of cultural power and normalization.'[16] The most dangerous and violent aspect of these practices is that dominant representations of the colonized are also internalized by the colonized: 'They (the colonizers) had the power to make us see and experience ourselves as the 'Other'... It is one thing to position a subject or set of peoples as the 'Other' of a dominant discourse. It is quite another to subject them to that knowledge.'[17] It is in this sense that power is productive. It produces knowledge.

That Palestinians are made the (unseen and irrelevant) 'Other' of a long-term Zionist paradigm and are made subject to that knowledge and image of themselves is not difficult to see. Since their early encounters with Zionist ideologies, the Palestinians have been the target of a concerted effort by Zionists and their supporters elsewhere to silence them, strip them of their right to know themselves, or to narrate their own politics, their own history and even acknowledge their existence. Edward Said, among other scholars, has consistently made this point, particularly in his essay 'Permission to Narrate,' which has since been copiously cited and referred to.[18] Had the Palestinians been granted, or allowed, the right to represent themselves and to narrate their own story, it might have been difficult, even impossible, for Zionism to normalize, if not legitimize, its own master narrative of Jewish people as a scattered, pioneering and victimized people responding to the call to 'redeem a desolate land that had no people.'[19]

But colonization means that the colonized — a population earmarked for transfer and dispossession — is always invisible and therefore voiceless. If this population does exist, then it should not be allowed to be seen or heard. It must be spoken for. Thus, under what can be called a Zionist paradigm, the ideology that has formed and informed the formation and persistence of the state of Israel, Zionism undertook to speak for Palestine and the Palestinians. Zionist ideology, as Said writes in *The Question of Palestine,*

has always been a blocking operation, by which the Palestinian cannot be heard from (or represent himself) directly on the world stage. Just as the expert Orientalist believed that only he could speak (paternally as it were) for the natives and the primitive societies that he had studied – his presence denoting their absence – so too Zionists spoke to the world on behalf of the Palestinians.[20]

Since its creation in 1948, Israel has been particularly adept at dominating the spaces of the Palestinians in different ways. But most relevantly it has managed to restrict the imaginative spaces of its subjects through a narrative of power that sought, according to Charles Tripp, to mould the imagination of its subjects as it was interwoven with and reinforced 'the material forms of power that are part of the landscape of domination.'[21] Working along the meta-narrative connecting the birth of Israel with the struggle for national and (Jewish) survival, the restrictions on the Palestinians' ability to excavate their imaginative spaces could only reinforce dominant representations and embed them in the mainstream Israeli and Western media. Rashid Khalidi writes that Israel's ability to ensure the hegemony of its narrative is partly due to the fact that it has more resources than its 'enemies' which allows it to propagate its version of reality, particularly as historians 'are forced to tell the story of the powerless (…) in the words of those who victimized them.'[22] That history is always written by the powerful is an old adage. But Israel's ability to ensure the dominance of its narrative is also because of the ways in which the mythologies associated with the meta-narrative and idea of itself have been reproduced, mediated and normalized through countless media genres, through various images and stories, productions and publications, limiting the ability to look beyond them and the ability to cast a different light on various events and truths. As a result, nationalist myths associated with Zionism and the founding of Israel have held a privileged place in mainstream Western media and public discourse, painting Israelis and Jews as victims suffering from long-term persecution. For the victim, as Ofer Zur writes, 'is always morally right, neither responsible nor accountable, and entitled to sympathy,'[23] and can appeal to transnational publics for sympathy, attention and money, or what Daniel Bensaïd has called capital victimaire.[24] Central to the narrative of victimhood is the assumption that Jewish victimhood is unique, surpassing all other narratives of suffering, an assumption that has been reproduced in Western mainstream media coverage of Palestine/Israel. Indeed, reports of violence often gloss over the number of Palestinians killed while telling personal narratives and stories about the lives of any Israeli victim.

Countering normalization

Israeli historian Ilan Pappé suggests that Israel's privileged place in the West and Western mainstream media is the result of Israeli-Zionist continuous efforts to manage and market an image of Israel as a state of what the West aspires for in the East — that of a modernizing and modern state championing Western-centric discourses of progress and civilization.[25] The images and narratives formulated by Zionist leaders and activists in the past, and Israeli Jewish intellectuals and academics in the present, have presented Israel as the inevitable, successful implementation of the European history of ideas. In his book, *The Idea of Israel: A History of Power and Knowledge*, Pappé writes:

> Ideas are the transformative agents that in any narrative of Western enlighten-
> ment lifted Western societies and in turn the rest of the world, out of medieval
> darkness and into the Renaissance, and helped restore civilisation following
> the Second World War.... Israel was one such transformative idea. To challenge
> it as such is to challenge the entire narrative of the West as the driving force of
> human progress and enlightenment..... In order to be marketed, the idea must
> be packaged as a narrative, a story that begins with the birth of the state and
> its raison d'être. The nation is born as an ideal that becomes a reality that must
> be maintained and protected.[26]

It would be a mistake to treat Israel's idea (narrative) of itself as a monolithic or unitary discourse that brings together all Jews and Israelis — there have been many challenges to this totalizing narrative by Israelis and Jews from outside and within.[27] In fact, given the focus on power and its dynamic relationship to knowledge, ideology and belief, it is not surprising that critical Israeli sociologists and historians have made valiant efforts to counter this narrative, bringing on themselves accusations of being anti-Zionist but also throwing into question the very legitimacy of the state of Israel.[28] However, as we have seen in the reporting and the images of Palestinians and of Gaza in particular, there is no doubt that those that continue to seek to normalize ideas and narratives by and large continue to base their views on a denial of the complexity and of the validity of the Palestinian experiences and perspectives. Said, long disturbed by the silencing and sidelining of the Palestinians as well as by images and representations of the Palestinians (often seen as terrorist/ guerrilla fighters or as destitute refugees) in mainstream Western media and discourse, suggested that the problem (of the closure of representation) partly lay with the refusal by Israel and the United States to 'see' the Palestinians or to take seriously their claims for justice and human rights. In his book *After the Last Sky*, published in 1986, Said movingly questions such images and juxtaposes them with other images of Palestinian everyday lives. He aptly notes:

> for all the writing about them, the Palestinians remain virtually unknown. Especially in the West, particularly in the United States, Palestinians are not so much a people as a pretext for a call to arms. It is certainly correct to say that we are less known than our co-claimants to Palestine, the Jews. Since 1948, our existence has been a lesser one.... Many of us have been killed, many permanently scarred and silenced, without a trace. And the images used to represent us only diminish our reality further. To most people, Palestinians are visible principally as fighters, terrorists, and lawless pariahs. Say the word 'terror' and a man wearing a kaffiyeh and mask and carrying a kalashnikov immediately leaps before one's eyes. To a degree, the image of a helpless, miserable-looking refugee has been replaced by a menacing one as the veritable icon of "Palestinian".[29]

The 'icon of Palestinian' Said refers to in his elegant and moving book has changed not simply because circumstances have changed since he wrote his book, but also because of real and perceptible transformations in global attitudes towards Palestine and the Palestinians, manifest in the use of the image of Palestine as the global symbol of resistance to power in different parts of the world; the emergence of an increasingly powerful global politics of solidarity with Palestine as well as new affirmative directions in the literature on Palestine and the Palestinians. This literature, situated within and between disciplines, and some of it written by Palestinians, seriously disturbs and challenges official hegemonic narratives, such as the Israeli one, and makes visible the damaging role official histories have had in silencing colonized subjects.

But the most important and most powerful transformation in the Palestine/Israel context is evident in the ways in which ordinary Palestinians are consciously and semi-consciously challenging the stereotypical and harmful images of themselves through creating and disseminating a broader range of narratives of the quotidian as well as images of themselves and their lives even at times of destitute (ab)normalcy. These images and stories are nowhere more uplifting and, dare I say powerful, than in the stories and images by and of ordinary Palestinians in Gaza and elsewhere that, in themselves, produce meaningful representations and knowledge about subjects as agents and actors challenging, and resisting, normalization practices. For it is true that power and resistance go hand in hand. And it is true that although the tradition of the oppressed, as Benjamin poignantly wrote shortly before his tragic death in 1940 'teaches us that the state of emergency in which we live is not the exception, but the rule.... we must attain to a conception of history that is in keeping with this insight.'[30]

Even during, but mostly following, the relentless bombardment against Gaza in the summer of 2014, ordinary people in Gaza have used different tools and spaces, indeed whatever is available to them, to tell their stories, live their lives and remain in place, thus challenging the narratives of those imposing a state of permanent war and opening up the regimes of representations. In their mundane practices, Palestinians are producing images and discourses of their present, thus reclaiming their past and dismantling the myth of the Zionist/Israeli narrative and testifying to the power of the traditions of the oppressed. Countless stories and images have emerged from and about Gaza, forcing us to turn our gaze to the young and the old, the men and the women who make up Gaza's fabric and what they do with what remains of their lives following the inhumane violence waged against them in the summer. There are young boys and girls carrying mattresses, blankets, chairs, dishes among the rubble; women cooking with whatever cooking utensils have survived of their kitchenware; men clearing roads with makeshift brooms and children smiling to the camera as they read from their books, all determined to go on.[31] These images and others tell us that Palestinians are, in fact, intervening and disrupting normalization practices and forcing us in our complacency to watch and listen to their stories and to question and challenge the totalizing narratives of history.

Crucially, these images tell us that Gaza is an image and presence that, along with other parts of historic Palestine, will continue to define the relationship to Israel. Edward Said knew as much back in 1986 when he wrestled with and conveyed the ineluctable fact that it is the Palestinians' very existence and presence that matters in this equation. As he wrote:

> To the Israelis, whose incomparable military and political power dominates us, we are at the periphery, *the image that will not go away*. Every assertion of our nonexistence, every attempt to spirit us away, every new effort to prove

that we were never really there, simply raises the question of why so much denial of, and such energy expended on, what was not there? Could it be that even as alien outsiders we dog their military might with our obdurate moral claim, our insistence (like that of Bartleby the Scrivener) that 'we would prefer not to,' not to leave, not to abandon Palestine forever?[32]

THINKING GAZA

GAZA AT THE FRONTIERS OF ZIONISM[1]

Darryl Li

In January 2008, Palestinians in the Rafah refugee camp took down the metal barrier marking the border between the Gaza Strip and Egypt. Thousands surged into Egypt in search of supplies. Without an Israeli garrison present and with Hamas newly in control of the local administration, the possibility of an open border emerged. A dream for some, however, is often a nightmare for others: Israel announced plans to send in thousands of animal vaccines to prevent possible outbreaks of avian flu and other epidemics due to livestock and birds entering Gaza from Egypt.[2] Medicines for human beings, on the other hand, were among the supplies that barely trickled in to Gaza after the border was resealed.

More than an act of enlightened self-interest — or, more bluntly, a recognition that 'the virus doesn't stop at the checkpoint'[3] — the reported animal vaccine shipment is a clue to how Israel has reconfigured its control over the Gaza Strip since removing permanent ground forces and colonies remains from the territory in 2005. It persists in the moments between the sporadic and spectacular onslaughts — 'Cast Lead,' 'Pillar of Cloud,' 'Defensive Edge' — that occasionally draw the world's attention.

The story of the post-disengagement Gaza Strip has often been understood as a form of siege, whose severity is conveyed largely through statistics: the staggering number of shuttered businesses, families dependent on food aid, jobs lost. Journalists and NGOs have rendered individual portraits of ruined farmers, bankrupted merchants and trapped medical patients. But the stranglehold on Gaza is not simply a stricter version of the closure imposed since the early 1990s; it also reflects a qualitative shift in Israel's technique for management of the territory. The contrast between Israel's expedited transfer of animal vaccines to Gaza and its denial of medicine for the human population is emblematic of this emergent form of control, that, for lack of a better term, we may call disengagement.

'Disengagement' is, of course, the name Israel gave to its 2005 removal of colonies and military bases from the Gaza Strip. But disengagement was not a one-time abandonment of control; rather, it is better understood as an ongoing process of controlled abandonment, by which Israel is severing ties forged with Gaza over decades of direct domination without allowing any viable alternatives to emerge, all while leaving the international donor community to subsidize what remains. The effect is to treat the Strip as an animal pen whose denizens cannot be domesticated and so must be quarantined. Disengagement is a form of rule that sets as its goal neither justice nor even stability, but rather survival — as we are reminded by every guarantee that an undefined 'humanitarian crisis' will be avoided.

From Bantustan to Internment Camp to Animal Pen

Since its beginnings over a century ago, the Zionist project of creating a state for the Jewish people in the eastern Mediterranean has faced an intractable challenge: how to deal with indigenous non-Jews — who today comprise half of the population living under Israeli rule — when practical realities dictate that they cannot be removed and ideology demands that they must not be granted political equality. From these starting points, the general contours of Israeli policy from left to right over the generations have been clear: first, maximize the number of Arabs on the minimal amount of land, and second, maximize control over the Arabs while minimizing any apparent responsibility for them.

On the first score, Gaza is a resounding success: although it covers only 1.5 percent of the area between the Jordan River and the Mediterranean Sea, it warehouses one out of every four Palestinians living in the entire country. But on the second count, Gaza's density has made it very difficult to manage and its poverty makes it an eyesore before the world community. Thus, Palestinian resistance and, to a lesser extent, international constraints have forced Israel to revise its balance of responsibility and control several times. Each phase of this ongoing experiment can be understood through spatial metaphors of increasingly constricted scope: Bantustan, internment camp, animal pen.

From 1967 to the first *intifada* of 1987–1993, Israel used its military rule to incorporate Gaza's economy and infrastructure forcibly into its own, while treating the Palestinian population as a reserve of low-wage migrant workers. It was during this stage of labor migration and territorial segregation that Gaza came closest to resembling the South African 'Bantustans' — the nominally independent black statelets set up by the apartheid regime to evade responsibility for the indigenous population whose labor it was exploiting.[4]

During the Oslo phase of the occupation of the Gaza Strip (1993–2005), Israel delegated some administrative functions to the Palestinian Authority (PA) and welcomed migrant workers from Asia and Eastern Europe to replace Palestinians. A new infrastructure of movement controls also emerged. Permits for travel to Israel and the West Bank, once commonly granted, became rare. Ordinary vehicular traffic ceased. In the second half of the 1990s, Israel erected a fence around the territory and commenced channeling non-Israeli people and goods through a handful of newly built permanent terminals like the ones that came to the West Bank a decade later. It was during this period that Gaza under Israeli management most resembled a giant internment camp. The detainee population was, to a certain extent, self-organized, and appointed representatives to act on its behalf (the PA) who nevertheless operated under the aegis of supreme Israeli military authority, within the framework of agreements concluded by Israel and a largely defunct Palestine Liberation Organization (which are now basically agreements between Israel and itself).

The failure of the settlement enterprise and the ferocity of the armed resistance during the second *intifada* beginning in the autumn of 2000 undoubtedly contributed to the decision to remove settlements and withdraw soldiers. Aside from buying Israel crucial political cover to push ahead with its colonization plans in the West Bank and Negev, disengagement has also drastically reduced vulnerability to Palestinian armed groups. From 2000 to 2005, Gaza contained less than 1 percent of the Jewish population of Israel-Palestine but accounted for approximately ten percent of Israeli *intifada*-related fatalities (and more than 40 percent of all Israeli combatant deaths). At the same time, the threat was almost entirely located within the territory, against soldiers and settlers. Gaza's hermetic closure largely neutralized the threat of suicide bombs, leaving

Palestinian armed groups in Gaza with few effective means of harming Israel.[5] Even as the armed groups continued to improve the reach of their rockets, their strengths remained primarily defensive. The number of Israeli civilians killed by rockets fired over the Green Line in the decade after disengagement was dwarfed by the number of soldiers killed in under three weeks of ground combat during the 2014 onslaught.

Critics have been quick to point out that disengagement did not change Israel's effective control over Gaza and hence its responsibility as an occupying power under international humanitarian law. At the military level, Israel continued to patrol Gaza's airspace and coast, and ground troops operated, built fortifications and enforced buffer zones inside the Strip so regularly that the major difference seems to have been a mere relocation of their barracks a few kilometers to the east.[6] With the removal of permanent military bases, however, critics also tended to decry Gaza's ongoing dependency on Israel as evidence of control. The taxation system, currency and trade remained in Israel's hands; water, power and communications infrastructure continued to depend on Israel; and even the population registry was still kept by Israeli authorities.

Israel's response has been simple, if disingenuous: if responsibility for Gaza arises from Gaza's dependency on Israel, then it would be more than happy to cut those ties once and for all. And this is exactly what Israel started doing after Fatah's military defeat in Gaza at the hands of Hamas in June 2007. This effectively ended the Oslo experiment in indirect rule in the Gaza Strip. Israel instead began to treat the territory less like an internment camp and more like an animal pen: a space of near total confinement whose wardens are concerned primarily with keeping those inside alive and tame, with some degree of mild concern as to the opinions of neighbors and other outsiders.

The difference is most apparent in the question of electricity. In 2006, Israel responded to the capture of one of its soldiers and the killing of two others by bombing Gaza's only power plant, which, even after some repair, now operates at roughly one third of capacity.[7] A year later, after the Hamas takeover, Israel sought to accomplish the same deprivation through cutting the electricity that it supplies directly to Gaza, compounding the daily blackouts that were already common. These reductions, as approved by the Israeli Supreme Court in 2008, have been calibrated to ensure that the 'essential humanitarian needs' of the population are met.[8] This shift in Israel's approach from 2006 is akin to the difference between clubbing an unruly prisoner over the head to subdue him and taming an animal through careful regulation of leash and diet.

Disengagement and 'Essential Humanitarianism'

In order to understand the management differences between an internment camp and an animal pen, it may help to start with the place where Israel's control over Gaza is most physically manifest: the crossings.

During the Oslo phase of the occupation, Karni crossing was the sole official transit point for commercial traffic between the Gaza Strip and Israel, a highly fortified facility straddling the frontier on the site of an old British military airfield near Gaza City. Karni had approximately thirty lanes for handling different types of cargo — from shipping containers to bulk goods — needed to meet the diverse needs of a modern economy. Karni was a creature of the Oslo period, concretizing its logic of impressive spectacle and laborious inefficiency in order to balance Israeli control with the image of Palestinian autonomy. The crossing operated on the wasteful principle of 'back-to-back' transport (as opposed to the more typical 'door-to-door' method): goods were left by one party in a walled-off no man's land and then picked up by the other without direct contact, significantly raising shipping costs.

In 2007, Israel completely shut down Karni (except for occasional shipments of wheat grain and animal feed, which were discontinued later on) and demolished part of the non-functioning facility in 2012. Israel instead started to channel goods mostly through the Kerem Shalom crossing further south. While Karni operated as a 'back-to-back' facility, Kerem Shalom uses an even more inefficient 'double back-to-back' method: trucks from the Israeli side enter the crossing, unload their palletized wares, and leave. A 'sterilized' truck — so-called because it never leaves the crossing — then moves the goods to the Palestinian side of the terminal, where they are then picked up again for onward transport into the Gaza Strip. Under this method, goods are unloaded and loaded at least six times over the course of a single journey, raising transport costs even further and exposing cargo to additional risk of damage. The language of a 'sterilized' crossing here gestures to how disengagement manages Gaza as a source of potential contagion, whose needs are to be addressed as biological rather than economic.

The sheer redundancy of Gaza's economy in Israel's eyes is most obvious in the context of the Israeli Supreme Court decision approving fuel cuts to Gaza on the basis that if it is possible to ration the remaining fuel for hospitals and the sewage network, then Gaza's economy need not play a role: 'We do not accept the petitioners' argument that "market forces" should be allowed to play their role in Gaza with regard to fuel consumption.'[9] The logic of the Court's decisions on fuel and electricity suggests that once undefined 'essential humanitarian needs' are met, all other deprivation is permissible.

In practice, the neat distinction between vital needs and luxuries is often impossible to implement since it ignores the enormous swath of human activities and desires in between that are no less important simply because they can be temporarily deferred. This has been most poignant in the case of permits to leave Gaza for medical treatment, which are now granted only to those with 'life-threatening' conditions.[10] Under the scheme, even procedures such as open-heart surgery have been treated as mere 'quality of life' treatments that do not qualify for travel permits, leading to patient deaths. In the case of the electricity cuts, the Supreme Court blithely acted as if Palestinians in Gaza could easily redirect remaining power to hospitals and sewage networks despite clear evidence to the contrary.[11] To the extent that electricity can be redistributed within areas, technicians must physically go to substations several times per day and manually pull levers that are designed to be operated only once a year for maintenance purposes. As a result, there have been numerous breakdowns and multiple instances of engineers being electrocuted.

Even if it was possible to implement and was done with the best of intentions, the logic of 'essential humanitarianism' (it is unclear what would constitute the 'inessentially' humanitarian) promises nothing more than turning Palestinians in Gaza one and all into beggars — or rather, into well-fed animals — dependent on international money and Israeli fiat. It allows Israel to keep Palestinians and the international community in perpetual fear of an entirely manufactured 'humanitarian crisis' that can be induced at the flip of a switch (due to the embargo, Gaza's power plant only has enough fuel at any one time to operate for a few days). And it distracts from, and even legitimizes, the destruction of Gaza's own economy, institutions and infrastructure, to say nothing of ongoing colonization elsewhere in Israel-Palestine. The notion of 'essential humanitarianism' reduces the needs, aspirations and rights of 1.8 million human beings to an exercise in counting calories, megawatts and other abstract, one-dimensional units measuring distance from death.[12]

The Names of Inequality

As Israel has experimented with various models for controlling Gaza over the decades, the fundamental refusal of political equality that undergirds them all has taken on different names, both to justify itself and to provide a logic for moderating its own excesses. During the Bantustan period, inequality was called coexistence; during the Oslo period, separation; and during disengagement, it is reframed as avoiding 'humanitarian crises,' or survival. These slogans were not outright lies, but they disregarded the unwelcome truth that coexistence is not freedom, separation is not independence, and survival is not living.

Disengagement, however, is not merely the latest stage in a historical process; it is also the lowest rung in a territorially segregated hierarchy of subjugation that encompasses Palestinians in the West Bank, East Jerusalem and within the Green Line. Half of the people between the Mediterranean and the Jordan live under a state that excludes them from the community of political subjects, denies them true equality and thus discriminates against them in varying domains of rights. Israel has impressively managed to keep this half of the population divided against itself — as well as against foreign workers and non-Ashkenazi Jews — through careful distribution of differential privileges and punishments and may continue to do so for the foreseeable future. Of course there is always the possibility of occasional, dramatic acts of resistance like the breaching of the border — which temporarily transformed a desolate stretch of demolished houses into a giant open-air market — and incremental technocratic changes in local administration. But between these two paths, the inexorable governing logic of controlled abandonment seems likely to remain intact.

It is telling that despite all of the talk of separation, even the most remote and isolated segment of the Palestinians living under Israeli control are still close enough to Israeli Jews for the introduction of livestock and fowl from Egypt to prompt rapid public health action. For the transfer of animal vaccines speaks not only to Israel's control over Gaza and its disclaimer of any responsibility for the people living there, but is also a tacit reminder of the intimacy that persists through nearly a half-century of domination. The people of the southern Israeli town of Sderot, too, were unpleasantly reminded of this intimacy when, one morning in 2005, they awoke to find hundreds of leaflets on their streets warning them in Arabic to leave their homes before they were attacked.[13] The Israeli military had airdropped the fliers over neighboring parts of the northern Gaza Strip in an attempt to intimidate the Palestinians there, but strong winds blew them over the frontier instead.

CONCENTRATION-PLACE

Ariella Azoulay

To concentrate is to direct or bring to one place either one's attention, a mass of things or of people. When it comes to people, the act of concentrating them in one place and denying them permission or possibilities to leave it implies the use of force — namely confinement. Concentration differs from imprisonment in that no crime has been committed by those concentrated in a given place, and therefore, the incarceration is not a post factum, measured punishment for a given crime, but rather enforced in the pursuit of a certain goal or policy, often as a preventive measure, anticipating certain deeds or demands of the incarcerated people. The concentration ensures that the inmates be prevented from appearing freely in public spaces and may act and interact with people living outside solely through their status as inmates, that is, deprived of the freedom to participate like others in the production of meaning of their condition, situation and actions.

In *Israel, Army and Defense: A Dictionary* published in 1976, under the entry 'Gaza Strip,' the author writes: 'The Gaza Strip served as a concentration-place (*Mekom Rikuz*) for Arab refugees from Jaffa and the south. To the 100,000 local inhabitants, 130,000 refugees were added.'[1] The process of channeling people by the tens of thousands to the Gaza Strip is often reported in less than a single line of text. Accounts of the 'silent propaganda' of fear, and need — agreed upon by David Ben Gurion and Yosef Weitz — to maintain a fear campaign in order to achieve the departure of Palestinians living along what in militaristic language was called the 'Faluja-Majdal axis,' is discussed, as well as the moment after, namely their life as refugees. But a lacuna is produced regarding the passage from fear to departure and arrival at specific destinations.[2] Miraculously, we are made to believe, tens of thousands of people who had lived in different cities, towns or villages, knew how to navigate and find their way, as in a funnel, directly to a place such as Gaza. It is certainly not the only lacuna, but it is symptomatic of the particular temporality imposed by the constitution of differential sovereignty — its violent imposition that requires immediate acknowledgment of its existence as a *fait accompli* by both the governed population and the international community. Places, things, institutions, and most importantly differentiated roles — citizens, refugees, infiltrators, soldiers, terrorists, violators — should be performed as already established and their attribution to the different actors should be assumed definitive. The swift establishment of this sovereign discursive grid is conditioned by the reduction to bare minimum of the information about the fabrication of new statuses, roles, institutions names and places. They should be made available for immediate use by everyone, inside and out, as simple designations. From a country with a majority of Palestinians, Palestine was turned into the sovereign State of Israel, and the constant evocation of 'Arabs threatening to destroy it' replaces and conceals the destruction its imposition had perpetrated. Israeli sovereignty imposes itself as if it had always been there until the invasion of Palestinians/Arabs determined to destroy it. From citizens under the British Mandate, the Palestinians were turned into 'refugees' or 'infiltrators' and their forms of habitat were naturally turned into either tents or 'nests' — of 'brigands' or 'terrorists.' Internal and external 'concentration-places' were created to make sure that their extraction from and differentiation within the body politic is physically embodied.

The word 'concentration' clearly recalls the Nazis' concentration of Jews in Nazi camps in Europe, but it also echoes and reiterates a series of other variations on concentration forms from the long history of slavery and imperialism. The word 'place' — instead of camp — used by Israelis in 1948 and which remained in use in the 1970s, may be understood as an effort to distance the immediate association with Nazism, but the common use of the word 'ghetto' since 1948 onward, naming other forms of concentration of Palestinians alongside Jewish neighborhoods in what became Israel, as well as the attempt to create 'model villages' of working Arabs in the 1950s, weakens this hypothesis.[3] After all, many were the violent procedures of population manipulation that the Nazis adopted from the available repertoire of imperialism. The Allies, too, as well as future sovereign states, continued to use such models after the collapse of the Nazi regime, as part of the promise of a new world order.[4] The term 'concentration-place' was more accurate than concentration camp to describe the internal as well as the external enclosures that were created by Israel.

They were managed differently and simultaneously by various states and bodies — after all most of the concentration-places were located outside of the territory that the Israeli forces wanted to appropriate as the locus of their sovereignty. The conditions of incarceration and the scale of freedom in them and from them to the outside world and back were not the same as in camps. All of them were and, in some ways, still are concentration-places that are under Israel's direct or indirect rule, and exposed to various degrees of its interventions. They are maintained as concentration-places due to the constant refusal of the State of Israel to acknowledge the Palestinians as political subjects who have a claim to the way they should be ruled in their homeland. Within Israel, the concentration-places were mainly in the Galilee and 'Triangle' areas, where the majority of the remaining Arab population was concentrated and put under martial rule until 1966. Other concentration-places for Palestinians who were uprooted from their homes and forced to leave were fixed outside mandatory Palestine — in Syria, Jordan or Lebanon — or in territories then not yet conquered by Israel, such as the Gaza Strip. In archival documents, as well as in captions of photos, the expellees are often already referred to as 'refugees' — the status that would be enforced on them once they reached their destination in the concentration-place. From the moment of expulsion on, they would be referred to with this status that erases the actual process of imposing it upon them, as well as the process of socializing the Jews to experience their citizenship as justifying the preservation of Palestinians who were expelled from their homes as inmates, or as Palestinians are often referred to — 'refugees'.

Once the newly constituted State of Israel successfully excluded the Palestinians — who just a few months earlier had other political aspirations for their homeland — from the international arena of 'ceasefire agreements' to be achieved solely between sovereign states, the transformation of Palestinians into 'refugees' was completed, and with it, the determination of the Israeli regime as a differential sovereignty. By definition, differential sovereignty constantly produces a particular type of disaster — what I have presented elsewhere as a regime-made disaster.[5] Regime-made disasters' principal traits are as follows: differential manipulations of the population are made into law, the direct victims are deprived of the position of political subjects, citizens are deprived of the capacity to encounter the direct victims of the differential rule outside of the phenomenal field fabricated by the regime and therefore deprived of the capacity to recognize their own deeds and contribution to the perpetuation of the regime-made disaster.

The military logic of the multiple campaigns against the Gaza Strip since its creation as a concentration-place, as if waged from the outside on an external enemy, as well as the perverse logic of Israel's 'disengagement plans' regarding the Gaza Strip — rule without acknowledging its rule — are manifestations of this regime-made disaster. Its disastrous aspects are visibly amplified every once in a while, as in the summer of 2014, in the massive ruination of parts of the concentration-place, but the chronicles of the regime-made disaster consist of smaller scale ruination events that hold Gazans in their concentration-place, and Israelis protected from acknowledging its lasting effects as direct outcome of their differential citizenship. The expulsion of Palestinians as refugees, already embodying the figure of refugee even while still in the transit concentration-places in their towns and villages, and their persecution already in 1948 as 'infiltrators' — those who threaten the sovereignty of Israel — is the other side of the constitution of Israeli Jews as citizens whose citizenship has nothing to do with the existence of Palestinians as inmates in those concentration-places.

Telling are the accounts written by Israeli soldiers who conquered the Gaza Strip in 1956 several years after the 1948 expulsion, when for the first time they entered those concentration-places created by their fellow citizens, perceiving them, however, as somehow self-made. Beyond the personalized style of different writers, the language of differential regime and colonial differentiation is blatant and allows the authors to distinguish themselves in terms of their civil status, human traits, and knowhow. Writes Avi Oded:

> We settled in the middle of the city surrounded by houses populated by refu-gees and local inhabitants. The habitat of the refugees is similar to transit camps [mainly for Jews who migrated from Arab countries] but they are bet-ter and more well-organized. The dwellings are arranged according to districts of origin: Jaffa refugees, Jabalya, Manshye, Ibne, Jassir, Aqir, etc., each district is under the responsibility of one Mukhtar who receives 10 Egyptian pounds

a month. Their life is inactive, the men do nothing and the women collect firewood and seem highly active. Their main activity is limited to the household. Childcare is not part of it; dirty children are roaming around, abandoned and hungry, and they observe their parents in the process of degeneration.[6]

In his imagination, the author rescues one extremely pretty girl — Fahima — from her fate of being raised by her negligent parents in such deplorable conditions. Neither he nor the other writers recognize these concentration-places as the imprint of the Israeli regime they proudly represent.

The externality of Gaza as a concentration-place was anchored in the fact that until 1967 and, with the exception of a few months of Israeli rule in 1956, Gazans were officially and internationally under Egyptian rule. In actual fact, Israel acted as one of the guardians of the Gaza concentration-place. Since Israel refused to let the expellees return, borders became necessary to seal the Gaza Strip off. Israel erected fences, made sure that the inmates would not leave the territory, killed those who tried to return to their homes, continued to expel Palestinians and incarcerate them in Gaza even though the Egyptians were not asked for their permission (the several waves of transfer of Palestinian population from neighboring al-Majdal is a typical example[7]), and conducted recurrent military operations against 'infiltrators' not solely within Israel but in the Gaza Strip itself, under the general appellation of 'retaliation campaigns.' Israeli citizenry was recruited to a total campaign against 'infiltrators' in body, language, habitat, school curricula, and otherwise.

Part of the campaign against the Palestinians targeted Israeli Jews whose approval of government policy was required in order to persecute 'infiltrators' and keep Palestinians in concentration-places. All means were acceptable. Moshe Sharett made it clear in a government meeting on 28 July 1949:

There was a time when we too assumed that uprooting these Arabs is temporary and not for generations, and that it would be natural for the Arab to return to his village. This was the assumption among our people [...] When the Ministry of Foreign Affairs began to speak publicly against the return – it emphasized that it was speaking not only outwardly and that it was first and foremost attempting to construct [internal] public opinion against the return [...] In time, the public realized what had happened, got accustomed to it and understood that a mass return would be disastrous, and so this opposition to it had formed.[8]

In 1955, a year before the conquest of the Gaza Strip, Ben Gurion made public the guidelines of the new government: 'The goals facing the State of Israel will be attained not only by force of rule, apparatus, law and budget. The government must nurture the youth's pioneering values and encourage mass voluntarism in all walks of life to help the new immigrants, integration, and state security.' For clarity's sake, he proceeded to state that these are not just pompous words but a concrete call upon Jewish citizens to prove resilience in the upcoming military campaigns: 'When the bugle sounds, our settlements' resilience is no less important than our army's might.'⁹ Palestinians embodied the existential threat and Israeli Jews embodied those who could face them fearlessly. On 3 April 1956, David Ben Gurion and Moshe Dayan — in person — paid a visit to Jewish settlers in *Mivtachim* ('Protective Haven', one of many settlements built as part of the campaign against 'infiltrators') and helped them dig trenches and fortify the border. The settlers were often new immigrants brought to Israel to act as 'human shields' in proximity to borders made dangerous.¹⁰ Most of them were unfamiliar with life in Palestine prior to 1947, and received their citizenship together with the knowledge that the Arab is the enemy. Ben Gurion and Dayan were accompanied by photographers to make sure the message was also visually transmitted.

Since 1948, the Gaza Strip as a concentration-place has been essential for the protection of Israeli Jews from its inhabitants as well as for the reproduction of the differential principle of the Israeli regime. As long as Gazans are incarcerated and the gates tightly guarded, their existence is controlled and mediated by the military and political elites' interests, and filtered to the public as an unavoidable outcome of the security situation. Once the Palestinians are out of the concentration-place and roaming freely, their encounter with Jewish Israelis outside of the political and military arenas pre-fabricated by the regime might enable the public articulation of a different meaning of what Jewish Israelis did to them. Jewish Israelis might be finally faced with the imprint and the meaning of their crimes unfiltered. The concentration localities designated for Palestinians enable the preservation of Jewish Israelis in a particular type of mental concentration camp — a Jewish Israeli hall of mirrors. In this hall of mirrors, the meaning of the deeds they are encouraged and driven to commit by the government is reflected as an expression of their good citizenship.

It is not solely the exposure of the entire Gaza Strip to catastrophe that recurs every now and then, but a wholesale regime-made disaster. The

Benjamin Gepner (ed), 1957. *The Book of the Sinai Campaign*, Le'Dory Publishing House

almost total absence of a call — internally and internationally — to overthrow a political regime that is based on concentration-places for Palestinians and differential rule, and the concentration of the discourse on 'occupation,' instead of the Israeli regime in its entirety, is the greatest achievement of the Israeli regime and a guarantor of its reproduction as well as the catastrophe it perpetuates. The fabricated conflation between state, regime, and people that is produced internally and reiterated in the international discourse in relation to the 'existential threat' to destroy all of the above, made any attempt to question the legitimacy of the regime created in 1948 and any call to overthrow it equivalent to calling for the destruction of the state and the annihilation of the Jews living in it. Since 1948 has Israel promoted these ominous phantasms in the name of which it perpetuates regime-made disaster. It is not out of solidarity with Gazans, and Palestinians in general, that Israeli Jews who are second-generation perpetrators — descendants of those who created the concentration camps — should protest against 'the occupation,' but out of partnership with Palestinians, with whom they are differentially ruled. They should call for the overthrow of the political regime that rules them together differentially and claim their right not to be kept perpetrators, guardians of the fences of concentration-places and external spectators of the ruination of Gaza.

REPETITION

Nimer Sultany

The Israeli onslaught against Gaza in the summer of 2014 left more than 2000 Palestinians dead. As we have seen these scenes before, the invocation of repetition comes naturally. This essay provides a brief examination of the meanings of repetition and its effects in a colonial setting. Part I starts with a brief examination of the different meanings of, and internal tensions within, repetition: sameness vs. complexity; context-emphasizing vs. context-erasing; tragic v. responsibility-highlighting; and rhetorical vs. structural. Part II connects the idea of repetition to structural features of the international laws of war that make them more prone to repetition, and hence facilitate war. These features are: the stipulation of formal equality between belligerents; the potential indeterminacy of the basic legal categories; and the reliance on state practice and enforcement. Parts III and IV apply the discussion to the categories of civilians and retaliation. The legalization of warfare is accompanied with the demise of the former and the expansion of the latter. Finally, Parts V and VI enquire about the meaning of oppressive practices in colonial contexts for notions of peace, justice and morality. As the stronger colonial powers seek to appropriate moral and legal discourse — *contra* Nietzsche — the weaker natives are not likely to find refuge from politics and power in law. Throughout the essay I contextualize the question of Palestine in the wider context of colonial occupations and colonial wars.

I. Repetition Outside Context

'Once again' is a commonly used phrase when it comes to death and suffering under occupation in Palestine, and specifically in Gaza.[1] The list of Israeli military attacks in recent years includes: 'Operation Defensive Shield' in March–May 2002; 'Operation Rainbow' in May 2004; 'Operation Days of Penitence' in September–October 2004; 'Operation Summer Rains' in June 2006; 'Operation Cast Lead' in December 2008–January 2009; 'Operation Pillar of Defense' in November 2012; and 'Operation Protective Edge' in July–August 2014. The sense of *déjà vu* is inescapable. 'Once again' can be a rhetorically deployed knee-jerk reaction (as in: once again Israel is killing Palestinians; or: once again Israel has to defend itself against Palestinian attacks). It can also be deployed by a well-meaning third party that perceives the rhetorical deployment of 'once again' as a propaganda war between two parties involved in a tragic conflict. Accordingly, repetition is equated with futile death.

Repetition, however, does not imply sameness. Repetition is complex and dynamic, not static, and thus, if viewed in abstraction it conceals its variability and obscures the process of evolution.[2] 'Once again' is not a mere rhetorical gesture nor is it symptomatic of tragic despair. It connotes a recursive power dynamic and a structural relationship between an occupier and an occupied. It should serve as a reminder of context rather than an erasure of context. An example of this erasure of context is the dismissal of an attempt to bring context into the discussion as mere 'talking points', as Jake Tapper of CNN accused Diana Buttu of doing.[3] Indeed, context is confusing and destabilizes simplifications. The CNN anchor proceeded in his questions to the representative of the 'Palestinian view' to deploy his own (though unacknowledged as such) talking points by invoking the alleged culture of hate and martyrdom amongst Palestinians. The erasure of context renders Palestinian violence irrational.[4] Hence there is a need for an alternative context in which cultural and religious explanations are paramount. This alternative framing does not scrutinize the Israeli side in a similar fashion, even though antecedent events like the kidnapping and the killing of a Palestinian minor could have provoked such reflections (as it did in some Israeli circles like *Ha'aretz*).[5] Such a reflection would seem pertinent given long-term processes of production of hate and prejudice in Israeli society that are not limited to crisis moments.[6] It could also have been linked to settlers' systematic and violent assault on the Palestinians in the West Bank and the Israeli state's legal and institutional complicity, as detailed in many reports, but it did not.[7] It could have reminded the viewers of the rejectionism of Benjamin Netanyahu's government and its foot-dragging over the peace process as part of the context, but it did not.[8] It did not because context is abstract and remote (more than sixty years). Violence is concrete and immediate (the Hamas rockets).

There is nothing 'rhetorical' or 'tragic' about the repeated deaths in Palestine. Rhetorical accounts reduce the materiality of death and suffering to image production for political gains. In 'tragic' accounts political responsibility disappears from view behind lamentations of 'unnecessary deaths.' These accounts distort the political responsibility of the parties (including the absolution of third parties' complicity in the continuation of oppression). In these views, the focus on cultural and 'leaders' personality' explanations pushes away structural explanations of power dynamics.[9] Lacking proper context, the responsibility is either equally shared by two symmetrically opposed agents of violence or the stronger party bears no responsibility because it is merely responding to the weaker party's irrational violence, the latter bearing ultimate responsibility for death and suffering.

II. Repetition and the Laws of War

The current situation in Gaza revives questions regarding the utility of the laws of war, the legalization of political discourse and inversion of moral discourse. The loss of proper context is aided by the basic dichotomy in international law between justifications for launching a war and conduct during war. The former is more readily open to the political (after all people disagree on the propriety of war, e.g. whether it is in self-defense or not). The latter is presumably more contained and can be confined with a *prima facie* professional language. But repetition in the historical evolution of the laws of war is subversive.

Writing in 1874, H. Edwards, author of *The Germans in France*, enumerated what he called 'the three great principles of invaders' law':

1. For every offence punish someone; the guilty, if possible, but someone.

2. Better a hundred innocent should suffer than one guilty man escape.

3. When in doubt shoot the prisoner.[10]

Edwards sought a descriptive account, not a critique. Yet, he recognized that these principles 'proceed naturally from the fact that the invader has to deal with a population unanimously opposed to him...'[11] The fact that there are general principles that produce a general law emanating from a basic condition of violence and opposition is another manifestation of the repetitive nature of the structure.

But repetition can also be a sign of failure, on the one hand, and of despair, on the other hand. Repetition becomes a removal of contingency and a confirmation of 'objective' reality.[12] Those who see historical time as a matter of linear progression will find no comfort in this repetitive pattern. From today's perspective, little progress appears to have been made since Edwards' nineteenth century account despite the evolution of the laws of war post-WWI and WWII. The evolution of the laws of war is supposed to be an answer to the Athenian invaders' retort to the weak Melians in the Peloponnesian war à la Thucydides in his *History of the Peloponnesian War*. In that account, the Melians question the meaning of the pre-invasion negotiations: 'Your military preparations are too far advanced to agree with what you say, as we see you are come to be judges in your own cause, and that all we can reasonably expect from this negotiation is war, if we prove to have right on our side and refuse to submit, and in the contrary case, slavery.'[13] The Athenians describe to the Melians how the world works when there is no symmetry of power: 'You know as well as we do that right, as the world goes, is only in question between equals in power, while the strong do what they can and the weak suffer what they must.'[14] The Athenians proceed to explain to the Melians the advantage of submission: 'You would have the advantage of submitting before suffering the worst, and we should gain by not destroying you.'[15] If the Athenian challenge has not been effectively answered then the project of limiting power is not successful.

The failure of the laws of war is structural and not merely incidental. Despite law's intertwinement with politics, international law flees from contested substantive and political judgments. As observed by Martti Koskenniemi, '[m]odern international law is an elaborate framework for deferring substantive resolution elsewhere: into further procedure, interpretation, equity, context, and do so on.'[16] Hence, it is simplistic to understand the role of law simply as a limit on power, or to understand history as the evolution of the rules that equalize power relations in the pursuit of fairness. Both international law and liberal constitutionalism play a simultaneously limiting and empowering role.[17] Yet, the limits they impose are often on the excesses of power rather than on its normal operation. And although they formally stipulate equality of power ('equality of belligerents'), that equality does not correspond to reality and hence merely reproduces the asymmetry of power.

This presumption of formal equality is part and parcel of the flight from substance. For the purposes of international humanitarian law — *jus in bello*, the rules governing conduct during 'armed conflict' — on which international lawyers rely to make the critiques of proportionality and distinction between civilians and combatants, it does not matter who started the war. It does not matter if Israel's claim to self-defence is genuine. It does not matter if Hamas is trying to impose *shari'a* law on Israel or if it is a liberation movement. It does not matter who is the weak or the strong. It does not matter who the good guys and the bad guys are. Israel and Hamas are equal.

It is true that *jus ad bellum*, the rules governing the recourse to war, or theories about just wars, do prevent aggression or breaches of the peace. However, these rules neither outlaw war as such, nor influence the legal obligations on the parties during the conflict, nor impose liability on ordinary soldiers.[18] International law does not prevent the powerful from crushing the weak, if it is done legally, that is, without the perpetration of war crimes and crimes against humanity. It does not even prevent the killing of civilians if it is unintentional and proportional. It obliges both sides — the strong and the weak — to abide by the same rules of the game. Lady Justice is blind in order to have egalitarian scales, but her sword is double edged; law plays a double function: on the one hand, it limits recourse to wars and conduct during wars, and, on the other hand, it enables war. It tells us what kinds of violence are permissible, what targets are legitimate, and which killers are immune from prosecution.[19]

In any case, international law is keen on separating the rules governing conduct during war from the rules governing recourse to war. Scholars argue that the attempt to maintain the separation reflects a statist bias. When a state is engaged in an armed conflict with a non-state actor, international humanitarian law applies if the non-state actor acquires state-like qualities like effective control and hence this becomes an international conflict.[20] The same was true when liberation movements were relegated in Protocol I in 1977 to the category of international conflicts and hence international humanitarian law became applicable. Their goal is statehood and territorial integrity just like states.[21] Thus, they are treated like states for the purposes of international humanitarian law even though they are not states yet. This means they lose their distinction as a liberation movement and as guerrilla fighters. The state and the non-state actor are both similarly situated agents of violence, and equally potentially liable.[22]

This de-contextualization and de-politicization is evident in the Goldstone Committee's report on Gaza. The committee accepted Israel's claim for self-defense and focused on violations of proportionality and the distinction between civilians and combatants. Moreover, the very mandate of the committee distorted reality by focusing on and recommending actions against the 'exceptional' outburst of violence while Israel is consistently pursuing the strangulation of Gaza and the colonization of the West Bank and Jerusalem and thus providing the breeding ground for violence. This focus on what is perceived as 'exceptional' implicitly renders other periods in the life of the occupation normal.[23]

A second structural feature of the laws of war is their openness to manipulation and conflict. The separation between *jus in bello* and *jus ad bellum* is unstable given the ideological influences on legal interpretation. As Karma Nabulsi argues, the failure to distinguish between lawful and unlawful combatants, as well as between *jus in bello* and *jus ad bellum*, is not accidental. It is a product of 'the ideological framework within which the laws of war were embedded.'[24] This indeterminacy is structured as it allows the articulation of competing views within the international legal framework. This shows the futility of the previous structural feature (the flight from politics) given the need to make substantive political judgments at every turn. It also shows that the legal framework is incoherent as it houses competing views. For Koskenniemi, this is not an 'externally imposed distortion in the law' as it follows from the 'formality of international law' and its flight from substance.[25]

The intertwinement of law and politics comes to light in Israel's actions and its ability to act with impunity. Yet, it is important to keep in mind that the openness to manipulation is both external (for the purposes of international law and relations) and internal (for domestic purposes and conflicts of interest). An example of the latter is the indeterminacy of the legal category of war itself. The Israeli government refused initially to declare the attack on Lebanon in 2006 as a war. The reason seems to be the difference in monetary consequences within domestic law. For if it declares it a 'war' more citizens will be able to demand compensation for their losses during the war. The Israeli Supreme Court affirmed the state's decision arguing that there is no need for a formal declaration of war; that the decision to declare a war is intertwined with political and international considerations; and that the government has a wide discretion in issues related to security and foreign relations.[26] Thus, the Court made a political choice not to intervene in what it considers a political question, even though the question has legal consequences for citizens. Despite the judicial stamp of approval, however, the state reversed its decision within months. In March 2007 the state recognized the operation as a war.[27] Similarly, in the summer of 2014 the state refused to call Operation Protective Edge a war, arguing that domestic private law addresses questions of compensation without recourse to the official label of war.[28]

This is related to a third structural feature of laws of war: they find their genesis in treaties and state practice and they rely on international enforcement. Throughout its history, Israel sought to both justify its actions in legal terms and to change international law through violations. As George Bisharat argues, Israel is a 'legal entrepreneur' that seeks to exploit the elastic nature of international legal norms and the practice-based structure of customary international law to legalize its violent actions.[29]

Thus, the failure of the laws of war is related to their facilitation of war and to their distortion of the reality of war that accompanies the assumption of symmetry. The failure of international political actors to mobilize those potential resources of limitation and accountability in international humanitarian law magnifies this distortion. Consequently, this failure may generate a sense of helplessness. The weaker party is weaker both in warfare and in lawfare because the law's limited potential is suppressed. Accordingly, repetition is merely the sign for the oppressed to surrender to fate. Either they accept their suffering or they unleash more suffering. It is their choice.

Although the occupied did not choose to be invaded and occupied — and cannot control how they will live under the occupation regime — they are asked to choose between slow death and immediate death, between the 'normality' of oppression and the 'exceptionality' of spectacular suffering, between proportional suffering and disproportionate suffering. Life under an advanced colonial occupation, argues Achille Mbembe, is a permanent experience in pain and a continual subjection to the power of death.[30] Palestine — and Gaza specifically — have been subjected to long-term policies of economic exploitation and de-development, geographical encirclement, and violence.[31] Generally, colonial law has always been concerned with proportional violence and the prevention of unnecessary suffering (as in India and Egypt under British colonial law).[32] This is also true in Palestine. The Israeli Supreme Court is very fond of the proportionality doctrine.[33] It applies the doctrine 'within a colonial prism.'[34] Hence, it advances a 'colonial regime.'[35]

But that is the order of things in normal times. In exceptional times, in moments of violent encounter, in moments of resistance, such as the recent 'wars,' the colonial power unleashes disproportionate suffering. This disproportionate suffering sets the parameters and foundations for the continuation of the proportionate suffering. Colonial wars are a necessary condition for the maintenance of colonial rule. After all, war is not merely the continuation of politics by other means. Rather, war is essentially about governance: it creates the conditions for policy-making.[36]

III. Repetition and Civilian Suffering

These impossible choices between colonial rule and colonial wars are underscored by a legalization of modern discourse. It is quite bizarre how legal nomenclature dominates public discourse, especially during violent encounters in 'conflict' zones. This legalization has bad effects as it substitutes a full acknowledgment of the political and moral consequences of violence. Legal rhetoric may hinder the acknowledgment of responsibility by perpetrators of crimes and quell their anxiety as to the consequences of their actions. In accordance with legal justifications, these actions are perceived as consistent with legal rules.[37] In turn, the legalization and humanization of warfare makes wars more acceptable and more likely.[38]

Concretely, this legalization reconciles parties to the conflict and participants in wider public debates with the horrors of civilian suffering and massive injustices. The distinction between civilians and combatants in the laws of war, alongside the principle of proportionality, is supposed to provide minimal protections to the civilians who are caught up in a 'conflict' zone. Yet, Israeli military onslaughts against Lebanon in 2006 and against Gaza in 2009 deliberately sought to erode the distinction by attacking the 'civilian infrastructure' supporting the 'combatants' and expanding the latter's definition (to include for example the police force).[39]

The repetition in the context of colonial history, imperial wars and the legalization of modern warfare is quite striking. This is evident in US and Israeli warfare. Both the US and Israel learned a great deal from the British Empire's experience in colonial asymmetric wars.[40] A most recent example is the US drone war in Yemen which has inflicted a similarly expansive suffering by making all young men 'military age' men and hence potential targets.[41] The US did the same in the Vietnam War by inflicting massive suffering on civilians to subdue those modern Melians who reject conditions of enslavement and hence risk destruction.[42] In Palestine, like in Vietnam during the war, we have two groups: on the one hand, a US/Israel-supported group ruling despite lack of democratic legitimacy (South Vietnam; Palestinian Authority), and on the other hand, a group opposed to US/Israeli policies (North Vietnam; Gaza). Ideologies behind opposition may differ. Hamas' Islamism, however, should not distract from this structural situation, in the same way that the Viet Cong's communism does not. In both cases, we have a superior army relying on aerial bombing and heavy bombardment of civilian areas. In both cases, we have a weaker party trying to balance this weakness by digging tunnels to escape the bombing (Gaza's tunnel network; Củ Chi tunnels in Vietnam).[43] In both cases, we have an anti-colonial struggle in which the natives are seeking independence from foreign domination. In both cases, the civilian suffering is disproportionately on the native side.

Given this structural similarity, it is unsurprising that the war rhetoric is also similar. US Air Force Chief of Staff General Curtis Emerson LeMay commented in the mid-1960s that the US should bomb North Vietnam 'back into the Stone Ages'.[44] Echoing these comments, Interior Minister Eli Yishai said of Israel's onslaught against Gaza in 2012 that the 'goal of the operation is to send Gaza back to the Middle Ages. Only then will Israel be calm for forty years.'[45] Yet, 'calm' was not achieved and Israel bombarded Gaza again two years later. Moreover, Israel's claims to be handling the war effort in a moral and humane way echo American claims decades earlier that 'the bombing of the North [of Vietnam] has been the most accurate and the most restrained in modern warfare.'[46]

Similarly, some of the Israeli methods (warning shots on the rooftops, leaflets, collective punishment) seem to be directly derived from the British colonial textbook for counter-insurgency methods in Oman against the Dhufari revolutionaries. These included, *inter alia*, in 1969:

A warning rocket or gun strike would suffice to give warning of bombing run. Alternatively, a few leaflets dropped could explain why we were going to destroy the town "within five minutes" so that there would be no time to alert the air defense units.[47]

Attacks on civilians are not novel then. However, it seems now that the erosion of the distinction between civilians and combatants is complete in some parts of the public discourse. This is evident in media reports (like in *Ha'aretz*) on the death of 'noncombatants' in Gaza.[48] If the reference point is the combatants rather than the civilians, then civilians are defined as a negation. They are an afterthought. Rather than being the norm, they become the exception. The expectation and fear that Edwards expressed is still lingering beneath the categories that define and represent the reality of the oppressed: they are against the invader and hence are suspected of being combatants until proven otherwise. The Israeli reaction to every report of civilian casualties is representative of this view. Often, this reaction indicates that the fatal strike that led to civilian deaths targeted a combatant. Or, that the civilian deaths are the product of Palestinian combatants' disregard for their own people's lives.[49] More bluntly, Giora Eiland, a former head of Israel's National Security Council, wrote during 'Protective Edge' on 5 August 2014 that there are no 'innocent civilians' in Gaza:

> … why should Gaza's residents suffer? Well, they are to blame for this situation just like Germany's residents were to blame for electing Hitler as their leader and paid a heavy price for that, and rightfully so. Hamas is not a terror organization which came from afar and forcibly occupied Gaza. It's the authentic representative of the population there. It rose to power following democratic elections and built an impressive military ability with the residents' support. Its power base has remained stable despite the suffering.[50]

Consistent with this approach, the Israelis contested the number of the killed 'civilians' immediately following the conclusion of the massive onslaught.[51] The 'civilian', then, is a suspicious category that requires proof.

These arguments and positions, however, seek to justify the infliction of suffering on civilians, to punish them, and force them into submission. Writing in 1965, in the context of the guerrilla wars in Vietnam and Algeria, Eqbal Ahmad explained that revolutionaries — far from disregarding their people's lives — have high regard for the 'human factor.'[52] The popular support for the combatants, he added, originates in the 'moral alienation' from the colonial rulers.[53]

IV. Repetition and Retaliation

Nevertheless, it is not merely innocent suffering that expands (point 2 in Edwards' list above), but punishment and retaliation that does (point 1 in Edwards' list). Retaliation is not confined to violent actions that require mobilizing military or police power which may entail the use of brute force and infliction of corporal injuries. These can be understood as disciplinary mechanisms that the colonizer inflicts on the body politic of the colonized.

Consider the following examples. When Hamas won the 2006 elections the Israeli government withheld Palestinian tax money as a punishment (and released it, as if a reward, after current Palestinian Authority President Mahmoud Abbas (Abu Mazen) fired the Hamas government, leading to the split with Gaza.[54] When the UN General Assembly voted to make Palestine a non-member observer state in 2012, the Israeli government declared three thousand new housing units (and processed an additional thousand permits) in East Jerusalem and the West Bank.[55] More recently, when the Palestinians declared on June 2014 a unity agreement between Fatah and Hamas, Israel responded by initiating housing units in the settlements.[56] In January 2015, Israel withheld the transfer of Palestinian tax revenue following the Palestinian authority's request to join the International Criminal Court.[57]

This expansion of the idea of punishment obscures the prolonged nature of the occupation; a temporality not foreseen by the laws of war. No wonder then that international lawyers in recent years have questioned whether the Israeli occupation should be considered 'illegal' *tout court* or simply a '*de facto* annexation'.[58] This expansion of punishment also obscures the settler colonial nature of the occupation by concealing the decades-long colonization project, and the state's investment in it. Policies advancing the colonial project are presented as a reaction rather than an action, and as a punishment rather than the norm. However, this form of punishment does not seek to deter or rehabilitate those who deviate from the norm. Rather, it seeks to advance the norm: the colonization of Palestine.

V. Repetition and Justice

The repeated failure of the deployment of the laws of war to protect the weak seems to make Israel a Nietzschean state. But that is only partially true. Nietzsche, like Thrasymachus (in Plato's *Republic*) and Callicles (in

Plato's *Gorgias*) before him, saw justice/law as the will of the stronger.[59] In the *Genealogy of Morals* Nietzsche critiques the weak for blackmailing the stronger with moral chatter about equality, justice, tolerance, un-egoism, humility, patience, forgiveness, etc. The weak cannot defeat the powerful so he tries to undermine the powerful's ability to express his will to power ('the essence of life'[60]) and dominate th e weak. This slave morality represents weakness and subjection as strength and virtue, and it turns humans from spontaneous and aggressive beings into tamed and civilized ones.[61] The condemnation of suffering undermines the powerful by making them ashamed of their instincts and feel 'guilty' because of the pangs of 'conscience'. Nietzsche writes:

> To see others suffer does one good, to make others suffer even more: this is a hard saying but an ancient, mighty, human, all-too-human principle... let me declare expressly that in the days when mankind was not yet ashamed of its cruelty, life on earth was more cheerful than it is now that pessimists exist. The darkening of the sky above mankind has deepened in step with the increase in man's feeling of shame *at man*.... I mean the morbid softening and moral-ization through which the animal 'man' finally learns to be ashamed of all his instincts.[62]

Interestingly, however, there is a reversal of the Nietzschean prism in the context of the Israeli occupation of Palestinian territories. Here we witness an occupier who wants to have both the unleashing of destruction that comes with relatively unlimited power, and the mentality or discourse of the weak/slave morality. The stronger and aggressive party, who seeks to undermine internal legal norms that restrict its actions against the Palestin-ians, appropriates the slave morality discourse. It deploys the rhetoric of victimhood in which Israeli suffering is magnified even if comparatively negligible, and Palestinian suffering is justified and de-valued. More impor-tantly, this morality seeks to shame Palestinians for using violence, for resisting, for rejecting a complete surrender. It does not matter from this perspective if some Palestinians exhibited signs of willingness to surrender (as in the Palestinian Authority and its security cooperation with Israel).[63] So long as there are groups who are unwilling to surrender, or occasionally resist, there is sufficient justification to invoke the moral arm hand-in-hand with military might.

This appropriation of morality is a familiar trope in colonial contexts. Frantz Fanon described the colony as 'a Manichean world' because the settler s eeks to subdue the colonized both physically and morally.[64] In accordance with what Fanon terms 'the totalitarian character of colonial exploitation', the colonizers associate the natives with evil and the negation (rather than, merely, the absence) of values or ethics.[65] This is why it becomes easier to deny them the 'civilian' status and its concomitant protection. The natives become suspicious of the colonial invocation of values given the violence that accompanies their deployment.[66] C.L.R. James famously declared, in the context of the Haitian revolution, that 'it was easier to find decency, gratitude, justice, and humanity in a cage of starving tigers than in the councils of imperialism.'[67]

VI. *The Unholy Trinity: War, Peace, Morality*

In short, war, peace, and morality are united at the moment against Palestinians' quest for freedom. The war machine crushes Palestinian daily life as well as their actions of resistance. The peace process is conditioned on their abdication of their right to resist an unjust foreign occupier and is conditioned on their subordination of demands on behalf of justice for the sake of peace. But they are trapped. Because the relative justice they are willing to accept is increasingly relative to the extent it becomes indistinguishable from unconditional surrender.[68] In the gradual nature of a prolonged 'peace process', the fundamental issues are continuously deferred at the same time that facts on the ground are being created (e.g., an increasing number of settlements and settlers in the West Bank and Jerusalem; the fragmentation of the territories; the continued denial of the refugees' right to return; stripping Jerusalemites of their residency permits; the exploitation of natural resources; etc.). This deferral is a product of the structure of the negotiations process: the absence of a guiding substantive principle/outcome reduces the process to procedural questions that are determined by power relations.[69] Thus, any Palestinian move, diplomatic or otherwise, effective or meaningless, has to be confined to the bilateral logic of the process. Otherwise, it is deemed harmful to the peace efforts and considered a unilateral move that may justify Israeli unilateral moves or punishments. And of course, any 'violations' of the process and agreements justify mobilizing the war machine.

Repetition is endemic to the process. Repetition here does not merely signify inertia but also that the process gains a semi-autonomous existence. The process of negotiations is repeated despite apparent failure and futility: 'A decent chance of success has never been a prerequisite for US-led talks. The peace process offers its own rewards, quite independent of its ostensible purpose.'[70] According to this prism, 'rising instability is almost always taken as evidence of the necessity of new talks'.[71] Rather than questioning the process, its premises, and its connection to instability, it is perpetuated *ad infinitum*.

Indeed, the Oslo peace process itself has served as a justification for an Israeli shift in the deployment of force vis-à-vis the Palestinians. Under the Oslo process, Israel redeployed its military forces from areas in the West Bank. These redeployments reduced direct Israeli military presence in areas that were transferred to the Palestinian Authority's administrative and security control. The unilateral disengagement plan from Gaza in 2005, in which Israel withdrew from Gaza and dismantled the settlements, exemplified a similar pattern. This 'withdrawal' conceals the continued reality of occupation and allows Israel to treat the territories as 'external' areas to which it has no responsibility.[72] Rather than policing activities to maintain order in an occupied territory, Israel responds with a military assault. As Levine and Hajjar write:

> ... since the redeployments agreed to under the Oslo Accords, and particularly since the start of the second intifada, Israel has asserted its right to wage war on Palestinians in Gaza and the West Bank, deploying military force at levels unprecedented since 1967, including the deployment of tanks, helicopter gunships, and snipers. In response to international criticism about the excessive use of force, officials asserted that, because the army was "out" of Palestinian-inhabited areas, riot control and policing were no longer options, and therefore a militarized response was necessary and legitimate to defend against a foreign "armed adversary". Israel asserted its self-defence right to attack an "enemy entity", while denying that those stateless enemies had any right to use force, even in self-defence.[73]

Peace, from this perspective, warrants and enables war. War becomes the exception to the general condition of peace (which is reduced to a process with no definite endpoint) and seeks to restore it (as a process). Resistance is a violation of the process, which is predicated on its abdication, and war on resistance is a restoration of the condition of the (peace) process. In other words, war is peace.[74] Peace is surrender.[75] Surrender is the right thing to do (à la the morality of the powerful). The right thing to do is to wage war on those whose very existence and resistance is a reminder of the conditions of absence of freedom.

This reasoning is of course flawed. It is based on blurring the distinction between peace and war. Peace is equated with lack of hostilities (that is, colonial rule) rather than with genuine conditions for human flourishing and self-determination. The prolonged nature of the occupation contributes to this conflation. The redeployments ('peace') conceal the occupation's reality despite continued control. Additionally, the repeated wars make the condition of war common rather than exceptional. Ultimately, colonial wars are part and parcel of maintaining colonial rule/peace.

Clearly, so long as this reasoning and conflation is the dominant political discourse and practice, the repeated deaths in Gaza will be meaningless. Only eventual freedom will give meaning to the deaths of Palestinians. Only a proper contextualization will bring freedom back to the discussion. Only changing the power structure is likely to prevent repetition.

GAZA:
NO SE PUEDE MIRAR — 'ONE CANNOT LOOK':[1]
A BRIEF REFLECTION
Sara Roy

'I am living in minutes. I need one more minute.'

From a friend in Gaza

Summer 2014

I have long been warned about making any kind of comparison between the Jewish victims of the Holocaust and the Palestinians living under Israeli occupation. Some friends have told me, some screaming at me, that I weaken my argument with such comparisons and de-legitimize myself. More importantly, they say, I defile the memory of the six million — among whom are my grandparents, aunts and uncles — by invoking their names alongside Palestinian ones.

I listen to their arguments very carefully because I am a child of survivors and my family history is one I would never knowingly dishonour. My mother and father survived Auschwitz among other horrors. My life has been defined by the Holocaust and the unimaginable losses it inflicted on our family (throughout my life I heard stories about individuals I came to love but never knew). Yet, with those losses came lessons that were drummed into me by my parents, lessons burned into my soul, which I promised never to forget.[2] The Holocaust is not a shield beyond which you cannot look, my mother and father taught me; rather, it is a mirror with which to reflect and examine your actions, a mirror you must always carry with you.

While there is no equivalence between the Holocaust and the occupation — just as there is no equivalence between the occupier and the occupied — there are parallels. After nearly fifty years of occupation, twenty-one years of closure, eight years of blockade, and three wars waged against it in six years — Gaza pleads for those parallels to be made.

Where civilians do not exist

Today, Gaza finds itself in an unknown and precarious place, deprived of the ordinary and comprehensible. Perhaps for the first time since the occupation began, Palestinians in Gaza see no horizon or future beyond the panorama of destruction that now confronts them. Over my three decades of involvement with Gaza, I have witnessed the deliberate and purposeful disablement of this vibrant place and its gentle people — and now its large-scale destruction. And I continue to ask myself, why? Yet, among all the stories that Gazans could tell, one continues to preoccupy them more than all the others — an entreaty that still remains unheard: the quest for human dignity.

This quest is constant and unrelenting, as ferocious in its insistency as are the attempts by Israel to extinguish it. There is a voice that has always been present through all my years of research among Palestinians and it speaks these words: we, too, are mothers and fathers, sisters and brothers, professors and lawyers, fishermen and factory workers. We, too, are human beings with individual histories and stories that must be recounted by the living, not only buried with the dead.

Gaza is a place, Israel argues, where innocent civilians do not exist. The presence of such civilians in Gaza is suspect, they say, because Palestinians elected a terrorist organization to represent them. Retired Israeli Major General Giora Eiland stated, '[T]hey [the citizens of Gaza] are to blame for this situation just like Germany's residents were to blame for electing Hitler as their leader and paid a heavy price for that, and rightfully so.'[3] According to this logic there is no such thing as a civilian home, school, hospital, mosque, church or playground in Gaza; all these places are therefore legitimate targets of Israeli bombs since every home is a non-home; every kindergarten, a non-kindergarten; and every hospital, a non-hospital.

During Operation Cast Lead (OCL), Israel's 2008–9 offensive against Gaza, Reserve Major Amiram Levin stated, 'What we have to do is act systematically with the aim of punishing all the organizations that are firing the rockets and mortars as well as the civilians who are enabling them to fire and hide.' The IDF spokesperson, Major Avital Leibowitz, argued that 'anything affiliated with Hamas is a legitimate target.'[4] Not surprisingly the UN-commissioned Goldstone Report whose mandate it was to investigate all violations of international human rights and humanitarian law that might have been committed during OCL found that the 'humiliation and dehumanization of the Palestinian population'[5] were Israeli policy objectives in its assault on Gaza, an assault that was nothing less than 'a deliberately disproportionate attack designed to punish, humiliate and terrorize a civilian population, radically diminish its local economic capacity both to work and to provide for itself, and to force upon it an ever increasing sense of dependency and vulnerability.'[6]

That the area being bombed was urban with over 20,000 human beings per square kilometer does not weigh on the majority of Jewish people. That my friends and their children were among those being bombed, people who have always welcomed me as a Jew into their homes in Gaza, is of no consequence. For General Eiland, Majors Levin and Leibowitz and for too many others, there are no parents in Gaza, there are no children, there are no deaths to mourn. Gaza is a place where words are mimed and screams are mute. Even the wars against Gaza are silent: soundless tanks, soundless drones, soundless bombs. Rather, Gaza is where the grass grows wild and must be mowed from time to time.[7]

' [T]o be able to give, one has to possess.'[8]

The desolation inflicted on Gaza is powerfully seen in the almost complete destruction of Khuza'a in 2014, a village once known as Gaza's orchards. Writes a UN colleague:

> Khuza'a was very difficult. There are whole stretches with every dwelling smashed, and untouched land between them. People are living in two-and three-walled rooms. There is almost no sign of the neighborhood economy until you drive some blocks back—but also no sign of transport for people to reach the trading. We saw only one little micro-enterprise cart of the kind that normally fills neighborhoods. It feels as though they are miles away from any kind of community, and I can't begin to imagine the impact of staring at

jagged wreckage day after day. When they see the big UN car, everyone drifts toward it, sometimes hailing it and sometimes angry or just desperate to tell someone what they are living through.

What had been a lively neighborhood has been reduced, so suddenly, to complete dependence. They fell through the floor of any kind of humane standard ... there is a fragility in these areas that I find frightening.[9]

The devastation of Khuza'a (and Beit Hanoun, Shejaiya, Beit Lahiya) conceals an even greater theft that has been imposed on Palestinians, especially in Gaza: the desecration of daily life. Professor Nadera Shalhoub-Kevorkian writes that Palestinians live in 'a zone of non-existence' where one finds 'new spaces of obscenity in the politics of day-to-day lives.'[10] These obscene spaces are defined by a maimed reality where engaging in normal, everyday acts of living and working — building a home, going to school, visiting relatives, planting a tree, playing in a park or sitting on a beach — are treated as criminal activities, punishable even by death.

Simone Weil argues that the 'future brings us nothing, gives us nothing; it is we who in order to build it have to give it everything, our very life. But to be able to give, one has to possess; and we possess no other life, no other living sap, than the treasures stored up from the past and digested, assimilated and created afresh by us.'[11] How are Palestinians to create a future out of their disfigured present and dismembered past, a future Israel and the Jewish people more generally have taken from them — an act that speaks to our own inability to live a life without the walls we are constantly asked to build? This begs the question, can Jews as a people be ordinary, an essential part of our rebirth after the Holocaust?

As I have written elsewhere: 'Is it possible to be normal when we [as a people] seek refuge in the margin, and remedy in the dispossession and destruction of another people? How can we create when we acquiesce so willingly to the demolition of homes, construction of barriers, denial of sustenance, and ruin of innocents? How can we be merciful when, to use [Jacqueline] Rose's words, we seek "omnipotence as the answer to historical pain?"'[12] Instead we celebrate the slaughter of Palestinian children while remaining the abused, 'creating situations where our victimization is assured and our innocence affirmed.'[13] As seen in the words of General Eiland: 'Because we want to be compassionate towards those cruel people [in Gaza], we are committing to act cruelly towards the really compassionate people — the residents of the State of Israel.'[14] In this way,

Gaza speaks to the unnaturalness of our own condition as Jews. For in Gaza, we seek resolution and comfort in the agony of another people.

Gaza, Israel, and the end of Holocaust consciousness

One of the most powerful works of Holocaust literature I have read is Yehiel De-Nur's *Shivitti: A Vision*. He signed this book, as he did his others, not with his name but with the number he was given in Auschwitz: Ka-Tzetnik 135633 (K.Z. being the initials of 'concentration camp' in German and pronounced 'ka-tzet'). He did so in memory of every camp inmate who was known by 'Ka-Tzetnik Number . . . ,'[15] the number itself branded into the flesh of the left arm, as was my father's.

In what is perhaps the most memorable passage of the book, De-Nur describes how he hid in a coal bin inside a crematorium truck, which was parked and locked in a garage. Reliving the moment when he escaped from the truck, De-Nur, covered in coal dust, encounters a stunned garage superintendent who is an SS officer, and screams at him, 'I'm a human being. No evil spirit! No demon! I am human and I want to live! I am a human being! Human!'[16] — words I hear cried in Gaza, words meant to affirm existence and self-worth.

During Israel's last assault in the summer of 2014, known as Operation Protective Edge, Raji Sourani, a prominent human rights lawyer in Gaza, wrote me: 'Gaza is a totally unsafe place. Day and night the same: shock and terror . . . Airplanes do not leave Gaza's skies and they are throwing death to children and women. I visited the intensive care unit at Shifa Hospital and you cannot imagine the scene; most of them will die soon. Even medicines do not exist .... The hospital is full of women and children; many lost [body] parts and limbs . . . People here have nothing to lose except misery and humiliation . . . We want to live a normal life, with dignity.'[17]

Another friend, Sami Abdel Shafi, a political analyst and the then Gaza representative of the Atlanta-based Carter Center, sent me the following during some of the worst days of the bombing: 'Gaza is being slaughtered. Innocents who are in favour of peace are being slaughtered . . . My God. My God, the God of all good people.'[18]

In another distressing email to me, Sami recounted the following: 'I am barely sleeping from utter worry and fear, a new kind I haven't had [since] 2008/09. Stories of civilian targeting on the streets and at home are [terrifying]. Unbelievable. So often, I spend my time running from one place to the other around the house fearing what may come. I started mistaking the sound of boiling water on the stove as though it is something descending from the sky . . . You don't know when it will start, where, for what reason or how long it will [last]. Sheer paranoia.'[19]

As I pictured Sami running from one room to another trying desperately to find a place of safety, a family story from the Holocaust immediately pressed its way into my memory, a story I try hard not to recall because of the pain it always inflicts. The Nazis came to the *shtetl*[20] where my grandparents lived. All of their nine children — my mother, aunts and uncles — were adults and no longer lived at home except for my aunt Frania (who told me this story) and my aunt Sophie who was only 12 years old. Before emptying the town of its Jewish inhabitants, the Nazis decided to take children first. On the day they came for Sophie, my grandfather and grandmother frantically ran through the rooms of their home searching for a place — a closet, a chest, a cupboard — to hide Sophie from the destruction that ultimately claimed her. My grandparents succeeded at first but eventually she was taken — as they were — and never seen again.

How can I not think of those innocents murdered in Gaza last summer — among them over 500 children — alongside my grandfather, grandmother, and Sophie? Refusing any such association or bond, as I have been told I must do, is not only the end of Holocaust consciousness, it is the end of Jewish ethical history[21] — shattering the mirror I promised my parents always to use.

GAZA AS ARCHIVE[1]

Sherene Seikaly

A man and his young son sit on two cement blocks, surrounded by piles of rubble that were once their home, on the edges of what was once their street. Their postures mirror one another. With thin arms dangling over knees, fingers clasped, and eyes downcast, they survey the losses. They ponder the next step.

It was 16 July 2014, eight days after the Israeli military commenced its onslaught on the Gaza Strip. This image, like many, would circulate through multiple venues around the world. The photographs left Gaza, even when the Palestinians could not.[2] People consumed, read and circulated these images to express the singular desperation of the Gaza Strip, to compile a database of the present.[3] But these snapshots of loss and displacement are not exceptional. They are instances of the historical experience that is the Palestinian condition.

Beginning at nine in the evening on 19 July Israeli tanks, artillery, and missiles pounded the residents of one of the Gaza Strip's poorest and most overcrowded neighborhoods, Shejaiya.[4] The Israeli army and its cohorts in the Israeli, European, and US media scripted these people as 'human shields.'

With the adjective 'shield' these pundits rendered 1.8 million people 'killable.'[5] The 'shield' in this phrase acted as a protective armour for Israeli aggression. It is a semiotic and legal ruse that Israel uses to conduct drone and F-16 attacks with impunity. If the people in Gaza were simply civilians, Israel's aggression would, according to international law, constitute a war crime.[6] Through the technique of the 'human shield', Israel and its supporters pretended to attend to international law: the same domain Palestinians have sought refuge in, the same domain which has time and again bound and constrained them.[7]

With the adjective 'shield' Israel and its supporters found new ways to claim authority and to redefine the genres of the human.[8] The 'shield' alleged to account for the vulnerability of its predicate the human, precisely by negating it. For the unquestioning consumers of this cynical slogan, what remained of the 'human' was an icon of the ungrievable.[9]

Yet the technique of the 'human shield' was itself a repetition. Israel has, since Hamas' electoral victory in 2006, constructed the Gaza Strip as an insurgent zone. Blurring the line between civilian and combatant was crucial to this effort. Gaza became a 'liminal space' in which Israel has full discretion and authority to exercise brutal force.[10]

Thus in 2014, as in so many instances before, the Israeli Goliath would incite, overpower, and punish its enemy, while all the while claiming the sacred role of the victimized David. Israel scripted this enemy as Hamas, but the real enemy is the Palestinian people, indeed the very idea of a Palestinian people. The original sin, then, of the 'human shields' in Gaza is that they were born Palestinian.[11] Their mere existence as Palestinians living on the remaining shards of Palestine effectively renders them non-human.

The cruel work of the phrase 'human shield' came to light on the morning of 20 July as corpses and body parts lined the streets of Shejaiya.[12] A matriarch with a blood-spattered headscarf cried in shock: my son is dead. A young man lay immobilized in the debris; he called out to God just before an Israeli sniper killed him.[13] The people that remained fled in terror, racing for their lives under ongoing assault. A dark cloud hung over them as they walked, drove, or rode away in wheelchairs leaving their homes behind.

On the afternoon of 24 July people taking shelter at a United Nations school in Beit Hanoun gathered in the yard to evacuate. Minutes later a barrage of Israeli artillery shells thundered into the school killing sixteen people and wounding 200. The Israeli army claimed it had given evacuation orders, while UN spokesperson Chris Gunness insisted that the UN had called for a lull in the fighting to facilitate evacuation.[14] It was the fourth time Israel had hit a UN facility since it had began its assault. In the summer of 2014, to live in Gaza was to live in perpetual search of refuge.

On 27 July the Palestinians in Gaza had a reprise from bombardment. They began sifting through the piles of wreckage to search for the dead. Surrounded by the smell of decomposing bodies, they uncovered another

150 people. A young adolescent, dressed in green, gaunt and resolute, gathered her books in the debris that was once her room. She searched, like so many, for the remnants of biography.

These are but a few of the scenes of Gaza 2014. They express the agony of this singular moment. They express the will to live in the midst of destruction and profound loss. They are painful in their immediacy. But it is their familiarity that is the deepest source of injury. They do not belong to this time or this place alone. To apprehend Gaza 2014, to resist understanding the Palestinian home and the Palestinian body as somehow continuous with violence, we must better attend to historical repetition.

Gaza 2014 is not simply an indicator of an ongoing struggle or an inimitable resistance. It is an instance in what is now a century-long confrontation with colonialism. It is part of an archive that is the Palestinian condition.

Gaza 2014 conjures formative catastrophes. It reminds, repeats, and rehearses the meta-moments of displacement that shape what it means to be a Palestinian. It echoes 1948. It echoes that year when eighty percent of Palestine became Israel; when Zionist forces destroyed or depopulated over 400 villages; when 800,000 Palestinians became stateless refugees denied their internationally recognized right to return;[15] when 150,000 Palestinians in what was now Israel became 'present-absent' strangers on their own land.[16]

Gaza 2014 conjures the ongoing catastrophes that have defined what it means to be Palestinian since 1948. It echoes brutal instances of indiscriminate death at the hands of a superior military force, often acting under the guise of retaliation, and always enacting collective punishment.[17] Gaza 2014 conjures the Qibya massacre of 1953 when a young Ariel Sharon killed sixty-nine residents and reduced forty-five homes to rubble.[18] It conjures Sabra and Shatila in 1982 when the Israeli army shelled the refugee camps and lit the way for Lebanese Phalangists to 'mop up' the Palestinians inside.

Gaza 2014 conjures other more mundane instances, micro-moments of the colonial experience. It reiterates the house demolitions, the land expropriations, and the targeted assassinations that have shaped what it means to be a Palestinian since the 1930s, if not before. It echoes the relentless technologies of Israel's targeting of land, livelihood, and life since 1948. Israel's most recent incursion in 2014 resulted in the designation of forty-four percent of the Gaza Strip's land as a 'buffer zone'.[19] This is a historical repetition of a staple Israeli strategy: the ongoing expropriation of land has aimed at and resulted in an ever-shrinking Palestine.

For the Palestinians living under occupation in the West Bank, for the Palestinians living in Israel, for Palestinian refugees, for the Palestinians in diaspora, Gaza 2014 is not exceptional. Exodus, displacement, grief, and searching for refuge are not specific to this moment. Gaza 2014 is but another historical repetition in the confrontation with Zionism's settler colonial enterprise. That enterprise has with all of its technologies and adaptations continued its conquest of land and everything that this conquest necessitates: most crucially the erasure of the Palestinians. Gaza 2014 belongs to the archive of colonialism.

On 2 July Israeli police found the tortured and burnt sixteen-year-old body of Mohammed Abu Khdeir in a Jerusalem forest.[20] Six young Israelis had kidnapped him on his way to prayer. They forced him to drink gasoline and lit him on fire. Those one and a half million people subjected to the injurious and colonial label 'Israeli Arab' took to the streets from the south in the Naqab to the north in Haifa. Throughout the non-contiguous bantustans of the West Bank, Palestinians rose up. On both sides of the green line that partitions historic Palestine, there were pitched battles with Israeli forces. One side threw rocks. The other side threw tear gas, rubber coated bullets, live fire, and toxic water called 'skunk.' During those days of uprising, it was hard to distinguish between Nazareth and Ramallah, between Tulkarm and Baqa.

The profound power of these demonstrations was to defy the militarized lines separating the Palestinians from one another. These include the always shifting 1967 border across which the definition of the Palestinian moves from second-class 'citizen stranger' to colonial subject; the multiple divides within the West Bank itself which isolate Palestinians into various enclaves; and the walls that render Gaza territorially isolated from the rest of Palestine. During those days of uprising, resisting bodies erased, if only ephemerally, Israel's machinations of separation.

These uprisings too, do not belong to their time alone. They conjure other instances in the history of Palestine. They belong to the rebels of 1936–1939 who for a brief moment liberated the cities of Palestine from British rule; to the *fedayeen* of the Palestinian revolution in the 1960s and 1970s; to the strikers and marchers who stood up against land confiscation inside Israel on Land Day in 1976; to the revolutionaries of the first *intifada* who faced brutality with civil disobedience; to the stone throwers whose time in Israeli prisons became rites of passage.[21] Gaza 2014 belongs to the other part of the archive that is the Palestinian condition: the one of decolonization.[22]

In launching its military experiment on its favorite laboratory,[23] the Gaza Strip, Israel banked on and delivered historical repetition. The Palestinian death toll mounted. But in return, the Palestinians delivered historical rupture. For the first time since 1993 and the launching of the Oslo process, the Palestinians insisted to the many forces much stronger than them that they would not fall prey to the logic of 'agree now, negotiate later'. They refused the choice between slow or immediate death.[24] They demanded an end to the siege of Gaza, a siege that Israel has administered since 2006, a siege that is itself an act of war.[25]

In contradistinction to Israel's last two assaults on Gaza, Hamas inflicted higher costs than ever before on Israel's far superior military power, killing sixty-six soldiers, a security coordinator, and four civilians.[26] Previously narrating Hamas as irrational and irrelevant, Israeli commentators confronted Hamas' steadfastness in the face of a devastating power imbalance. That steadfastness shifted, if only momentarily, the terms of political discourse across Palestinian political factions from the swamp of 'negotiations' to a revitalized focus on resistance. Gaza 2014 was a rupture in the historical record.

And in response to this rupture, in response to the unified call to end the debilitating siege of Gaza, Palestinians — once again and across territorial separations — took to the streets. On the evening of 24 July and in the thousands, they braved live fire and rubber coated bullets. In Ramallah they marched to Qalandia. In Nablus, they marched to Huwwara. In Hebron, in Bethlehem, in Tulkarm, they confronted Israeli forces. In the Jerusalem suburb of Abu Dis, young men chipped at the Wall. The symbolic destination was Jerusalem. The concrete outcome was a refusal to submit and a rejection of the bifurcation of Palestine and Palestinians into isolated shards of land and experience.

To designate these mobilizations as 'pro-Gaza' is to misread history. Of course these Palestinians stood with Gaza. But they understood Gaza as part of their reality, as part of their ongoing confrontation with colonialism. They seized the rupture and they demonstrated for Gaza and also for Palestine, beyond, before, and across Israel's machinations of separation. But it is not their acts alone that resist and transgress Israel's relentless drive to keep Palestinians apart.

The accumulation of these acts and experiences also does this work. The archive and the archiving of these moments of destruction and uprising, of death and life, of loss and accumulation, of hope and despair, resist Zionism's separations and its attempts to render Gaza 2014 as distinct, as exceptional, as isolated.

By the end of its assault on the Gaza Strip in 2014, the Israeli military machine had killed 2,131 and injured over 11,000 Palestinians.[27] That machine destroyed 18,000 homes. That machine, at the height of its assault, displaced 425,000 Palestinians, who by the end of those bloody and hot summer months sought refuge in various shelters. That machine rendered 1,000 children permanently disabled. That machine destroyed twenty-eight schools, damaged an additional 118, and targeted the Islamic University in Gaza. Because of that machine, 20 to 30 percent of Palestinian households in Gaza remain today unable to access clean water.[28]

In the face of this tremendous loss, of life, of livelihood, of basic needs, it is counterintuitive to ponder accumulation. Yet we can reflect on those fifty days of assault as the latest instance of historical accumulation.

Taken alone, Gaza 2014 and its abundant repository of loss appear fleeting. It resembles the fragility of a sand sculpture. On 17 July, an Israeli

'Tomorrow I Will Be Fine.' Palestinian students at the UNRWA school in Canada Camp, Rafah, 1988. Image by Randa Shaath.

gunboat shelled and killed four boys playing on the beach: Ismail Bakr and his cousins Ahed, Zakariya, and Muhammad.[29] The sand sculpture commemorating the boys was delicate, temporary, and transient. It was a poignant gesture that reflected the conditions of the moment. But we must see this sculpture, this work of memory and commemoration, as one of many. We must suture this sculpture with other gestures, with other commemorations that the imminence of the present blurs. We must collect, document, and read the repetitions and ruptures of the Palestinian condition. The Palestinian archive resists settler colonialism's imperative to isolate, to separate, and to erase. The Palestinian archive is expansive and flexible. It is not the historian alone who conducts the labor of compiling and reading it.

At the thin intersections of popular memory and archival practices, people tell their stories to make sense of the everyday. They weave these stories to shape the present, to build connections to the past, and to stake claims to the future. They draw on continuities. They distinguish ruptures. They attend to that pit of possibility and danger that is historical contingency. They sift through repetition to identify the singular, the new. And they build and nourish an archive: one that keeps a record of colonization and guards the will to decolonize. Gaza 2014, in its continuities and its ruptures, is an instance of the archive that is the Palestinian condition.

NOTES

INTRODUCTION

1. Mahmoud Darwish, 'Silence for Gaza.' Translated by Sinan Antoon, *Hayrat al-'A'id* (The Returnee's Perplexity) (Beirut: Riyad al-Rayyis, 2007). http://mondoweiss.net/2012/11/mahmoud-darwish-silence-for-gaza, last accessed 7 January 2016.
2. Atef Abu Saif, *The Drone Eats With Me: Diaries from a City Under Fire* (Manchester: Comma Press, 2015), p. 45.
3. See Jean-Pierre Filiu, *Gaza: A History* (London: Hurst, 2014).
4. Mahmoud Darwish, 'Silence for Gaza.' (op. cit.).

1. GAZA AS LARGER THAN LIFE

1. Ghassan Kanafani, 'Letter from Gaza,' *Short Story & Essay Writing*, 1991, pp. 77–80.
2. By relying on the strength and flexibility of the human body and whatever exists in the (usually urban) surroundings, parkour is akin to a military obstacle course training mixed with gymnastics and street dance. Whether performed individually or in groups, it requires a performer to move around, across, through, over and under the features of his environment. See for example the Facebook site of Gaza Parkour and Free Running: https://www.facebook.com/Gaza.PKT, last accessed 7 January 2016.
3. Marah Majed Elwadia's Instagram is available at: https://instagram.com/marahgaza/
4. Two recent examples include: Refaat Alareer (ed.), *Gaza Writes Back: Short Stories from Young Writers in Gaza, Palestine* (Chrlottesville, VA: Just World Books, 2014); Atef Abu Saif (ed.), *The Book of Gaza: A City in Short Fiction*, (Manchester: Carcanet Press Ltd., 2014).
5. See for example the Pinterest site of Sarah Al-Khatib: https://www.pinterest.com/sarahsos946/my-paintings/, last accessed 7 January 2016.

6. See http://www.dailymail.co.uk/news/article-2734142/People-Gaza-turn-RUBBLE-bucket-challenge.html, last accessed 7 January 2016.

7. There are at least two versions: https://www.youtube.com/watch?v=nFtG3ZZKCSk and https://www.youtube.com/watch?v=S4gu27QVzOc

8. See https://www.youtube.com/watch?v=a5LuoVzNCXM, last accessed 7 January 2016.

9. This is a onomatopoeic word for the sound of a drone, a term which, as far as I know, is unique to Gaza.

10. The local pronunciation of a Kalashnikov.

11. See for example: Mia Grondahl, *Gaza Graffiti: Messages of Love and Politics* (Cairo: The American University in Cairo Press, 2010); Bill Rolston, 'Messages of allegiance and defiance: the murals of Gaza,' *Race & Class* 55(4), 2014, pp. 40–64; and Julie Peteet, 'The writing on the walls: The graffiti of the Intifada,' *Cultural Anthropology* 11(2), 1996, pp. 139–159.

12. As commander of the southern front after the 1967 war, Ariel Sharon earned the nickname 'The Bulldozer' as he ordered the bulldozing of thousands of homes to create pathways through the tight alleyways of refugee camps and allow for easier access of tanks and armored personnel carriers. I have heard people living in the Rafah refugee camp refer to these as 'Sharon's boulevards.' Tens of thousands of Palestinians were made homeless during these bulldozing sprees. The same practice was used inside Rafah and especially the border zone with Egypt, see note 13.

13. This is a fourteen-kilometer-long border zone by Rafah, established as a demilitarized buffer zone between Israel and Egypt in their 1979 Peace Treaty, during which they agreed that it would be controlled by Israel. It has been the site of immeasurable violence as this is the area where tunnels are dug from Gaza into Egypt, and where the Israeli military has been razing homes and expanding the buffer zone (on the Palestinian side) since the 1990s.

14. One can obviously read the historical 'in reverse' as it were: that human history shows time and again that oppression does not end but takes on new forms; that losers do not eventually or necessarily win, no matter how just their cause might be. As such, perhaps Palestinians are nothing short of delusional. This line of argument can keep spiraling, for one can equally read that the historical 'losers' have been the Jews and that Israel has been the result of 'righting' certain historical wrongs.

15. See Helga Tawil-Souri, 'Digital Occupation: Gaza's High-Tech Enclosure,' *Journal of Palestine Studies* 41(2), 2012, pp. 27–43

16. See Helga Tawil-Souri 'The Technological End Between the "Inside" of Gaza and the "Outside" of Gaza,' *7iber*, September 2014, http://www.7iber.com/2014/09/the-technological-end-between-the-inside-of-gaza-and-the-outside-of-gaza/. Last accessed 7 January 2016.

17. Lisa Taraki, 'Urban Modernity on the Periphery: A New Middle Class Reinvents the Palestinian City,' *Social Text* 26(2), 2008, pp. 61–81.

18. Similarly, Joseph Massad argues that Palestinians should be called *mankubin* meaning 'catastrophe-d or disaster-ed people'. Joseph Massad, 'Resisting the Nakba,' *Al-Ahram Weekly* 897 (15–21 May, 2008). http://weekly.ahram.org. eg/2008/897/op8.htm

19. Israel Ministry of Foreign Affairs, 'Agreed Documents on Movement and Access from and to Gaza,' 15 November 2005.

20. Maps of rocket threats have been made by Israeli and foreign news sources alike, as well as by a range of Israeli official bodies. A map first published in the *Jerusalem Post* can be found here: http://www.cameraoncampus.org/blog/ wp-content/uploads/2013/05/map.jpg, last accessed 7 January 2016; one from the IDF's Twitter feed is available here: http://www.idfblog.com/wp-content/ uploads/2014/07/Map-Amlach-new-EN1.jpg, last accessed 7 January 2016; the IDF also tweeted various images of tunnels dug between Gaza and Israel with fighters teeming like ants in underground networks during the 2014 summer war: https://kristiann1.files.wordpress.com/2014/07/10466976_8124234121138 64_7528886616213082666_o.jpg and http://honestreporting.com/wp-content/ uploads/2014/07/IDF-tunnels.jpg, last accessed 7 January 2016.

21. Israeli Chief of Staff Moshe Ya'alon said of Gaza in 2002 that it is a 'cancer [...] that constitutes an existential threat ... [where] it's necessary to apply [...] chemotherapy,' quoted in Baruch Kimmerling, *Politicide: Ariel Sharon's War Against the Palestinians* (New York: Verso, 2003), p. 165. During the summer 2014 war, a flurry of misogynistic and violent rhetoric circulated implying the need to rape Gazan women, see David Sheen 'Israel's War Against Gaza's Women & Their Bodies' (23 July 2014): http://muftah.org/israels-war-gazas-women-bodies/#, last accessed 7 January 2016.; for a longer historical view of the targeting of Palestinian women's bodies and sexuality as structurally part of the Israeli settler colonial project's racialized logic of elimination, see: Nadera Shalhoub-Kevorkian, Sarah Ihmoud and Suhad Dahir-Nashif, 'Sexual Violence, Women's Bodies, and Israeli Settler Colonialism,' Jadaliyya (17 November 2014): http://www.jadaliyya.com/pages/index/19992/sexual-violence-women%E2%80%99s-bodies-and-israeli-settler, last accessed 7 January 2016.

22. Atef Abu Saif, *The Drone Eats With Me: Diaries from a City Under Fire* (London: Comma Press, 2015), p. 76.

23. Eyal Weizman, 'The Art of War,' *Frieze* 99, May 2006, http://www.frieze.com/ issue/article/the_art_of_war/, last accessed 7 January 2016.

24. It must be noted that despite the political, economic, military, and symbolic asymmetries, Israel is also a state in siege.

25. See for example Michael Dahan, 'The Gaza Strip as Panopticon and Panspectron: The Disciplining and Punishing of a Society,' *Proceedings Cultural Attitudes Towards Technology and Communication*, 2012, pp.25–37, http:// sammelpunkt.philo.at:8080/2136/, last accessed 7 January 2016.

26. Paul Virilio, *Desert Screen: War at the speed of light* (London: A&C Black, 2005). As an example, see John Collins, *Global Palestine* (London: Hurst Publishers, 2011).

27. See for example Lisa Bhungalia, 'Im/Mobilities in a "Hostile Territory": Managing the Red Line,' *Geopolitics*, 17(2), 2012, pp. 256–275.

28. Achille Mbembe, 'Necropolitics,' *Public Culture* 15(1), 2003, pp. 11–40.

29. Stephen Graham, *Cities Under Siege: The new military urbanism* (London: Verso Books, 2011).

30. Derek Gregory, 'Defiled Cities,' *Singapore Journal of Tropical Geography* 24(3), 2003, pp. 307–326.

31. Saskia Sassen, 'When the city itself becomes a technology of war,' *Theory, Culture & Society* 27.6 (2010): 33–50.

32. Eyal Weizman, *The Least of all Possible Evils: Humanitarian Violence from Arendt to Gaza* (London: Verso Books, 2012), p.96.

33. The most comprehensive analysis of the similarities and differences between Ferguson and Gaza is: David Palumbo-Liu, 'Ferguson and Gaza: The definitive study of how they are and are not similar,' *Salon* (22 August 2014), http://www.salon.com/2014/08/22/ferguson_and_gaza_the_definitive_study_of_how_they_are_and_are_not_similar/, last accessed 7 January 2016.

34. I am purposefully playing with Joe Sacco's book title, and in particular a passage in which he states: 'History can do without its footnotes. Footnotes are inessential at best.' Joe Sacco, *Footnotes in Gaza: A graphic novel* (London: Macmillan, 2009), p. 8.1

2. DIARY, 20 JULY 2014

1. This is an edited version of a diary published on *Al-Jazeera*, 21 July 2014, http://www.aljazeera.com/indepth/opinion/2014/07/diary-an-israeli-war-2014721102859370216.html, last accessed 7 January 2016.

2. This is an edited version of an article published in *Electronic Intifada*, 12 July 2014, http://electronicintifada.net/content/gaza-signposts-road-liberation/13554, last accessed 7 January 2016.

3. Edward Said, 'Permission to Narrate,' *London Review of Books* 6(3), 1984, http://www.lrb.co.uk/v06/n03/edward-said/permission-to-narrate, last accessed 7 January 2016.

4. I have made a similar argument elsewhere: http://electronicintifada.net/content/gaza-2009-culture-resistance-vs-defeat/8063, last accessed 7 January 2016.

3. GHAZEH EL SUMUD: CONFRONTING ISRAELI MASS TORTURE

1. For a deeper understanding of the concept see Lena Meari's excellent analysis. Lena Meari, 'Sumud: A Palestinian Philosophy of Confrontation in Colonial Prisons,' *South Atlantic Quarterly* Vol. 113(3) (2014), pp. 547–578.

2. United Nations Office for the Coordination of Humanitarian Affairs occupied Palestinian territory — OCHAoPt. (2014a), *Gaza Initial Rapid Assessment (August 27, 2015)*. Last accessed 3 February 2015 from http://www.ochaopt.

org/documents/Gaza_MIRA_report_9September.pdf

3. Ari Yashar, 'Israel among the ten most powerful nations in world,' Arutz
    Sheva, 24 January 2014. Last accessed 3 February 2015, from http://www.
    israelnationalnews.com/News/News.aspx/176683#.VCb_vkuEPVI

4. Al Mezan Center for Human Rights, 'Press release 1 September 2014'. Last
    accessed 3 February 2015, from http://www.mezan.org/en/details.php?id=195
    14&ddname=IOF&id2=9&id_dept=9&p=center

5. OCHAoPt (2014a), Gaza Initial Rapid Assessment, op. cit., p. 2

6. Ibid, p. 2.

7. See note 4.

8. United Nations Office for the Coordination of Humanitarian Affairs occupied
    Palestinian territory—OCHAoPt. (2014b). *Gaza Emergency Situation Report
    (4 September 2014)*. Last accessed 3 February 2015, from http://www.ochaopt.
    org/documents/ocha_opt_sitrep_04_09_2014.pdf

9. Darryl Li, 'The Gaza Strip as Laboratory: Notes in the Wake of Disengagement,'
    Journal of Palestine Studies Vol. 35(2) (2006), pp. 38–55.

10. Ibid., p. 38.

11. Ibid., p. 39.

12. Ibid., p. 39.

13. Darryl Li, 'From Prison to Zoo: Israel's "Humanitarian" Control of Gaza,'
    Adalah's Newsletter, Vol. 44 (January 2008), p. 3. Last accessed 3 February 2015,
    from http://www.adalah.org/uploads/oldfiles/newsletter/eng/jan08/jan08.
    html

14. See also Li in this volume. Jeff Halper, 'Israel's message to the Palestinians:
    Submit, leave or die,' 12 July 2014. Last accessed February 2015, from http://
    www.intifada-palestine.com/2014/07/israels-message-palestinians-submit-
    leave-die/

15. Ibid.

16. Li, 'The Gaza Strip', op. cit., pp. 43–48.

17. Opall-Rome, 2004 as cited in Atef Abu Saif, *Sleepless in Gaza: Israeli drone
    war on the Gaza Strip*, Rosa Luxemburg Stiftung, Regional Office Palestine,
    2014. Last accessed 3 February 2015, from http://www.rosalux.de/fileadmin/
    rls_uploads/pdfs/sonst_publikationen/Sleepless-in-Gaza-by-Atef-Abu-Saif-
    RLS-Palestine.pdf

18. Russell Tribunal on Palestine: The Gaza War (2014) under International
    Law: An Inquiry into Israel's Crimes, Responsibility, and the Response of the
    International Community. Extraordinary session: Brussels, 25 September
    2014. Last accessed 3 February 2015, from http://www.alterinter.org/spip.
    php?article4258

19. Amira Hass, '2,279 calories per person: How Israel made sure Gaza didn't
    starve,' *Ha'aretz*, 17 October 2012. Last accessed 3 February 2015, from http://
    www.haaretz.com/news/diplomacy-defense/2-279-calories-per-person-
    how-israel-made-sure-gaza-didn-t-starve.premium-1.470419

20. Institute of Middle East Understanding, 'Putting Palestinians "on a diet": Israel's siege and blockade of Gaza,' 14 August 2014. Last accessed 3 February 2015, from http://imeu.org/article/putting-palestinians-on-a-diet-israels-siege-blockade-of-gaza

21. Michael Schwartz, Salma Abdelaziz, Josh Levs, 'Israel drops leaflets warning Gaza residents to evacuate ahead of strikes,' CNN, 13 July 2014. Last accessed 3 February 2015, from http://edition.cnn.com/2014/07/13/world/meast/mideast-tensions

22. Noam Chomsky, 'The Real Reason Israel "Mows the Lawn" in Gaza,' AlterNet, 9 September 2014. Last accessed 3 February 2015, from http://www.alternet.org/noam-chomsky-real-reason-israel-mows-lawn-gaza

23. Joe Burgess and Karen Yourish, 'The growing reach of Hamas's rockets,' New York Times, 13 July 2014. Last accessed 3 February 2015, from http://www.nytimes.com/interactive/2014/07/13/world/middleeast/the-growing-reach-of-hamas-rockets.html?_r=0

24. Abu Saif, Sleepless in Gaza. Last accessed 3 February 2015, from http://www.rosalux.de/fileadmin/rls_uploads/pdfs/sonst_publikationen/Sleepless-in-Gaza-by-Atef-Abu-Saif-RLS-Palestine.pdf

25. Martin E. P. Seligman & Steve F. Maier, 'Failure to escape traumatic shock,' Journal of Experimental Psychology: Animal Behavior Processes, Vol. 74 (1967) pp. 1–9. See also J. Bruce Overmier & Martin E. P. Seligman, 'Effects of inescapable shock upon subsequent escape and avoidance responding,' Journal of Comparative and Physiological Psychology, Vol. 63 (1967), pp. 28–33.

26. Haggai Matar, 'Report details "double tap" bombings that hit first responders in Gaza,' 972Mag, 21 January 2015. Last accessed 3 February 2015 from http://972mag.com/report-details-idf-double-tap-bombings-that-hit-first-responders-in-gaza/101627/

27. Helga Tawil-Souri, 'The Technological End Between the "Inside" of Gaza and the "Outside" of Gaza,' 7iber, 9 September 2014. Last accessed 3 February 2015, from http://www.7iber.com/2014/09/the-technological-end-between-the-inside-of-gaza-and-the-outside-of-gaza/

28. 'Gaza: Israel drops leaflets against the resistance' (Arabic), Al-Quds, 23 August 2014. Last accessed 3 February 2015, from http://www.alquds.com/news/article/view/id/520634

29. Rachel Avraham, 'Israeli broadcast in Gaza: Hamas causes your death,' Jerusalem Online, 28 July 2014. Last accessed 3 February 2015, from http://www.jerusalemonline.com/news/middle-east/israeli-palestinian-relations/israeli-broadcast-in-gaza-hamas-causes-your-death-6765

30. United Nations: Convention against Torture and Other Cruel, Inhuman or Degrading Treatment or Punishment (1984). Last accessed 3 February 2015, from http://www.hrLast accessed.org/legal/cat.html

31. http://www.ochaopt.org/documents/Gaza_MIRA_report_9September.

pdf. Hernán Reyes, 'The worst scars are in the mind: psychological torture,' *International Review of the Red Cross*, Vol. 89(867) (2007), pp. 591–616. Last accessed 3 February 2015, from https://www.icrc.org/eng/assets/files/other/irrc-867-reyes.pdf

32. Ibid., p. 595.

33. As cited in ibid., p. 600.

34. See note 8.

35. See note 31.

36. Ibid., p. 612.

37. See note 18.

38. Ali Abunimah, 'How many bombs has Israel dropped on Gaza?' *Electronic Intifada*, 19 August 2014. Last accessed 3 February 2015, from http://electronicintifada.net/blogs/ali-abunimah/how-many-bombs-has-israel-dropped-gaza

39. Angela Ebert & Murray J. Dyck, 'The experience of mental death: The core feature of complex PTSD,' *Clinical Psychology Review* (2004). Last accessed 3 February 2015, from http://www98.griffith.edu.au/dspace/bitstream/handle/10072/16910/33579_1.pdf?sequence=1

40. Lilla Hárdi & Adrienn Kroó, 'Psychotherapy and psychosocial care of torture survivor refugees in Hungary,' *Torture* Vol. 21(2) (2011), pp. 84–97.

41. Ibid., p. 87.

42. Security Council Meeting on the 'Caesar' report concerning mass torture perpetrated by the Syrian regime (15 April 2014). Last accessed 3 February 2015, from http://www.diplomatie.gouv.fr/en/country-files/syria-295/the-un-and-syria/article/security-council-meeting-on-the

43. Alice K. Ross & Jack Serle, 'Get the data: What the drones strike,' *Bureau of Investigative Journalism*, 23 May 2014. Last accessed 3 February 2015 from http://www.thebureauinvestigates.com/category/projects/drones/drones-graphs/

44. International Human Rights and Conflict Resolution Clinic at Stanford Law School, & Global Justice Clinic at NYU School of Law, *Living Under Drones: Death injury and Trauma to Civilians from US Drone Practices in Pakistan*, (2012). Last accessed 3 February 2015 from http://www.livingunderdrones.org/wp-content/uploads/2013/10/Stanford-NYU-Living-Under-Drones.pdf

45. Metin Başoğlu, 'Drone Warfare or Mass-Torture? – A learning theory analysis,' (2012). Last accessed 3 February 2015 from http://metinbasoglu.wordpress.com/2012/11/25/drone-warfare-or-mass-torture-a-learning-theory-analysis/

46. Ibid. See also Metin Başoğlu and Susan Mineka, 'The role of uncontrollable and unpredictable stress in posttraumatic stress responses in torture survivors,' in in Metin Başoğlu (ed.), *Torture and its Consequences: Current Treatment Approaches*, (Cambridge: Cambridge University Press, 1992), pp. 182–225.

47. See note 45.

48. See note 24.
49. See note 9.
50. This quote is often inaccurately attributed to David Ben Gurion, though it does capture the spirit of his Zionist ideology and its policies during the 1948 war (*Nakba*). See Asa Winstanley, "'The old will die and the young will forget' — Did Ben-Gurion really say it?', *Electronic Intifada*, 23 August 2013. Last accessed 3 February 2015 from http://electronicintifada.net/blogs/asa-winstanley/old-will-die-and-young-will-forget-did-ben-gurion-say-it

4. GAZA AS A METAPHOR FOR UNSUSTAINABILITY

1. This article first appeared in *Foreign Policy* in a slightly different version; 'In the Eye of a Man Made Storm,' *Foreign Policy*, 26 September 2014, http://foreignpolicy.com/2014/09/26/in-the-eye-of-a-man-made-storm/, last accessed 7 January 2016.
2. See Peter Beaumont, 'Gaza reconstruction plan "risks putting UN in charge of Israeli blockade"', *The Guardian*, 3 October 2014, http://www.theguardian.co.uk/world/2014/oct/03/gaza-reconstruction-plan-un-israel-blockade, last accessed 7 January 2016.

5. ISRAEL MOWS THE LAWN

1. This is an edited version of a piece previously published in the *London Review of Books*, http://www.lrb.co.uk/v36/n15/mouin-rabbani/israel-mows-the-lawn, last accessed 7 January 2016.
2. Noura Erakat, 'No, Israel Does Not Have the Right to Self-Defense In International Law Against Occupied Palestinian Territory', 11 July 2014, *Jadaliyya*, http://www.jadaliyya.com/pages/index/8799/no-israel-does-not-have-the-right-to-self-defense-, last accessed 7 January 2016.
3. Lisa Hajjar, 'Is Gaza Still Occupied and Why Does it Matter?' *Jadaliyya*, 14 July 2014, http://www.jadaliyya.com/pages/index/8807/is-gaza-still-occupied-and-why-does-it-matter, last accessed 7 January 2016.
4. The death toll at the time of writing on 18 July 2014.
5. See Conal Urquhart, 'Gaza on brink of implosion as aid cut-off starts to bite,' http://www.theguardian.com/world/2006/apr/16/israel, last accessed 7 January 2016.
6. Nathan Thrall, 'How the West Chose War in Gaza,' *New York Times* 17 July 2014, http://www.nytimes.com/2014/07/18/opinion/gaza-and-israel-the-road-to-war-paved-by-the-west.html?_r=0, last accessed 7 January 2016.

6. ON WAR AND SHIT

1. Translated by Ghada Mourad and Tyson Patros.

8. FROM FENCE TO FENCE: GAZA'S STORY IN ITS OWN WORDS

1. Firqat Al-Rawabi, *Hajamu ('they Attacked')* N.d. *Soundcloud*, last accessed, 28 March 2015. https://soundcloud.com/adel-r-odeh/6i8xnqtkthgv?in=adel-r-odeh/sets/thwar; The verses are from the song *Hajamu ('they Attacked')* by Firqat al-Rawabi. In the first *intifada*, the songs of al-Rawabi echoed with the rise of the Palestinian resistance movement whose ideology was Islamist (i.e. Hamas and Islamic Jihad).

2. Ilana Feldman, 'Gaza's Humanitarianism Problem,' *Journal of Palestine Studies* 38.3 (2009) p. 23.

3. For example, such metaphors appear in two articles that were published in Gaza: 'The Residents of Gaza Are Looking Forward to the Ceasefire and Are Concerned from a Potential Backstab by the Zionist Occupation,' *The Palestinian Information Center*, 19 June 2008. Last accessed, 22 March 2015. https://www.palinfo.com/site/pic/newsdetails.aspx?itemid=65180; 'From Fence to Fence. They Walk through Gaza by Foot,' *Alresalah.ps*, N.p., 5 March 2012, last accessed, 22 March 2015. http://alresalah.ps/ar/index.php?act=post&id=48202

4. Laleh Khalili, *Heroes and Martyrs of Palestine: The Politics of National Commemoration* (Cambridge: Cambridge UP, 2007), p. 2.

5. Ibid., p. 2.

6. 'Life in the Gaza Strip,' *BBC News*, N.p., 14 July 2014, last accessed, 28 March 2015. http://www.bbc.com/news/world-middle-east-20415675

7. 'Population,' Palestinian Central Bureau of Statistics, last accessed, 20 March 2015. http://www.pcbs.gov.ps/site/lang__en/881/default.aspx#Population

8. 'Where we work,' *United Nations Relief and Works Agency for Palestine Refugees in the Near East*, last accessed, 20 March 2015. http://www.unrwa.org/where-we-work/gaza-strip

9. 'Gaza in 2020, a liveable place?', UNCT for oPt, Jerusalem, August 2012, last accessed, 19 March 2015. http://www.unrwa.org/userfiles/file/publications/gaza/Gaza%20in%202020.pdf

10. Jan Nederveen Pieterse and Bhikhu C. Parekh, 'Metaphors and the Middle East: Crisis Discourse on Gaza,' in *The Decolonization of Imagination: Culture, Knowledge and Power* (London: Zed, 1995).

11. Ibid.

12. Ibid.

13. Feldman, op. cit., p. 23.

14. Avi Shlaim, 'How Israel Brought Gaza to the Brink of Humanitarian Catastrophe,' *The Guardian*, 6 January 2009, last accessed, 19 March 2015. http://www.theguardian.com/world/2009/jan/07/gaza-israel-palestine

15. Ibid.

16. Adel Samara, 'Arab Nationalism, the Palestinian Struggle and an Economic Scenario for a Potential Arab Unity,' *Khamsin* 12 (1986): 53–86.

17. Jean-Pierre Filiu (trans. John King), *Gaza: A History* (NY, NY: Oxford UP, 2014), p. 79. It is worth noting that under the British Mandate, the district of Gaza covered the entirety of southern Palestine, while the area around Gaza City was demarcated as the Gaza sub-district.

18. 'Arif al-'Arif, *Tarikh Ghazzah* (Bayt Al-Maqdis: Maṭba'at Dār Al-Aytām Al-Islāmīyah, 1943), p. 298.

19. 'S/1264/Corr.1 of 23 February 1949.' *S/1264/Corr.1 of 23 February 1949.* N.p., n.d. Last accessed, 20 March 2015. http://unispal.un.org/UNISPAL.NSF/0/9EC4 A332E2FF9A128525643D007702E6

20. Ghazi Al-Sourani, *The Gaza Strip 1948–1957: A Historical, Political, and Social Study.* N.p.: n.p., n.d. Modern Discussion, 19 June 2013, last accessed, 13 February 2015. http://www.ahewar.org/debat/show.art.asp?aid=364924

21. Ibid.

22. Filiu, op. cit. p. 79.

23. Ibid., p. 79.

24. Ibid., p. 80.

25. Ibid., p. 81.

26. 'PREVENTION OF INFILTRATION (OFFENCES AND JURISDICTION) LAW, 5714-1954*.' Israel Law Resource Center, N.p., n.d. Last accessed, 25 March 2015. http://www.israellawresourcecenter.org/emergencyregs/fulltext/ preventioninfiltrationlaw.htm

27. Filiu, op. cit. p. 97.

28. Noam Chomsky, *Powers and Prospects: Reflections on Human Nature and the Social Order* (Boston, MA: South End, 1996), p. 165.

29. Gabriel Piterberg, *The Returns of Zionism: Myths, Politics and Scholarship in Israel* (London: Verso, 2008), p. 63.

30. 'Uthmān Muṣṭafá Ṭabbā', *Ithāf Al-a'izzah Fī Tārīkh Ghazzah* (Ghazzah: Maktabat Al-Yāzijī, n.d). Print. Vol. 1, 85.

31. Al-Arif, op. cit. p. 325.

32. Salīm 'Arafāt Mubayyiḍ, *Ghazzah Wa-qiṭā'uhā : Dirāsah Fī Khulūd Al-makān – Wa-ḥaḍārat Al-sukkān : "min Al-'aṣr Al-ḥajarī Al-ḥadīth Ḥattá Al-ḥarb Al-'ālamīyah Al-ūlá"* [Cairo]: Al-Hay'ah Al-Miṣrīyah Al-'Āmmah Lil-Kitāb, 1987. Print. p. 8.

9. GAZA: ISOLATION

1. http://thedailyshow.cc.com/videos/zlzdov/-500--crazies-of-summer#t=4m051s

2. Jonathan Whittall, Head of Humanitarian Analysis at Médecins Sans Frontières/Doctors Without Borders (MSF), 'Opinion and Debate: The limits of humanitarianism in Gaza,' 14 July 2014. http://www.msf.org.uk/article/opinion-and-debate-limits-humanitarianism-gaza, last accessed 7 January 2016.

3. Quoted in Ilana Feldman, *Governing Gaza: Bureaucracy, Authority, and the Work of Rule (1917–67)* (Durham, NC: Duke University Press, 2008).

4.   Egypt–Israel General Armistice Agreement, S/1264/Corr.1, 23 February 1949.
5.   Amira Hass, 'Israel's Closure Policy: an Ineffective Strategy of Containment and Repression,' *Journal of Palestine Studies*, Vol. 31, No. 3 (Spring 2002), pp. 5–20.
6.   *Jerusalem Post*, 22 July 2014.
7.   'Gaza refugees in search of freedom', http://www.alternativenews.org/english/index.php/special-reports/gaza/163-gaza-refugees-in-search-of-freedom
8.   Peter Beaumont and Patrick Kingsley, 'Devil and the deep blue sea: how Mediterranean migrant disaster unfolded,' *The Guardian*, 1 October 2014. http://www.theguardian.com/world/2014/oct/01/-sp-sea-mediterranean-migrant-disaster.

10. GAZA STRIP: THE LESSONS OF HISTORY

1.   See: http://www.plands.org/arabic/articles/018.html [Arabic]
2.   ICRC G59/I/GC, G 3/82, January 1949 Report, dated Gaza, 4 February, 1949. And Salman Abu Sitta and Terry Rempel, 'The ICRC and the Detention of Palestinian Civilians in Israel's 1948 POW/Labor Camps,' *Journal of Palestine Studies*, Vol. XLIII, No. 4 (Summer 2014), p. 11.
3.   Benny Morris, *Israel's Border Wars, 1949–1956* (Oxford: Clarendon Press, 1993), p. 416.
4.   http://www.savethechildren.org.uk/sites/default/files/docs/English_Gaza_Fact_Sheet_and_Citations.pdf, last accessed 7 January 2016.
5.   Cairo: Fajr Publishing, 1997.
6.   Joe Sacco, *Footnotes in Gaza* (London: Jonathan Cape, 2009).

11. GAZA: ENCYSTATION

1.   http://en.wikipedia.org/wiki/Cyst, last accessed 7 January 2016.
2.   The Israeli Ministry of Foreign Affairs asserts unequivocally that 'it cannot be clearly stated that the Palestinians' right to freedom of movement must take precedence over the right of Israelis to live' (http://securityfence.mfa.gov.il), (accessed April 2011, since removed).
3.   Frederick Boal, 'Encapsulation: Urban Dimensions of Ethnic Conflict,' in *Managing Divided Cities*, ed. Seamus Dunn, (Keele: Keele University Press, 1994), pp. 30–40.
4.   Mary Douglas, *In the Wilderness: The Doctrine of Defilement in the Book of Numbers* (Oxford: Oxford University Press, 2001).
5.   Whether these be buffered bulldozed strips of between twenty and forty meters in width containing two three-meter barbed wire topped fences, a ditch, another fence with electronic movement sensors, two raked sand 'trace strips', and a paved patrol road or eight-meter-high stretches of concrete wall crowned with smoked-glass windowed watchtowers protected by ditches, patrol roads and supplementary fences. Other 'walls' may be mobile such as the 'Closed Military

Areas' declared by Israeli soldiers or 'Border Police' to seal off sites of real or potential confrontation between Israelis and Palestinians.

6. Tarek Ibrahim documents the growing popularity in Israel proper (behind the 'Green Line') of municipalities and developers constructing (without the consent of the Palestinian communities) four-meter-high concrete walls between Jewish and Arab communities. Case studies are presented from Qisariya, Lid, and Ramle. See Tarek Ibrahim, *Behind the Walls: Separation Walls Between Arabs and Jews in Mixed Cities and Neighborhoods in Israel* (Nazareth: Arab Association for Human Rights, 2005).

7. Adriana Kemp, 'From Politics of Location to Politics of Signification: The Construction of Political Territory in Israel's Early Years,' *Journal of Area Studies* 12: (1998) 89–90, 92.

8. Ibid: 87.

9. Michel Warschawski, *On the Border*, Trans. Levi Laub (Cambridge, Massachusetts: South End Press, 2006) p. 12.

10. Sharon Rotbard, 'Wall and Tower (Homa Umigdal): the Mold of Israeli Architecture,' in *A Civilian Occupation: the Politics of Israeli Architecture*, eds. Rafi Segal & Eyal Weizman, pp. 39–56. (Tel Aviv and London: Babel and Verso, 2003), p. 52 and *passim*.

11. http://www.mfa.gov.il/mfa/mfa-archive/1950-1959/pages/law%20of%20return%205710-1950.aspx, accessed 5 February 2015.

12. http://www.jewishagency.org/aliyah, accessed 5 February 2015.

13. Vojin Dimitrijević, 'Ethnonationalism and the Constitutions: the Apotheosis of the Nation State,' *Journal of Area Studies* 3: (1993) 50–56.

14. Ulrich Raulff, 'Interview with Giorgio Agamben. Life, A Work of Art Without an Author: The State of Exception, the Administration of Disorder and Private Life,' *German Law Journal* V(5) (2004). (Translation Morag Goodwin, original *Suddeutsche Zeitung* 6 April 2004.) Retrieved 4 February 2015 at http://www.germanlawjournal.com/print.php?id=437, p. 610.

15. Giorgio Agamben, *Homo Sacer: Sovereign Power and Bare Life*, trans. Daniel Heller-Roazen. (Stanford: Stanford University Press, 1998).
_____ *State of Exception*, trans. Kevin Attell (Chicago: University of Chicago Press, 2005), p. 18.

16. Ibid: 88.

17. See Laurie King-Irani, 'Exiled to a Liminal Zone: Are We All Palestinians Now?' *Third World Quarterly*. XXVII(5) (2006): 923–36.

18. Yehouda Shenhav and Yael Berda, 'The Colonial Foundations of the State of Exception: Juxtaposing the Israeli Occupation of the Palestinian Territories with Colonial Bureaucratic History' in *The Power of Inclusive Exclusion: Anatomy of Israeli Rule in the Occupied Palestinian Territories*, eds. Adi Ophir, Michael Givoni & Sari Hanafi, 337–74. (Brooklyn, New York: Zone Books, 2009), p. 342. Avi Shlaim, *The Iron Wall: Israel and the Arab World* (London: Allen Lane, 2000).

19. Ibid: 355.

20. Neve Gordon, *Israel's Occupation* (Berkeley: University of California Press, 2008), p. 206. See also Neve Gordon, 'From Colonization to Separation: Exploring the Structure of Israel's Occupation,' *in Ophir et al. (eds), Inclusive Exclusion, op. cit* See also Avram Bornstein, *Crossing the Green Line: Between the West Bank and Israel* (Philadelphia: University of Pennsylvania Press, 2002). Gordon notes that during this period 'Israel invested considerable resources in closely monitoring the nutritional value of the Palestinian food basket in order to ensure that its policies were decreasing Palestinian susceptibility to disease and making inhabitants more useful in economic terms' (Gordon 2008: 207–8). See Baruch Kimmerling, *Politicide: Ariel Sharon's War Against the Palestinians* (London: Verso, 2003).

21. Shenhav and Berda, p. 338. Israeli policies of curtailing dependence on Palestinian labor and importing immigrant workers to replace it undermines parallels between Israel and South Africa. South Africa's apartheid regime, and the neo-liberal systems that have replaced it, reflect that country's dependence on black labor; Israel, in the wake of the first *intifada*, no longer needs its Palestinian population, and this puts that population at greater risk than simple exploitation.

22. Gordon, 2008, 206.

23. Gordon, 2008, 206–7.

24. See Rabbani, this volume.

25. Glenn Bowman, 'Israel's wall and the logic of encystation: Sovereign exception or wild sovereignty?' *Focaal - European Journal of Anthropology* 50 (2007): 127–36.

26. Only 2 percent of promised interim withdrawals from 13 percent of the West Bank were carried out after the Wye River Agreements, and these were reoccupied during Operation Defensive Shield.

27. Whereas the Oslo Accords of 1993 designated 316.9 square kilometers of the West Bank as Area A, the subsequent Oslo II Agreement (1995) reduced this to 96.3 square kilometers. See http://www.arij.org/atlas40/media/18.jpg and http://www.biu.ac.il/SOC/besa/books/maps.htm, both accessed 4 February 2015.

28. Israeli-Palestinian Interim Agreement on the West Bank and the Gaza Strip, Annex I: Protocol Concerning Redeployment and Security Arrangements, Article V.3 (Areas B and C); http://www.knesset.gov.il/process/docs/heskemb2_eng.htm, last accessed 3 February 2015.

29. See Akiva Eldar, 'West Bank outposts spreading into Area B, in violation of Oslo Accords', *Ha'aretz*, 18 February 2012. http://www.haaretz.com/print-edition/news/west-bank-outposts-spreading-into-area-b-in-violation-of-oslo-accords-1.413390, last accessed 4 February 2015.

30. http://www.ochaopt.org/documents/ocha_opt_area_c_factsheet_august_2014_english.pdf, last accessed 4 February 2015.

31. See UNOCHA 2006, 'Territorial Fragmentation of the West Bank', May 2006. http://www.ochaopt.org/documents/territorialfrag_18may06_Last accessed.pdf, accessed 4 February 2015.

32. CIA World Factbook, July 2014.

33. Bård Helge Kårtveit, *Dilemmas of Attachment: Identity and Belonging among Palestinian Christians* (Leiden: Brill, 2014).

34. Complete Diaries I, cited in Jacques Kornberg, *Theodor Herzl: From Assimilation to Zionism* (Bloomington: Indiana University Press, 1993), 166. See also Bowman, Glenn. "'Migrant Labor": Constructing Homeland in the Exilic Imagination', *Anthropological Theory* II(4): (2002) 456-463.

35. This position is elaborated by Ze'ev Jabotinsky, Zionist leader and founder of the clandestine anti-British militant organization Irgun, in his 1923 manifesto for a Jewish state, *The Iron Wall (We and the Arabs)*; see Shlaim 2000: 11–16. Vladimir Jabotinsky, '*O Zhelznoi Stene* (The Iron Wall — We and the Arabs)', 1923. In *Rassvyet* 4, http://www.marxists.de/middleast/ironwall/ironwall.htm, accessed 4 February 2015.

36. Baruch Kimmerling, *Politicide: Ariel Sharon's War Against the Palestinians* (London: Verso, 2003).

14. IN THE COMPANY OF FRANTZ FANON: THE ISRAELI WARS AND THE NATIONAL CULTURE OF GAZA

1. Jean-Paul Sartre, 'Preface', in Frantz Fanon, *The Wretched of the Earth* (London: Penguin Classics, 2001 [1963]), pp. 21, 7–26.

2. On the losses of the war and the human rights violations therein, see: http://www.amnesty.org/en/library/asset/MDE15/032/2014/en/613926df-68c4-47bb-b587-00975f014e4b/mde150322014en.pdf, accessed 23 December 2014.

3. See Jean-Pierre Filiu, *Gaza: A History* (London: Hurst, 2014).

4. Fanon, op.cit.

5. See Sigmund Freud, *Civilization and its Discontents* (London: Penguin Classics, 2002 [1930]).

6. Fanon, Op-Cit, p. 165.

7. See: https://www.youtube.com/watch?v=jlZnA40xCFk#t=507, accessed 23 December 2014.

8. Fanon, op. cit., p. 73.

9. Hannah Arendt, 'Understanding and Politics', in Tony Judt, *Reappraisals: Reflections on the Forgotten Twentieth Century* (London: William Heinemann, 2008), p. 77.

10. Laleh Khalili, 'A Habit of Destruction', http://societyandspace.com/material/commentaries/laleh-khalili-a-habit-of-destruction/, accessed 24 December 2014.

11. For example, see http://www.theguardian.com/world/2014/jul/31/israeli-polls-support-gaza-campaign-media, accessed 23 September 2014.

12. Freud, op. cit., p. 77.

13. Edward Said, *The Question of Palestine* (London: Random House, 1978).

14. David Grossman, *To the End of the Land* (London: Vintage, 2011), p. 173.

15. See the following Last accessedsite for an interesting piece on the Israeli poetry of solidarity with Gaza: http://alketaba.com/index.php/2013-10-30-09-55-50/item/2801-sdryg/2801-sdryg.html#.VJ8OJADAHA, accessed 23 December 2014.

16. Amos Oz, *Help Us to Divorce. Israel & Palestine: Between Right and Right* (London: Vintage, 2004), pp. 19–20.

17. John R. Gee, *Unequal Conflict: The Palestinians & Israel* (London: Pluto Press, 1998), p. 15.

18. Fanon, op. cit., p. 73.

19. Ibid., p. 169.

20. The Palestinian Information Center, which is close to Hamas, is particularly rich with literary and visual materials that embrace and eulogize the resistance on a constant basis.

21. http://www.aljazeera.net/news/cultureandart/2009/2/9/شعر-من-أجل-غزة , accessed 23 December 2014.

22. Ibid.

23. https://www.youtube.com/watch?v=jlZnA40xCFk#t=507, accessed 23 December 2014.

24. Fanon, op. cit., p. 6.

25. Silence for Gaza by Mahmoud Darwish, translated by Tom Clark: http://tomclarkblog.blogspot.co.uk/2014/07/mahmoud-darwish-silence-for-gaza.html, accessed 23 December 2014.

26. Ja'bari (1960–2012) was second in command of the military wing of Hamas, namely the 'Izz ad-Din al-Qassam Brigades. Israel assassinated him on 14 November 2012.

27. See: http://articles.islamLast accessed.net/media/index.php?page=maincategory&lang=A&vPart=992, accessed 24 December 2014.

28. See: http://www.english4arab.net/vb/t25399.html, accessed 24 December 2014.

29. Fanon, op. cit., p. 175.

30. For the poem, see https://www.youtube.com/watch?v=pmezHGfBgnA , accessed 24 December 2014.

31. Fanon, op. cit., p. 69.

32. See https://www.youtube.com/watch?v=pmezHGfBgnA , accessed 24 December 2014.

33. See Atef Alshaer, *Poetry and Politics in the Modern Arab World* (London: Hurst, 2015), particularly the chapter on the poetry of Hamas and Hizbullah.

34. Fanon, op. cit., pp. 140–141.

35. See for example Sharif Nashashibi's article on Al-Jazeera and also Marwan Bishara's: http://www.aljazeera.com/indepth/opinion/2015/01/palestine-wasted-time-at-un-20151111418591168.html; http://www.aljazeera.com/indepth/opinion/2014/12/unsc-failing-test-palestine-2014123131249943495.html, both accessed 2 January 2015.

36. Edward W. Said, *The End of the Peace Process: Oslo and After* (London and New York: Random House, 2003), p. 7.

37. Fanon, op. cit., pp. 54–55.
38. See Jeff Halper, 'The Problem with Israel', in William A. Cook, ed., *The Plight of the Palestinians: A Long History of Destruction* (London: Palgrave Macmillan, 2010), pp. 135–159, p. 151.
39. Jean-Paul Sartre, op. cit., p. 11.
40. Fanon, op. cit., p. 113.

15. CAN THE PEN BE MIGHTIER THAN THE SWORD? PERMISSION TO NARRATE GAZA

1. Taken from a Last accessed source on Lytton; see: http://www.lang.nagoya-u.ac.jp/~matsuoka/Bulwer-Lytton.html, last accessed 7 January 2016.
2. Edward Said, 'Permission to Narrate', *Journal of Palestine Studies*, vol. 13, no. 3, Spring 1984, pp. 27–48.
3. Noam Chomsky, *The Fateful Triangle: the US, Israel and the Palestinians* (London: Pluto, 1999).
4. There is now a journal devoted to this area of inquiry: *Settler Colonial Studies.*
5. These laws are well documented on the Last accessedsite of the leading legal Palestinian NGO in Israel, Adalah; see http://adalah.org/eng/, last accessed 7 January 2016.
6. Raphael Lemkin, 'Genocide as a Crime under International Law', *American Journal of International Law*, Vol. 41, No. 1 (1947), pp. 145–151. See also John Cooper, *Raphael Lemkin and the Struggle for the Genocide Convention* (London: Palgrave Macmillan, 2008).
7. See the European Court of Human Rights' Last accessedsite.
8. See Noam Chomsky and Ilan Pappé, *Gaza in Crisis: Reflections on Israel's War against the Palestinians* (Chicago: Haymarket Books, 2010), pp. 171–194.
9. The five groups are: the Palestinian citizens of Israel; the Palestinians in the West Bank; the Palestinians in the Gaza Strip; the Palestinians in the refugee camps and the Palestinians in the exilic communities.
10. These violations and many others are also documented on Adalah's website.
11. See the reports by Mossawa on http://www.mossawacenter.org/en/, last accessed 7 January 2016.

16. GAZA: IMAGE NORMALIZATION

1. Fawaz Turki, 'To be a Palestinian', *Journal of Palestine Studies*, 3(3), 1974.
2. Mainstream in this essay refers to those media that are widely disseminated to their audiences via various channels (for example, the BBC reaches 70 percent of television audiences in the UK via various genres); those media that are seen to generally reflect dominant discourses; those media that are closest to policy makers and elites; and those media that are broadly seen to set the public agenda and influence public debate. Examples include the BBC, CNN, CBS and the *New*

York Times.

3. For example, on 21 July 2014 BBC News at Ten presenter Huw Edwards asked a colleague live on air: '...the Israelis saying they'll carry on as long as necessary to stop the Hamas rocket attacks. Do you detect any signs at all that there's a hope of a coming together in the next few days or weeks, or not?'. On the BBC's News at Ten (23 July), reporter Quentin Sommerville commented (at 14:31): 'The kidnapping and murder of three Israeli teenagers, blamed on Hamas, sparked this conflict.' *The Guardian* readers' editor, Chris Elliott — ostensibly the newspaper's watchdog on bias in language and presentation — echoed Israeli propaganda, describing Israel's current attack as a 'counter-offensive'.

4. https://www.opendemocracy.net/arab-awakening/raef-zreik/longing-for-normalcy, last accessed 7 January 2016.

5. Salim Tamari, 'Normalcy and Violence: The Yearning for the Ordinary in Discourse of the Palestinian-Israeli Conflict,' *Journal of Palestine Studies*, Vol. XLII (4), summer 2013, p. 48.

6. Ibid.

7. Ibid., p. 50

8. Ibid., p. 48.

9. Achille Mbembe, 'Necropolitics', *Public Culture*, 15 (1), 2003, p. 23.

10. Ibid.

11. Ibid.

12. Michel Foucault, *Discipline and Punish: The Birth of the Prison* (New York: Vintage Books, 1995).

13. Walter Benjamin, 'Theses on the Philosophy of History', in *Benjamin, Illuminations, Essays and Reflections*, Hannah Arendt, ed., trans. Harry Zohn (New York: Schocken Books, 1978), p. 257.

14. Greg Philo and Mike Berry, *More Bad News from Israel* (London: Pluto Press, 2004/2011).

15. Howard Friel and Richard Falk, *Israel/Palestine on the Record* (London: Verso, 2007).

16. Stuart Hall, 'Cultural Identity and Diaspora', in Patrick Williams and Laura Chrisman, eds., *Colonial Discourse and Post-Colonial Theory: A Reader* (London: Harvester Wheatsheaf, 1994), p. 394.

17. Ibid.

18. Edward Said, 'Permission to Narrate'. *Journal of Palestine Studies*, 13 (3), Spring, 1984, pp. 27–48.

19. Nur Masalha, *The Politics of Denial: The Struggle for Palestinian Self-Determination* (London: Pluto Press, 2003), p. 11. Masalha uses a quote from a speech former Israeli Prime Minister Yitzhak Shamir made at the Madrid peace conference in 1991. The quote draws on Zionist concepts of land redemption and land conquest, according to Masalha.

20. Edward Said, *The Question of Palestine* (London: Vintage, 1980), p. 252.

21. Charles Tripp, *The Power and the People: Paths of Resistance in the Middle East* (Cambridge: Cambridge University Press, 2013), p. 253.

22. Rashid Khalidi, *Palestinian Identity: The Construction of Modern National Consciousness* (New York: Columbia University Press, 1997), p. 117.
23. Dr. Ofer Zur, 'Reflections on a Culture of Victims & How Psychotherapy Fuels the Victim Industry,' http://www.zurinstitute.com/victimhood.html, last accessed 7 January 2016.
24. Khalidi, *The Iron Cage: The Story of the Palestinian Struggle for Statehood* (New York: Columbia University Press, 2007), p. 35.
25. Rabinowitz makes a similar claim.
26. Ilan Pappé, *The Idea of Israel: A History of Power and Knowledge* (London and New York: Verso, 2014), pp. 4–5.
27. See for example, Ilan Pappé, ed., *The Israel/Palestine Question: A Reader* (London and New York: Routledge, 2009); Eugene Rogan and Avi Shlaim, eds, *The War for Palestine: Rewriting the History of 1948* (Cambridge: Cambridge University Press, 2007); Oren Yiftachel, *Ethnocracy: Land and Identity Politics in Israel-Palestine* (Philadelphia, PA: University of Pennsylvania Press, 2006) and Laurence Silberstein, *The Postzionism Debates: Knowledge and Power in Israeli Culture* (New York: Routledge, 1999).
28. See Chaim Waxman, 'Critical sociology and the end of ideology in Israel', *Israel Studies* 2/1 (1997) pp. 194–210.
29. Edward Said, *After the Last Sky: Palestinian Lives* (London: Vintage, 1986), p. 4.
30. Benjamin, 'Theses on the Philosophy of History.'
31. http://www.telegraph.co.uk/news/worldnews/middleeast/israel/10982394/Israel-Gaza-conflict-in-pictures-Fighting-continues-as-UN-seeks-to-broker-truce.html?frame=2982372, last accessed 7 January 2016.
32. Said, *After the Last Sky*, op. cit., pp. 41–42.

17. GAZA AT THE FRONTIERS OF ZIONISM

1. An earlier version of this article was published in 2008 under the title 'Disengagement and the Frontiers of Zionism' in *Middle East Report Online*, a publication of the Middle East Research and Information Project (http://www.merip.org/mero/mero021608), last accessed 7 January 2016.
2. Associated Press, 30 January 2008.
3. This phrase (*ha-virus lo 'otzer ba-mahsom*) is the title of a 2002 book on the health care system in the West Bank and Gaza Strip whose English edition (Tamara Barnea and Rafiq Husseini, eds.) appeared under the more politically correct *Separate and Cooperate, Cooperate and Separate: The Disengagement of the Palestine Health Care System from Israel and Its Emergence as an Independent System* (London: Praeger, 2002). Thanks to Deema Arafah for this reference.
4. Dark visions of a Bantustan future for Gaza are as dated as they are irrelevant. As early as 1985, two authors noted 'Gaza is effectively a Bantustan — a dormitory for day laborers in the Israeli economy. It is for this reason that the much vaunted "two-state solution" has rather less appeal to the people of Gaza

than to some on the West Bank.' Richard Locke and Antony Stewart, *Bantustan Gaza* (London: Zed Books, 1985), p. 2.

5. More than 70 percent of Israeli fatalities in the Gaza Strip pre-disengagement were armed security personnel, as opposed to 50 percent in the West Bank and 15 percent inside the Green Line. Statistics on Israeli fatalities are culled from 'Victims of Palestinian Terror Since September 2000,' updated regularly by the Israeli Ministry of Foreign Affairs at http://www.mfa.gov.il/, and from the tallies kept by the Israeli human rights organization B'tselem at http://www.btselem.org/English/Statistics/Casualties.asp

6. See Palestinian Center for Human Rights and Internal Displacement Monitoring Center, 'Under Fire: Israel's Enforcement of Access Restricted Areas in the Gaza Strip' (January 2014).

7. For an overview of the effects of the strike and an assessment of its legality, see B'tselem, *Act of Vengeance: Israel's Bombing of the Gaza Power Plant and Its Effects* (September 2006).

8. Israeli High Court of Justice (HCJ) 9132/07, *Jabr al-Basyuni Ahmad v. The Prime Minister* (interim decision of 29 November 2007), para. I.4.

9. Ibid.

10. HCJ 5429/07, *Physicians for Human Rights-Israel v. The Minister of Defense.*

11. HCJ 9132/07, *Jabr al-Basyuni Ahmad v. The Prime Minister* (final decision of 30 January 2008). For more on the Court's dubious factual findings (including its reliance on a government claim that unnamed 'Palestinian officials' had assured them that redistribution of power to hospitals was feasible, despite multiple signed affidavits to the contrary from senior Palestinian utilities managers), see Gisha (Legal Center for Freedom of Movement), 'Briefing: Israeli High Court Decision Authorizing Fuel and Electricity Cuts to Gaza,' 31 January 2008.

12. In 2012, nearly four years after the original publication of this essay, the Ministry of Defense disclosed a 'red lines' document detailing calculations for the minimum number of calories Gaza residents required to avoid malnutrition. Amira Hass, '2,279 Calories Per Person: How Israel Made Sure Gaza Didn't Starve,' *Ha'aretz*, 17 October 2012.

13. *Ynet*, 27 September 2005.

18. CONCENTRATION-PLACE

1. Ze'ev Schiff and Eitan Haber, *Israel, Army and Defence: A Dictionary* (Tel Aviv: Zmora, Bitan, Modan Publishers, 1976), p. 395 [in Hebrew].

2. On the Ben Gurion–Yosef Weitz agreement see Benny Morris, *The Birth of the Palestinian Refugee Problem 1947–1949* (Tel Aviv: Am Oved Publishers Ltd, 1991), p. 326 [in Hebrew].

3. The public resentment of 'comparison' is a much later phenomenon, and government sensitivity to the use of certain terms has not been constant. Some of the unexpected adoptions and changes are not easily explained and require

further research. On the plans to create 'model villages' to re-locate Palestinians in Majdal see Benny Morris, *Jews and Arabs in Palestine/Israel 1936–1956*, (Tel Aviv: Am Oved Publishers Ltd, 2004), p. 164 [in Hebrew].

4. Especially on the procedure of forced migration and concentration prior to, during and after WWII, see Mark Mazower, *No Enchanted Palace: The End of Empire and the Ideological Origins of the United Nations* (Princeton: Princeton University Press, 2009).

5. On regime-made disaster see Ariella Azoulay, 'Regime-made Disaster: On the Possibility of Nongovernmental Viewing,' in Yates McKee and Meg McLagan, eds., *Sensible Politics: The Visual Cultures of Nongovernmental Politics* (New York: Zone Books, 2012), pp. 29–42.

6. Avi Oded, 'On Fedayeen and a young girl,' *The Book of the Sinai Campaign* (Tel Aviv: LeDory Publishing House, 1957), p. 221 [in Hebrew].

7. The transfer of the remaining Palestinians from al-Majdal in 1950 was pursued under endless lies and deceptions, and the expellees were sent there without coordination with the Egyptians who ruled Gaza. On some of these see Morris (2004), pp. 149–174. Ben Gurion contested Egypt's right to rule Gaza and claimed that 'the presence of Egyptian army in the Gaza Strip' contradicted UN resolutions. David Ben Gurion, *The Sinai Campaign* (Tel Aviv: Am Oved Ltd Publishers, 1959), p. 35 [in Hebrew].

8. Quoted in Morris, 1991, p. 375.

9. Ben Gurion, op. cit., pp. 48–49.

10. According to Ben Gurion, in 1955, out of the 283 agricultures settlements, 319 (83.5 percent) were created by new immigrants (Ibid., p. 49).

19. REPETITION

1. Nimer Sultany, 'Colonial Realities', *The Guardian*, 3 March 2008.

2. Gilles Deleuze, trans. Paul Patton, *Difference and Repetition* (N.Y.: Columbia University Press, 1994), pp. 20–21.

3. Interview is available at: http://thelead.blogs.cnn.com/2014/07/10/former-palestinian-adviser-mideast-tension/, last accessed 7 January 2016.

4. This erasure of context is paramount in legal narratives and not only popular and political accounts. See, for example, Nimer Sultany, 'The Legacy of Justice Aharon Barak: A Critical Review,' *Harvard International Law Journal Online*, vol. 48 (2007): 83, p. 91.

5. Editorial, 'Jewish hate of Arabs proves: Israel must undergo cultural revolution', *Ha'aretz*, 7 July 2014.

6. See, for example, Daniel Bar-Tal and Yona Teichman, *Stereotypes and Prejudice in Conflict Representations of Arabs in Israeli Jewish Society* (Cambridge: Cambridge University Press, 2009).

7. See, for example, Valentina Azarov, 'Institutionalised Impunity: Israel's Failure to Combat Settler Violence in the Occupied Palestinian Territory' (Al-Haq,

2013).

8. For a longer history of Israeli rejectionism that pre-dated Netanyahu, see: Noam Chomsky, 'Rejectionism and Accommodation,' in *The Chomsky Reader*, James Peck, ed., (New York: Pantheon, 1987), pp. 371–405.

9. Nimer Sultany, 'Roger Cohen Sheds No Tears', *Jacobin*, 16 July 2014, available at: https://www.jacobinmag.com/2014/07/roger-cohen-sheds-no-tears/, last accessed 7 January 2016.

10. H. Sutherland Edwards, *The Germans in France: Notes on the Method and Conduct of the Invasion; the Relations between Invaders and Invaded; and the Modern Usages of War* (London: E. Stanford, n.d.), available at: https://archive.org/stream/cu31924028337024#page/n7/mode/2up (pp. 285–286).

11. Ibid.

12. Stathis Kouvelakis, *Philosophy and Revolution: From Kant to Marx* (London: Verso, 2003), p. 72 (discussing Heine's ideas).

13. Thucydides, *History of the Peloponnesian War*, translation: Richard Crawley (2007), p. 337.

14. Ibid.

15. Ibid., p. 338.

16. Martti Koskenniemi, 'The Politics of International Law', *European Journal of International Law*, vol. 1 (1990): 4, p. 28.

17. See, for example, Scott Newton, 'Constitutionalism and Imperialism sub specie Spinozae', *Law and Critique*, vol. 17: 3 (2006), p. 325.

18. Nathaniel Berman, 'Privileging Combat? Contemporary Conflict and the Legal Construction of War', *Columbia Journal for Transnational Law*, vol. 43 (2004): 1.

19. Ibid., pp. 4–5, 9–12.

20. Ibid., p. 19.

21. Ibid., p. 22.

22. Ibid., p. 23; and Samera Esmeir, 'The Time of Engagement, Zaman al-ishtibak', *Law, Culture and the Humanities*, vol. 10: 3 (2014): pp. 397–407.

23. Goncalo de Almeida Ribeiro, Vishaal Kishore and Nimer Sultany, 'The risks of de-contextualizing Gaza war crimes', *Electronic Intifada*, 25 September 2009; Nimer Sultany, 'Roundtable on Occupation Law: Part of the Conflict or the Solution? (Part V: Nimer Sultany)', *Jadaliyya*, 22 September 2011.

24. Karma Nabulsi, *Traditions of War: Occupation, Resistance, and the Law* (Oxford: Oxford University Press, 1999), p. 242.

25. Koskenniemi, op. cit., p. 30.

26. H.C. 6204/ 2006 *Dr. Yossi Beilin et. al. v. Prime Minister of Israel et. al.* (delivered on 1 August 2006).

27. Moti Bassok, 'When is a war not a war? It's a question of money', *Ha'aretz*, 30 July 2004.

28. Revital Hovel and Gili Cohen, 'State asks High Court to not declare Operation Protective Edge a war', *Ha'aretz*, 13 August 2014.

29. George Bisharat, 'Violence's Law: Israel's Campaign to Transform International Legal Norms,' *Journal of Palestine Studies*, vol. XLII: 3 (2013): p. 70.

30. Achille Mbembe, 'Necropolitics', *Public Culture*, vol. 15: 1 (2003): p. 39.
31. See, for example, Sara Roy, 'De-development Revisited: Palestinian Economy and Society since Oslo,' *Journal of Palestine Studies*, vol. 28: 3 (1999): 64–82. Darryl Li, 'The Gaza Strip as Laboratory: Notes in the Wake of Disengagement', *Journal of Palestine Studies*, vol. 35: 2 (2006): pp. 38–55.
32. Samera Esmeir, *Juridical Humanity: A Colonial History* (Stanford, CA: Stanford University Press, 2012).
33. Nimer Sultany, 'Activism and Legitimation in Israel's Jurisprudence of Occupation', *Social & Legal Studies*, vol. 23: 3 (2014): 315–339.
34. Sharon Weill, *The Role of National Courts in Applying International Humanitarian Law* (Oxford: Oxford University Press 2014), p. 39.
35. David Kretzmer, *The Occupation of Justice: The Supreme Court of Israel and the Occupied Territories* (Albany, NY: State University of New York Press, 2002), pp. 75, 70. See also Sultany, op. cit.
36. Brian Orend, 'War', *Stanford Encyclopaedia of Philosophy*, 2005, available at: http://plato.stanford.edu/entries/war/, last accessed 7 January 2016.
37. David Kennedy, *Of War and Law* (Princeton: Princeton University Press, 2006).
38. Laleh Khalili, *Time in the Shadows: Confinement in Counterinsurgencies* (Stanford, CA: Stanford University Press, 2013), pp. 7, 10.
39. For a discussion of the 'Dahiya Doctrine' see paragraphs 62–64, 1194–1198, and 1304 in the Goldstone Report: A/HRC/12/48 Human Rights Council, Twelfth session, Agenda item 7, 'Report of the United Nations Fact-Finding Mission on the Gaza Conflict' (25 September 2009), available at: http://www2.ohchr.org/english/bodies/hrcouncil/docs/12session/A-HRC-12-48.pdf, last accessed 7 January 2016.
40. Khalili, op. cit., p. 64.
41. Joe Becker and Scott Shane, 'Secret "Kill List" Proves a Test of Obama's Principles and Will', *New York Times*, 29 May 2012.
42. See, for example, Nick Turse, *Kill Anything That Moves: The Real American War in Vietnam* (New York: Metropolitan Books, 2013).
43. Eado Hecht, 'Gaza: How Hamas tunnel network grew', BBC, 22 July 2014.
44. Alfonso A. Narvaez, 'Gen. Curtis LeMay, an Architect of Strategic Air Power, Dies at 83', *New York Times*, 2 October 1990.
45. 'LIVE BLOG: Day 4 of Israel-Gaza conflict 2012', *Ha'aretz*, 17 November 2012.
46. A statement by McGeorge Bundy as quoted in Noam Chomsky, 'The Responsibility of Intellectuals,' in *The Chomsky Reader*, James Peck, ed., (New York: Pantheon, 1987), p. 67.
47. A British document quoted in Abdel Razzaq Takriti, *Monsoon Revolution: Republicans, Sultans, and Empires in Oman, 1965–1976* (Oxford: Oxford University Press, 2012), p. 146.
48. Gili Cohen, 'Israeli army says the killing of 8 Gazan family members was in error', *Ha'aretz*, 10 July 2014.
49. Anne Barnard, 'Questions About Tactics and Targets as Civilian Toll Climbs in Israeli Strikes', *New York Times*, 21 July 2014 ('Not all the casualties are due to

mistakes,' [a senior Israeli military official] said. 'If Hamas are holding people inside the apartments while shooting from there, that's one of the tragedies they are making.'); Ben Hubbard & Jodi Rudoren, 'Questions of Weapons and Warnings in Past Barrage on a Gaza Shelter,' *New York Times*, 3 August 2014 ('In any war, there are malfunctions and mistakes,' General Shamni said. Hamas militants 'usually do things in order to attract' Israeli fire, he added, 'and hope that some mistake will cause a disaster in order to delegitimize Israel.').

50. Giora Eiland, 'In Gaza, there is no such thing as "innocent civilians",' *Ynet*, 5 August 2014, available at: http://www.ynetnews.com articles/0,7340,L-4554583, 00.html, last accessed 7 January 2016.
51. Jodi Rudoren, 'Civilian or Not? New Fight in Tallying the Dead From the Gaza Conflict,' *New York Times*, 5 August 2014.
52. Eqbal Ahmad, 'Revolutionary Warfare: How to Tell When the Rebels Have Won,' in *The Selected Writings of Eqbal Ahmad,* Carollee Bengelsdorf, Margaret Cerullo, and Yogesh Chandrani, eds., (New York: Columbia University Press, 2006), p. 15.
53. Ibid., pp. 17, 20.
54. Aluf Benn, 'Dichter: Israel to allow aid supplies, food into Gaza,' *Ha'aretz*, 15 July 2007.
55. Kevin Connolly, 'Israel to build 3,000 settler homes after UN vote,' BBC, 30 November 2012.
56. Isabel Kershner and Jodi Rudoren, 'Israel Expands Settlements to Rebuke Palestinians,' *New York Times*, 5 June 2014.
57. 'Israel freezes Palestinian tax funds over international criminal court move,' *The Guardian*, 3 January 2015.
58. Orna Ben-Naftali, Aeyal Gross and Keren Michaeli, 'Illegal occupation: Framing the occupied Palestinian territory,' *Berkeley Journal of International Law*, 23 (2005): pp. 551–614.
59. Nietzsche, 'On the Genealogy of Morals,' in *Basic Writings of Nietzsche,* trans. Walter Kaufmann (New York: Modern Library, 2000), p. 511.
60. Ibid., p. 515.
61. Ibid., pp. 478, 482.
62. Ibid., p. 503 (emphasis in original).
63. Nathan Thrall, 'Our Man in Palestine,' *New York Review of Books*, 14 October 2010.
64. Frantz Fanon, *The Wretched of the Earth* (London: Penguin Classics, 2001[1963]), pp. 31–32.
65. Ibid., p. 32.
66. Ibid., p. 33.
67. C.L.R. James, *The Black Jacobins* (London: Penguin Books,1980 [1938]), p. 229.
68. Nathan Thrall, 'Israel & the US: The Delusions of Our Diplomacy,' *New York Review of Books*, 9 October 2014 (on Kerry's efforts to revive the negotiations as a retreat from previous negotiations and commitment the Palestinian negotiators secured).

69. Azmi Bishara, '4 May 1999 and Palestinian Statehood: To Declare or Not To Declare?', *Journal of Palestine Studies*, vol. 28: 2 (1999): pp. 5–16.

70. Thrall, op. cit.

71. Ibid.

72. See, for example, Sari Bashi and Kenneth Mann, *Disengaged Occupiers: The Legal Statues of Gaza* (Gisha: Legal Center for Freedom of Movement, January 2007); Iain Scobbie, 'An Intimate Disengagement: Israel's Withdrawal from Gaza, the Law of Occupation and of Self-Determination', in Cotran and Lau, eds., *Yearbook of Islamic and Middle Eastern Law, Volume 11* (London: Brill, 2007), pp. 3–31.

73. Mark Levine and Lisa Hajjar, 'International law, the Gaza war, and Palestine's state of exception', Al-Jazeera, 21 November 2012; See also, Bisharat, op. cit., pp. 75–76.

74. Former Israeli ambassador to the U.S. Michael Oren wrote: 'To guarantee peace, this war must be given a chance'. In, 'Israel must be permitted to crush Hamas', *Washington Post*, 24 July 2014.

75. Edward Said writes, for example, with reference to the Bush administration's 'Road Map': 'The road map, in fact, is not a plan for peace so much as a plan for pacification: it is about putting an end to Palestine as a problem. Hence the repetition of the term 'performance' in the document's wooden prose – in other words, the way Palestinians are expected to behave. No violence, no protest, more democracy, better leaders and institutions – all this based on the notion that the underlying problem has been the ferocity of Palestinian resistance, rather than the occupation that has given rise to it'. Edward Said, 'A Road Map to Where?', *London Review of Books*, vol. 25: 12 (19 June 2003): pp. 3–5.

20. GAZA: *NO SE PUEDE MIRAR* — 'ONE CANNOT LOOK'[1]: A BRIEF REFLECTION

1. Cited in Mira Bartok, *The Memory Palace: A Memoir* (New York: Free Press, 2011), p. 60. Original: 'Francisco de Goya y Lucientes, inscribed below a print from his series *Disasters of War*.'

2. See Sara Roy, 'Living with the Holocaust: The Journey of a Child of Holocaust Survivors', *Journal of Palestine Studies*, Volume 32, No. 1 (Autumn 2002), pp. 5–12.

3. Giora Eiland, 'In Gaza, there is no such thing as "innocent civilians"', *Ynetnews. com*, 5 August 2014, http://www.ynetnews.com/articles/0,7340,L-4554583,00. html, last accessed 7 January 2016.

4. Sara Roy, *Hamas and Civil Society in Gaza: Engaging the Islamist Social Sector* (Princeton, NJ: Princeton University Press, 2011), p. 235.

5. Norman G. Finkelstein, *Method and Madness: The hidden story of Israel's assaults on Gaza* (New York: OR Books, 2014), p. 32. Also see Norman G. Finkelstein, *This Time We Went Too Far: Truth & Consequences of the Gaza*

Invasion (New York: OR Books, 2010).
6. Finkelstein (2014), p. 33.
7. 'Mowing the lawn [or the grass]' is a metaphor used by Israeli officials for periodic strikes on Gaza. See John Feffer, 'Mowing the Lawn in Gaza,' *Foreign Policy in Focus*, 14 July 2014, http://fpif.org/mowing-lawn-gaza; Efraim Inbar and Eitan Shamir, 'Mowing the grass in Gaza,' *The Jerusalem Post*, 22 July 2014, http://www.jpost.com/Opinion/Columnists/Mowing-the-grass-in-Gaza-368516, last accessed 7 January 2016;and Mouin Rabbani, 'Israel Mows the Lawn,' in this volume.
8. Simone Weil, *The Need for Roots: Prelude to a Declaration of Duties towards Mankind* (London: Routledge/Taylor & Francis e-library, 2005), p. 48.
9. Email correspondence, October 2014.
10. Nadera Shalhoub-Kevorkian, paper presented at a closed conference, Jerusalem, Autumn 2010. The conference papers are published in Mandy Turner and Omar Shweiki, *Decolonizing Palestinian Political Economy: De-development and Beyond* (London: Palgrave Macmillan, 2014). Part of this section is drawn from Sara Roy, 'Introduction to the Third Edition,' *The Gaza Strip: The Political Economy of De-development* (Washington, D.C.: Institute of Palestine Studies, 2015, forthcoming), which was first presented in a lecture, 'A Deliberate Cruelty: Rendering Gaza Unviable,' The Edward Said Memorial Lecture, The Palestine Center, Washington, D.C., 10 October 2012, http://www.thejerusalemfund.org/ht/display/ContentDetails/i/36415/pid/897, last accessed 7 January 2016.
11. Simone Weil (2005), p. 48.
12. Sara Roy, 'A Jewish Plea,' in Nubar Hovsepian (ed.), *The War on Lebanon: A Reader* (Northampton, MA: Olive Branch Press, 2008), p. 307.
13. Sara Roy (2008), p. 308.
14. Giora Eiland (August 5, 2014).
15. Ka-Tzetnik 135633, *Shivitti: A Vision* (San Francisco, CA: Harper & Row, 1989), jacket.
16. Ka-Tzetnik, p. 103.
17. Email correspondence, July 2014.
18. Email correspondence, July 2014.
19. Email correspondence, July 2014.
20. Small towns with large Jewish populations in pre-war Central and Eastern Europe.
21. See the works of Marc H. Ellis, particularly *Toward a Jewish Theology of Liberation: The Challenge of the 21st Century* (Baylor, TX: Baylor University Press, 2004); and *The End of Jewish History: Auschwitz, The Holocaust and Palestine* (London: Pluto Press, 2006).

21. GAZA AS ARCHIVE

1. This piece originally appeared in a special weeklong series on the Stanford

University Press blog. The entire 10-part series can be found on the SUP blog, http://stanfordpress.typepad.com/

2. Judith Butler, *Frames of War: When is Life Grievable?* (London: Verso, 2009), p. 9.

3. Marlene Manoff, 'Archive and Database as a Metaphor,' *Libraries and the Academy* 10: 4 (2010): 385–398.

4. Sharif Abdel Kouddous, 'Massacre in Shejaiya,' *The Nation*, 20 July 2014. http://www.thenation.com/article/180728/massacre-shejaiya, last accessed 7 January 2016.

5. Neve Gordon and Nicola Perugini, 'The Politics of Human Shielding,' paper presentation at *American Studies Association Annual Meeting*, 8 November 2014.

6. Ibid.

7. Noura Erakat, 'Who Is Afraid of the International Criminal Court?' *Jadaliyya*, 12 January 2015. http://www.jadaliyya.com/pages/index/20523/who-is-afraid-of-the-international-criminal-court, last accessed 7 January 2016.

8. Alexander G. Weheliye, *Habeas Viscus: Racializing Assemblages, Biopolitics, and Black Feminist Theories of the Human* (Durham, NC: Duke University Press, 2014).

9. Butler (2009), p. 24.

10. Lisa Bhungalia, 'A Liminal Territory: Gaza, Executive Discretion, and Sanctions Turned Humanitarian,' *GeoJournal* 75:4 New Directions in Critical Geopolitics (2010): 347–357.

11. Maya Mikdashi, 'Can Palestinian Men Be Victims? Gendering Israel's War on Gaza,' *Jadaliyya*, 23 July 2014. http://www.jadaliyya.com/pages/index/18644/can-palestinian-men-be-victims-gendering-israels-w, last accessed 7 January 2016.

12. *Shujayea: Massacre at Dawn* (Al Jazeera English Productions, 2014): http://www.aljazeera.com/programmes/specialseries/2014/2014/07/shujayea-massacre-at-dawn-201472621348901563.html, last accessed 7 January 2016.

13. Ali Abunimah, 'War Crime: Video Shows Sniper Killing of Wounded Gaza Civilian.' *Electronic Intifada*, 21 July 2014. http://electronicintifada.net/blogs/ali-abunimah/war-crime-video-shows-sniper-killing-wounded-gaza-civilian, last accessed 7 January 2016.

14. Sharif Abdel Kouddous, '"The Tank Shells Fell Like Rain": Survivors of the Attack on UNRWA School Report Scenes of Carnage and Destruction,' *The Nation*, 25 July 2014.

15. Walid Khalidi, *Before Their Diaspora: A Photographic History of the Palestinians 1876–1948* (Washington, D.C.: Institute for Palestine Studies, 1984); Rashid Khalidi, *The Iron Cage: The Story of the Palestinian Struggle for Statehood* (Boston: Beacon Press, 2006); Benny Morris, *The Birth of the Palestinian Refugee Problem 1947–49* (Cambridge: Cambridge University Press, 1987).

16. Shira Robinson, *Citizen Strangers: Palestinians and the Birth of Israel's Liberal Settler State* (Stanford: Stanford University Press, 2013).

17. Rashid Khalidi, 'Collective Punishment in Gaza,' *The New Yorker,* 29 July 2014

18. Avi Shlaim, *The Iron Wall: Israel and the Arab World* (New York: W.W. Norton and Company, 2000), pp. 90–93, 103.

19. United Nations Office for the Coordination of Humanitarian Affairs (OCHA), 'Occupied Palestinian Territory: Gaza Emergency Situation Report (as of 22 July 2014, 1500 hrs),' http://www.ochaopt.org/documents/ocha_opt_sitrep_23_07_2014.pdf, last accessed 7 January 2016.

20. 'Palestinian Boy Mohammed Abu Khdeir Was Burned Alive, Says Official,' *The Guardian,* 5 July 2014.

21. Julie Peteet, 'Male Gender and Rituals of Resistance in the Palestinian "Intifada": A Cultural Politics of Violence,' *American Ethnologist* (1994) 21 (1): 31–49.

22. Roger Heacock, 'Locating and Opening Palestinian Archives: A National Priority,' *Birzeit University Working Paper* 2 (2011).

23. Samera Esmeir, 'Colonial Experiments in Gaza,' *Jadaliyya,* 14 July 2014. http://www.jadaliyya.com/pages/index/8482/colonial-experiments-in-gaza-, last accessed 7 January 2016.

24. Nimer Sultany, 'Repetition and Death in the Colony: On the Israeli Attacks on Gaza,' *Critical Legal Thinking,* 11 July 2014.

25. See statement by Palestinian academics, public figures, and activists in Gaza: 'No Ceasefire Without Justice for Gaza,' *Electronic Intifada,* 22 July 2014.

26. OCHA, 'Occupied Palestinian Territory: Gaza Emergency Situation Report,' 4 September 2014. http://www.ochaopt.org/documents/ocha_opt_sitrep_10_08_2014.pdf, last accessed 7 January 2016.

27. Ibid.

28. Ibid.

29. 'Horror on Gaza Beach: New York Times Photographer Witnesses Israeli Killing of 4 Palestinian Boys,' *Democracy Now!,* 17 July 2014.

BIOGRAPHIES

Jehad **ABU SALIM** was born in and grew up in the city of Deir al-Balah in the Gaza Strip. Jehad attended Al-Azhar University in Gaza, receiving his Bachelor's degree in Business Administration. Afterwards, he attended the Islamic University-Gaza where he received a diploma in the Hebrew language. Jehad has worked in a number of civil society organizations, including PalThink for Strategic Studies, a local Palestinian think tank, the Birzeit Center for Development Studies, Save Youth Future Society, the Palestinian Center for Democracy and Conflict Resolution, the HADAF Center for Human Rights, and Swisspeace. Since the fall of 2013, Jehad has been a PhD candidate at New York University for the joint program in Hebrew and Judaic Studies and History. His research focuses on the influence of the Nakba on the Gaza Strip and how it radically changed the political, social, demographic, and economic realities of Gaza.

Salman **ABU SITTA** is a graduate of Cairo University and University College London in civil engineering. Abu Sitta is the founder and president of the Palestine Land Society and author of several books including the *Atlas of Palestine 1917–1966* (English and Arabic editions), *Return Journey*, and more than 300 papers and articles on Palestinian refugees and the Right of Return. He is also a member of the Palestinian National Council and the general coordinator of the Right of Return Congress.

Naim **AL KHATIB** was born in 1968 in a refugee camp in the Gaza Strip. He received his bachelor's degree in Computer Science with a minor in Theatre from the American University in Cairo in 1993 and his master's in Computer Science from the University of Colorado at Boulder in 2003. He published his first narrative collection, *Free Reign*, in 2010, and his second, *Stolen Alive*, in 2013 (both in Arabic). He has also tried his hand at screenwriting and playwriting, in addition to his passion for acting and directing.

Atef ALSHAER is a lecturer in Arabic Language and Culture at the University of Westminster. He has authored several publications on the Arab world in the fields of literature, politics and language. He was educated at Birzeit University in Palestine and SOAS, University of London, where he obtained his PhD and taught for a number of years.

Ariella AZOULAY is an assistant professor in the Department of Modern Culture and Media and the Department of Comparative Literature, Brown University. Her recent books include *From Palestine to Israel: A Photographic Record of Destruction and State Formation, 1947–1950*, (Pluto Press, 2011), *Civil Imagination: The Political Ontology of Photography* (Verso, 2012), *The Civil Contract of Photography* (Zone Books, 2008), and, co-authored with Adi Ophir, *The One State Condition: Occupation and Democracy between the Sea and the River* (Stanford University Press, 2012). She is a curator and documentary film maker. Among her recent projects are *Potential History* (2012, Stuk/Artefact, Louven), and *Civil Alliances, Palestine, 47–48* (2012).

Ramzy BAROUD is an internationally-syndicated columnist, media consultant, managing editor of *Middle East Eye* and the author of several books. Baroud founded the *Palestine Chronicle* and is currently completing his PhD studies at the University of Exeter. His latest book is *My Father Was a Freedom Fighter: Gaza's Untold Story* (Pluto Press, 2010).

Glenn BOWMAN is Reader in Social Anthropology at the University of Kent's School of Anthropology and Conservation. His research (1983–present) has predominantly concerned Israel/Palestine (particularly Jerusalem and Bethlehem District) where he has examined topics ranging from pilgrimage and inter-communal shrine sharing to nationalist mobilisation and the historic and contemporary practices of structured separation. He has carried out cognate research in Yugoslavia (1990–present) and Divided Cyprus (2009–present). Some recent publications include: 'A Place for the Palestinians in the *Altneuland*: Herzl, Anti-Semitism, and the Jewish State' in *Surveillance and Control in Israel/Palestine: Population, Territory and Power*, eds Elia Zureik, David Lyon & Yasmeen Abu-Laban (Routledge, 2010); 'Viewing the Holy City: An Anthropological Perspectivalism' in *Jerusalem: Conflict and Cooperation in a Contested City*, eds Madelaine Adelman & Miriam Elman (Syracuse University Press, 2012); 'Sharing and Exclusion: the Case of Rachel's Tomb,'

Jerusalem Quarterly 58 (2014); and 'Violence before Identity: an Analysis of Identity Politics,' *The Sociological Review* 62 (2014).

Selma DABBAGH is a British Palestinian writer of fiction who lives in London. Her first novel, *Out of It* (Bloomsbury, 2012) set between Gaza, London and the Gulf, was critically acclaimed and listed as a *Guardian* Book of the Year. She has also published short stories with Granta, International PEN, the British Council, Wasafiri, Telegram and *The Letters' Page*. She has been nominated for several awards for her stories. Her first play, *The Brick,* was broadcast by BBC Radio 4 in January 2014 and nominated for an Imison Award. She is currently working on her second novel. Selma also works as a lawyer in London, with a focus on international criminal law. She has previously worked for human rights non-governmental organisations in East Jerusalem, Cairo, and London and has spent her life shuttling between Europe and the Arab world. www. selmadabbagh.com

Haidar EID is Associate Professor of Postcolonial and Postmodern Literature at al-Aqsa University in Gaza. He has written widely on the Arab-Israeli conflict, with articles published on Znet, Electronic Intifada, Palestine Chronicle, and Open Democracy. He has published papers on cultural studies and literature in a number of journals, including *Nebula*, *Journal of American Studies in Turkey, Cultural Logic,* and the *Journal of Comparative Literature*. Eid received his PhD in English Literature and Philosophy from University of Johannesburg. He is the author of *Worlding Postmodernism: Interpretive Possibilities of Critical Theory* (Roman Books, 2014).

Omar EL QATTAA is a dedicated and energetic photographer with five years' extensive experience in photography including photojournalism, commercial, nature and portraits.

Ilana FELDMAN is Associate Professor of Anthropology, History, and International Affairs at George Washington University. Her research has focused on the Palestinian experience, both inside and outside of Palestine, examining practices of government, humanitarianism, policing, displacement, and citizenship. She is the author of *Governing Gaza: Bureaucracy, Authority, and the Work of Rule, 1917–67* (Duke University Press, 2008); *In the Name of Humanity: The Government of Threat and Care* (Duke University, 2010; co-edited with Miriam Ticktin); and *Police Encounters: Security and Surveillance in Gaza under Egyptian*

BIOGRAPHIES

Rule (Stanford University Press, 2015). She is currently working on a project, tentatively titled 'Life Lived in Relief: Palestinian Experiences with Humanitarianism Since 1948', which involves fieldwork and archival research in and about Jordan, Lebanon, Syria, the West Bank and Gaza. This project explores the dynamics of long-term humanitarianism and the politics of living in the humanitarian condition.

Tanya HABJOUQA is a photographer with a master's degree in Global Media and Middle East Politics from the University of London, SOAS. Habjouqa's photographs focus on gender, social, and human rights issues in the Middle East. Tanya is a founding member of the Rawiya photographer collective, the first all-female photographer collective in the Middle East. Her work has been widely exhibited, and her series 'Women of Gaza' was acquired by the Boston Museum of Fine Art in 2013 and in private collections. In 2014 she won a World Press Award for her series 'Occupied Pleasures' in which she documents many of the ludicrous moments of everyday life that the 47-year occupation of the West Bank, Gaza, and East Jerusalem has created. Habjouqa was a finalist for the 2014 *FotoEvidence Book Award*, and recipient of the *Magnum Foundation 2013 Emergency Fund*. Based in East Jerusalem, she is working on personal projects that explore identity politics, occupation, and subcultures of the Levant. www.tanyahabjouqa.com

Khaled HROUB is a professor in residence of Middle Eastern Studies and Arab Media Studies at Northwestern University/Qatar, and a senior research fellow at the Centre of Islamic Studies at the University of Cambridge where he founded and directed the Cambridge Arab Media Project (CAMP). He is the author of *Hamas: A Beginners Guide* (2006/2010), *Hamas: Political Thought and Practice* (2000), and editor of *Political Islam: Context versus Ideology* (2011) and *Religious Broadcasting in the Middle East* (2012). In Arabic he published *Fragility of Ideology and Might of Politics* (2010), and *In Praise of Revolution* (2012). He has also published literary collections and poetry, including *Tattoo of Cities* (literary collection, 2008) and *Enchantress of Poetry* (poems, 2008) — both in Arabic.

Pierre KRÄHENBÜHL is commissioner-general of the United Nations Relief and Works Agency for Palestine Refugees (UNRWA). Prior to joining UNRWA, he served as director of operations at the International Committee of the Red Cross, overseeing the organization's response to conflicts in Afghanistan, Iraq, Syria, Colombia and Libya, among others.

BIOGRAPHIES

He holds a BA in Political Science and International Relations from the University of Geneva.

Darryl LI is an anthropologist and attorney who has worked in the Gaza Strip for the Palestinian Center for Human Rights, Human Rights Watch, and B'Tselem.

Dina MATAR is senior lecturer in political communication at the Centre for Film and Media Studies at the School of Oriental and African Studies. She works on the relationship between culture, communication and politics, with a special focus on Palestine, Lebanon and Syria. She is author of *What it Means to be Palestinian: Stories of Palestinian Peoplehood* (IB Tauris, 2010); co-editor of *Narrating Conflict in the Middle East: Discourse, Image and Communication Practices in Palestine and Lebanon* (IB Tauris, 2013) and co-author of *The Hizbullah Phenomenon: Politics and Communication* (Hurst, 2014). Matar is co-founding editor of the *The Middle East Journal of Culture and Communication*.

Ilan PAPPÉ is Professor of History at the Institute of Arab and Islamic Studies and Director of the European Centre for Palestine Studies at Exeter University. He founded and directed the Academic Institute for Peace in Givat Haviva, Israel, between 1992 and 2000 and was chair of the Emil Tuma Institute for Palestine Studies in Haifa between 2000 and 2006. Professor Pappé was a senior lecturer in the department of Middle Eastern History and the Department of Political Science in Haifa University, Israel between 1984 and 2006. He was appointed as chair in the department of History at Exeter University from 2007–2009 and became a fellow of the IAIS in 2010. His research focuses on the modern Middle East and, in particular, the history of Israel and Palestine. He is the author of *The Ethnic Cleansing of Palestine* (2006); *The Forgotten Palestinians* (2011); *The Idea of Israel* (2014) and *The Israel-Palestine Question* (1999), among other books.

Mouin RABBANI is Senior Fellow with the Institute for Palestine Studies and Co-Editor of *Jadaliyya*. He is a policy advisor with Al-Shabaka, the Palestinian Policy Network, and contributing editor to *Middle East Report*. He has published and commented widely on Palestinian affairs and the Arab-Israeli conflict.

Sara ROY is a senior research scholar at the Center for Middle Eastern Studies, Harvard University. Her most recent book is *Hamas and Civil*

BIOGRAPHIES

Society in Gaza: Engaging the Islamist Social Sector (Princeton University Press, 2011, 2013).

Sherene SEIKALY is Assistant Professor of History at the University of California, Santa Barbara. She is the editor of the *Arab Studies Journal*, and co-founder and editor of the *Jadaliyya* e-zine. Seikaly's *Men of Capital: Economy and Scarcity in Mandate Palestine* (Stanford University Press, 2015) explores how Palestinian capitalists and British colonial officials used economy to shape territory, nationalism, the home, and the body.

Said SHEHADEH was born and raised in Jaffa, Palestine. He completed his doctorate in Clinical Psychology at Rutgers University in New Jersey. His dissertation research examined the application of psychoanalytic theory to the Arab self. Shehadeh developed a wide range of interests in various types of trauma, including sexual, political, and community violence trauma. His clinical training and work centered on the psychological assessment and treatment of emotional and physical trauma. Based in Ramallah and New York, Shehadeh's current research project focuses on Palestinian resilience under settler colonial occupation.

Nimer SULTANY is Lecturer in Public Law at the School of Law, SOAS, University of London. Previously he was a postdoctoral Fellow at SUNY Buffalo Law School. He holds an S.J.D. from Harvard Law School; an LL.M. from the University of Virginia; an LL.M. from Tel Aviv University; and an LL.B. from the College of Management. He has practised human rights law in Israel/Palestine, and was the director of the Political Monitoring Project at Mada al-Carmel — The Arab Research Center for Applied Social Research. His publications include: 'The State of Progressive Constitutional Theory: The Paradox of Constitutional Democracy and the Project of Political Justification' in the *Harvard Civil Rights — Civil Liberties Law Review*; 'Against Conceptualism: Islamic Law, Democracy, and Constitutionalism in the Aftermath of the Arab Spring' in the *Boston University International Law Journal*; 'Activism and Legitimation in Israel's Jurisprudence of Occupation' in *Social & Legal Studies*; 'Redrawing the Boundaries of Citizenship: Israel's New Hegemony' in the *Journal of Palestine Studies*; and *Citizens without Citizenship: Israel and the Palestinian Minority* (Mada, 2003). His op-eds have appeared in Arabic, Hebrew, and English in numerous media outlets, including *The Boston Globe*, *The Miami Herald*, *The Guardian*, *The Buffalo News*, *Ha'aretz*, and *Al-Quds al-Arabi*.

BIOGRAPHIES

Helga TAWIL-SOURI is a media scholar, photographer and documentary film-maker whose work focuses on issues of spatiality, technology, and politics in the Middle East. The bulk of her scholarship analyzes culture and technology in everyday life in Palestine/Israel, theorizing how media technologies and infrastructures function as control and bordering mechanisms, and how territorial/physical boundaries function as cultural spaces. She writes on contemporary Palestinian cultural politics, the internet, telecommunications, television, cinema, videogames, as well as physical markers such as ID cards, checkpoints and buffer/border zones. She is associate professor of Media, Culture, and Communication and director of the Hagop Kevorkian Center for Near Eastern Studies at New York University.